GARDEN
HANDBOOK

ESSENTIAL STEP-BY-STEP
TECHNIQUES

GARDEN
HANDBOOK

ESSENTIAL STEP-BY-STEP
TECHNIQUES

**A COMPLETE GUIDE TO PLANTING, PLANNING, PRUNING,
LOW-MAINTENANCE GARDENING AND SEASONAL TASKS
WITH MORE THAN 650 PHOTOGRAPHS AND ILLUSTRATIONS**

JACKIE MATTHEWS AND ANDREW MIKOLAJSKI

southwater

This edition is published by Southwater

Southwater is an imprint of
Anness Publishing Ltd
Hermes House, 88–89 Blackfriars Road,
London SE1 8HA
tel. 020 7401 2077; fax 020 7633 9499
www.southwaterbooks.com; info@anness.com

© Anness Publishing Ltd 2005

UK agent: The Manning Partnership Ltd
tel. 01225 478444; fax 01225 478440

UK distributor: Grantham Book Services Ltd
tel. 01476 541080; fax 01476 541061

North American agent/distributor:
National Book Network, tel. 301 459 3366
fax 301 429 5746; www.nbnbooks.com

Australian agent/distributor:
Pan Macmillan Australia
tel. 1300 135 113; fax 1300 135 103

New Zealand agent/distributor:
David Bateman Ltd
tel. (09) 415 7664; fax (09) 415 8892

A CIP catalogue record for this book is
available from the British Library.

Publisher: Joanna Lorenz
Editorial Director: Helen Sudell
Editor: Valerie Ferguson
Designer: Andrew Heath

Photographers: Peter Anderson, Sue Atkinson,
Jonathan Buckley, Derek Cranch,
Sarah Cuttle, David England, John Freeman,
Michelle Garrett, Jerry Hapur,
Janine Hosegood, Jacqui Hurst,
Andrea Jones, Simon McBride, Peter McHoy,
Andrew Mikolajski, Marie O'Hara,
David Parmiter, Debbie Patterson,
Howard Rice, Derek St Romaine,
Barbara Segall, Brigitte Thomas,
Juliette Wade, David Way, Jo Whitworth,
Polly Wreford

Text contributors: Pattie Barron, Susan Berry,
Richard Bird, Steve Bradley, Valerie Bradley,
Kathy Brown, Jo Chatterton, Joan Clifton,
Ted Collins, Stephanie Donaldson,
Tessa Evelegh, Lin Hawthorne, Hazel Key,
Gilly Love, Peter McHoy, Jackie Matthews,
Andrew Mikolajski, Barbara Segall

Garden designers: Declan Buckley,
Lara Copley-Smith, Sally Court,
Dennis Fairweather, Jacqui Gordon,
Alan Gray, Bernard Hickie, Jennifer Jones,
Elsie Josland, Robert Kite, Shari Lawrence
Garden Design, Christina Oates, Antony Paul,
Wendy and Michael Perry, Ben Pike,
Graham Robeson, Lucy Summers,
Paul Thompson, Mrs Winkle-Howarth,
Diane Yakely

Previously published in as part of a larger
volume, The Handbook of Gardening.

1 3 5 7 9 10 8 6 4 2

*Page 1: White arum lilies. Page 2: Pink
clematis. Page 3 left to right: Trillium,
snowflakes and geraniums.
Page 4: (left) A Mediterranenan-style garden and (right) using paving for drama.
Page 5 left to right: Osteospermum and
Californian bluebell.*

Contents

Introduction

Whatever your particular interests, this gardening handbook is designed to help you achieve your aims and enjoy your garden to the maximum. Here, you will find everything you need in order to create a lovely outdoor environment – and with the minimum of maintenance if that is your desire. The wealth of informative material has been divided into six chapters that will help you through the gardening basics.

In *Right Plant, Right Place* you will learn how to assess your garden as an assemblage of mini-sites, each with its own microclimate and soil conditions that will suit certain types of plant more than others. You will also learn how to prepare soil, sow seed, plant out and then look after your plants once they are in the garden. The chapter concludes with a chart of popular plants that lists their preferred growing conditions, main season of interest and best planting time.

Shade, Tone & Hue is an exploration of the many ways you can use colour to create a variety of different moods and atmospheres in your garden. The effects of each colour on our emotions are described, together with

Left: Oranges and blues are strongly contrasting colours that create drama.

advice on how to combine colours and groups of colours successfully.

Perfect Patios covers everything from planning (choosing a site, determing the size is suitable for the purpose), through the relative merits of different construction materials, to thinking about appropriate screening and suitable plants. Style and finishing touches such as lighting, water features, arbours, furniture and even heating are also discussed.

Gardeners keen on reducing the time they spend on chores will find the chapter on *Low-maintenance*

Below: Large clematis flowers are visually appealing.

Gardening essential reading. The labour-saving tips and advice cover everything you need to know from landscaping ideas to watering, discouraging weeds, and selecting beautiful easy-care plants.

Pruning Success clearly explains the basic principles, showing how you can keep all your plants the size you want and encourage them to perform superbly. General techniques and equipment are described, while a helpful chart list plants (including climbers) along with the best time and method of pruning.

The last chapter, *Seasonal Tasks*, details all the gardening jobs that need to be done through the year. Each season is broken down into early, mid and late, or roughly monthly sections, but the exact timing will depend on the climate in your area.

Above: *Some gardens give the appearance of blooming effortlessly.*

Right: *An all white garden creates calm.*

Below: *Old roses have delicious scent.*

RIGHT PLANT, RIGHT PLACE

Every year thousands of plants, lovingly and carefully planted, fail to thrive simply because they have been placed in the wrong spot. A little time spent checking the ideal conditions for the plant you want to buy, or better still identifying the conditions you can offer and then seeking the right plant, will pay dividends in a better display and longer-lived, healthier plants.

Left: *Gardens that thrive contain plants that are suited to their situation, soil and aspect.*

Choosing the Location

EVERY PLANT HAS A PREFERENCE ABOUT ITS IDEAL GROWING
CONDITIONS, AND PUTTING A PLANT IN THE RIGHT LOCATION AND
SOIL WILL ENSURE THAT IT HAS THE BEST POSSIBLE START
AND CHANCE OF LONG-TERM HEALTH AND VIGOUR.

PERFECT PLANT ENVIRONMENTS

Many factors influence the environment in your garden and conditions can vary considerably in different parts of it. The climate, type of soil, shelter and the amount of sunlight it receives all play a role.

Fortunately, many plants can cope with a wide range of climatic variation and soil, and grow surprisingly well in conditions far removed from their natural habitat. These plants are understandably popular and deserve to be considered for inclusion in many

Above: This fuchsia and clematis look good together, and the clematis also benefits from having its roots in the shade.

schemes. But to get the very best results in the long term, plants need to be carefully selected to suit the particular conditions that are to be found in your garden, as well as to suit the requirements of your design.

Above: A single garden can contain dozens of environments, each of which can be exploited by growing suitable plants.

ALTERING THE ENVIRONMENT

While it is always better to work with nature, rather than against it, sometimes you may want to influence it to allow you to grow particular plants. Altering the environment within your garden allows you to create microclimates specifically for certain types of plants to enjoy.

SOIL STRUCTURE

All soil consists of sand, silt, clay and humus (organic matter), and the proportions in which each is present will determine its structure – its consistency and water-retaining properties. The more large sand particles it contains, the more easily water will drain through it and the quicker it will warm up in spring, allowing earlier planting. Silt particles are smaller, so water is held for longer, but they retain little in the way of nutrients. Clay particles are the smallest of all. They hold on to nutrients and water very well, but in high percentages will produce a heavy, solid soil that is cold (slow to warm up in spring), and prone to damage if worked when too wet.

Chalky and limy soils, which overlie chalk or limestone, are shallow,

Above: Matching plants to the type of soil in your garden ensures that they will thrive and perform well.

free-draining and of moderate fertility. Loam is a perfect balance of all the elements. It is a crumbly soil, often dark in colour, which holds both moisture and nutrients well without becoming waterlogged. Unfortunately, this ideal soil is rare – most gardens have a soil that favours one particle size over the others and so needs help in the form of added organic matter.

Above: A small pond sunk into a patio allows water-loving plants to be grown in an otherwise dry situation.

GARDENER'S TIP

To find out the texture of your soil, pick up a handful of damp soil and roll it between your finger and thumb. If it feels rough and granular, but the grains don't adhere to each other, the soil is sandy. If it forms a ball when your roll it between your thumb and forefinger, it is a sandy loam. If it is rather sticky and makes a firm shape, it is a clay loam. But if you can mould it into shapes, it is a clay soil.

Above: Roses like a rich, fertile soil that does not get too dry, and most prefer slightly acid conditions.

SOIL PH

Whether a soil is acid or alkaline is defined by its pH level, which can vary considerably within even local areas, depending on where topsoil may have been brought in from or the nature of the underlying rock. Within a garden levels can vary depending on where manure, fertilizer, lime or even builder's rubble has been applied in the past.

Individual plants prefer different pH levels and some have quite specific requirements. It is a good idea to test the soil in your garden or border before selecting plants. You can then be sure to make an appropriate choice.

Altering pH levels

It is possible to influence the pH level in soil, although this is usually only worthwhile for growing vegetables when increasing yields is desirable. With ornamental plants it is usually more satisfactory to choose plants to suit the soil.

Raising soil pH is relatively easy and can have beneficial effects on a long-term basis, but lowering it is difficult, costly and usually only a short-term measure. If you really want to grow lime-hating plants and your soil has a pH reading of 7 or over, then the best option is probably to grow them in containers with a compost (soil mix) to suit.

Above: Foxgloves and many other cottage-garden plants are not fussy about the type of soil they grow in.

Above: Many plants, including ferns, will thrive in the moist area surrounding a fountain.

MOISTURE

Plants vary in the amount of moisture they require, and the amount of moisture available to plants in your garden will depend on a number of factors.

Rainfall can vary considerably within quite small areas depending on local topographical conditions, and even the direction in which the garden faces can affect the water it receives, depending on the prevailing wind relative to the house. Even though plenty of rain falls, it may not be falling on the soil where it is needed, but on the house, where it runs off down the drains.

How long the moisture is held within the soil, and therefore how long it is available for use by plants, is affected by the amount of sun or shade the plot receives as well as the soil type. A light, sandy soil loses its moisture quickly, while a heavy, clay soil is slower to

drain, making moisture available to the plants for a longer period of time. Warmth from the sun will not only cause the soil to dry out more quickly, but will encourage plants to grow and use up more water.

Additionally, having large established specimens already in situ can mean there is less water available for newly introduced plants. An older plant will have sent roots down to the lower levels within the soil, to take advantage of all the moisture it can, leaving little for a new plant that is still reliant on water much nearer the surface. A 5-year-old tree, for example, will take up in excess of 4 litres (1 gallon) of water every day. If the garden does not receive enough rainfall to support plants with this kind of requirement you may have to consider choosing plants that need a lower intake.

Above: Ebullient yellow mimulas contrast well with the restrained foliage of hostas. Both these plants like moist soil.

Choosing the Location

SUN AND SHADE

Light is essential to plants. It provides the energy needed by the plant to manufacture food during daylight hours, a process known as photosynthesis. The length of daylight also influences the time of year when flowers and fruit are produced and leaves fall.

The amount of light individual plants require varies. Although the majority of garden plants are sun loving, there are nonetheless plenty of shade-loving plants that will also thrive in darker conditions. Many even prefer to grow in shade. Mediterranean plants and roses grow best in direct sunlight, but rhododendrons like some shade. Ivies and periwinkles like heavily shaded areas.

Above: A sun-drenched border blazes with a breathtaking display of fiery reds and yellows.

WIND AND POLLUTION

Exposure to strong winds can be a problem for some plants, especially young ones or those with fragile stems. It can damage growth and cause desiccation. Conversely a gentle wind aids the dispersal of pollen and seed, can cool plants down in hot weather, and prevents the build-up of a stagnant atmosphere round plants, which can incubate disease. Where strong wind is a regular problem, it needs to be moderated by the installation of a windbreak of some sort.

Busy urban thoroughfares can become laden with fumes and particles that can be detrimental to many plants, especially in front gardens. Finding attractive specimens that can withstand this daily onslaught will ensure that an urban garden never looks drab.

Above: Many plants enjoy shady conditions, but they tend to lack colourful flowers. Here, a garden ornament adds interest.

Above: Clever use of plant colour and shape can create stunning effects in any location within a garden.

PLANNING YOUR PLANTING

Whether you are planning an entire garden or just designing a border, you will naturally begin by visualizing the effect you want to create, and listing favourite plants that you cannot do without. Before you go any further, and without compromising your initial vision, it is essential to check all their growing requirements and be realistic about what you can grow.

Hard surfaces, including raised beds and paths, and vertical elements, in the form of climbing plants, shrubs and trees, need careful consideration. These create microclimates, extending the range of plants you can grow.

Most plants look far better when planted in largish groups. Propagation is one of the easiest and cheapest ways to increase your stock of plants. But you will need to plan when to do this

in order to have plants ready for your garden at the correct time. Most propagation is done in the autumn by taking cuttings or collecting seeds.

HOW TO USE THIS CHAPTER

This chapter explains how to successfully match plants to the conditions in your garden, to maximize good results. The first section tackles the basics of ground preparation, sowing and planting as well as offering tips on plant maintenance. In *Different Soil Conditions,* you can learn about how your soil influences the types of plants you are likely to grow most successfully. In *Planting in Different Locations* are examples of different types of site likely to exist within a garden and suggestions for planting them. Finally, there is a chart of plants with information on preferred soil type, whether they like sun or shade, and sowing, planting and flowering times.

Above: Planting in groups gives solid patches of eye-catching colour.

Getting Started

WHATEVER PLANTS YOU CHOOSE, YOU NEED TO LOOK AFTER THEM CORRECTLY. CAREFUL SOIL PREPARATION, SOWING AND PLANTING WILL PAY DIVIDENDS. REGULAR CHECKING AND MAINTENANCE ONCE ESTABLISHED WILL ENSURE THRIVING SPECIMENS.

ANALYSING YOUR SOIL

Plant nutrients are held in solution in the soil where they are absorbed by the roots. Phosphorus, potassium, magnesium, calcium and sulphur are needed in fairly large quantities for plants to thrive. Trace elements including manganese and chlorine are also needed in smaller quantities. You can test the soil for major nutrients using a special soil testing kit to see if any are lacking.

The calcium content of soil is measured on a scale of pH, which ranges from 0 to 14. The most acid is 0 and 14 is the most alkaline. The scale of pH affects the solubility of minerals and therefore their availability to plants via the roots.

Testing for pH

Before selecting plants for your garden, it is worth testing your soil to see whether it is acid, neutral or alkaline. A pH soil testing kit is easy to use and readily available from a garden centre. Alternatively, you can use a pH meter, which has a probe for inserting into the soil and is more economical in the long term.

1 Take a sample of soil from the area to be tested from about 10 cm (4 in) under the soil surface. If it is wet, allow it to dry out. Place the sample in a screw-top jar or test tube.

2 Following the manufacturer's instructions, add the indicator chemical to the soil and then the liquid. Shake vigorously and allow the contents to settle. Repeat the shaking and allow to settle again. Compare the colour of the liquid to the chart accompanying the kit to find the pH level of your soil. It is best to test several samples from different parts of the garden, as pH can vary within quite a small area. It can also alter over time, so repeat the process every few years to give you an accurate reading of current conditions.

PREPARING THE SOIL

The best results are achieved by getting the growing site in as good a condition as possible before you even purchase or propagate a plant. Once plants are in the soil, it will be difficult to dig it over or add compost in bulk. The first task is to clear the ground. Weeds will be the most likely problem, but in many new gardens there will be builder's rubbish to remove.

Weeds have to be either totally removed or killed. If the soil in your garden is light and crumbly, it is possible to remove the weeds as you dig. On heavier soils you can either cover the ground with an impermeable mulch such as thick black polythene, for several months, or use a weedkiller.

Dig the soil over, adding as much well-rotted organic matter as possible. If you can, carry out the digging in the autumn and leave the ground until spring before planting. If you do this you will see, and be able to remove, any weeds that have re-grown from roots that were missed before.

For an existing bed top-dress the soil with a good layer of well-rotted compost or farmyard manure.

GARDENER'S TIP

Never attempt to work soil when the weather is very wet. Pressure on wet soil will compact it. If you do have to get on a border when it is wet, stand on a wooden plank, which spreads the load.

DIGGING A NEW BED

1 When the ground is cleared of weeds, dig the first trench to one spade's depth across the plot. Barrow the soil to the other end of the plot.

2 Fork a layer of well-rotted compost or manure into the bottom of the trench to improve the soil structure and provide nutrients for the plants. Break it up if it is in thick clumps.

3 Dig the next trench across the plot, turning the soil on to the compost in the first trench. Add compost to the new trench and then dig the next. Continue down the border until the whole surface has been turned. Fill the final trench with the earth taken from the first.

Sowing Seed in Soil

For bulk growing of the more common garden plants, sowing directly into the soil is far less bother and much less expensive because you will not need to buy pots and compost (soil mix).

Like annuals, many perennials can be sown where they are to flower, but for those that will not flower until the following year it is best to sow them in a nursery bed, if you have the space.

Sow the seed in spring, as the soil begins to warm up. You can bring this forward a few weeks if you cover the soil with cloches from early spring. Mark the ends of each row with labels so you know what you have planted. Do not let the bed dry out and keep it weeded. When the seedlings have grown to a manageable size, thin them to distances of at least 15cm (6in).

Most species will be ready to plant out in their flowering position during the following autumn while the ground is still warm.

EASY SEED FOR SOWING IN OPEN GROUND

Alcea
Aquilegia
Astrantia
Centranthus ruber
Delphinium
Foeniculum
Helleborus
Myosotis
Primula
Verbascum
Verbena
Viola

Sowing in Open Ground

1 Prepare the soil carefully, removing all weeds and breaking it down into a fine tilth with a rake.

2 Draw out a shallow drill with a corner of a hoe, about 1cm ($\frac{1}{2}$in) deep. Keep the drill straight by using a garden line as a guide. If the soil is dry, water the drill with a watering can and wait until the water has soaked in.

3 Sow the seed thinly along the drill. Larger seed can be sown at intervals to avoid the need for thinning later. Gently rake the soil back into the drill, covering over the seed. Tamp down the row with the base of the rake. Keep the drills moist until germination.

Sowing Seed in Pots

For small quantities of seeds, and those that can be difficult to germinate, such as parsley, sow in 9cm (3½in) pots or in a tray, then place in a sheltered spot, away from direct sun. Germination will usually take from a few days to a few weeks depending on the species, although some can take longer and may even require a winter's cold weather before germination will occur. Keep the pots watered. The seedlings are ready to prick out when they have developed their first true leaves or when they are large enough to handle. Keep them covered in a cold frame for a day or so, before hardening them off by gradually opening the frame more fully each day.

Most perennials can be sown in early spring. Some, however, such as primulas and hellebores, need to be sown as soon as the seeds ripen in late summer or autumn.

Sowing Seed in Containers

1 Fill a pot or tray with compost (soil mix). Tap firmly on the bench to settle the compost and lightly flatten the surface with the base of a pot. This will exclude air pockets which would hinder the growth of roots. Sow the seed thinly on top.

2 Cover the seed with a layer of sieved compost or fine gravel. Water the pot thoroughly either from above with a watering can fitted with a fine rose or from below by standing the pot in a tray of shallow water.

Pricking Out Seedlings

1 Water the pot an hour before gently knocking out the seedlings. Carefully break up the rootball and split into clumps. Dealing with one clump at a time, gently ease the seedlings away, touching only the leaves.

2 Hold a seedling over a pot by one or more of its leaves and gently trickle moist compost around its roots until the pot is full. Avoid touching the fragile stem or roots. Tap the pot on the bench to exclude any air pockets, then firm down gently with your fingertips and water.

BUYING PLANTS

Most plants are available in containers all year round. If you want good-quality plants that are accurately labelled, go to a reputable source.

Check your prospective purchase carefully and reject any plant that is diseased, looks unhealthy or is harbouring pests. If possible, knock it out of its pot and look at the roots. Again reject any that show signs of pests. Also reject any that are pot-bound, that is when the roots have wound round the inside of the pot, creating a solid mass. Such plants are difficult to establish.

If the plants are in a greenhouse or tunnel, harden them off when you get them home. Planting them straight out in the garden may put them under stress, from which they might not recover.

Above: Bulbs are invaluable for growing in borders as well as for naturalizing in grassy areas.

PLANTING BULBS

Much of the interest and colour in a spring garden comes from flowering bulbs. Daffodils, tulips, snowdrops, bluebells, crocuses, *Iris reticulata*, aconites and hyacinths can be used en masse in borders or singly under trees. Daffodils, crocuses, snowdrops, blue-bells and aconites can be naturalized in lawns. To plant in lawns remove a plug of grass and soil and replace after positioning the bulbs.

PLANTING BULBS IN A BORDER

1 Excavate a hole large enough to take a group of bulbs. If the soil is poor or impoverished fork in garden compost or well-rotted manure. You could also add a layer of grit or sand.

2 Space out the bulbs, not too evenly, planting at a depth that will leave them covered with about twice their own depth of soil.

3 To deter slugs and encourage the bulbs to flower sprinkle more grit or sand around them before returning the soil.

Planting Shrubs and Perennials

When you are planting a new border put all the plants, still in their pots, in their positions according to your planting plan. Stand back to assess the result and make any necessary adjustments. When you are satisfied with the positions of the plants you can begin to plant.

Water the plants before planting out. Start planting at the back or one end of a border and move forwards. When you have finished planting, cover the soil between the plants with a layer of mulch to keep the weeds down and preserve moisture. Be prepared to water regularly in dry weather for at least the first few weeks after planting. If you are planting isolated plants in unprepared soil, add plenty of well-rotted organic matter to the soil.

If you decide that a plant is in the wrong spot you may have to leave it in place for the growing season, otherwise you might damage the roots, but in autumn or spring, you can lift it and move it to a better position.

SPRING BULBS

Crocus
Cyclamen coum
Eranthis hyemalis
Galanthus nivalis
Hyacinthoides
Hyacinthus
Iris reticulata
Narcissus
Tulipa

Planting Out

1 Dig a hole with a trowel or spade, and with the plant still in its pot, check that the depth and width is right. The plant must be placed in the soil at the same depth that it was in the pot or just a little deeper.

2 Knock the plant out of its pot, tease out some of the roots, to help them become established in the ground more quickly, and place it in the planting hole. Fill around the plant with soil and then firm it with your hands or a heel to expel large pockets of air. Water thoroughly unless the weather is wet. Mulch the surface with chipped bark, gravel, leaf mould or compost.

23

Different Soil Conditions

SOILS VARY WIDELY IN THEIR LEVEL OF ACIDITY OR ALKALINITY AND THE STRUCTURE OF THEIR PARTICLES, WHICH RANGE FROM LIGHT SAND TO HEAVY CLAY. THESE FACTORS DETERMINE HOW MUCH MOISTURE AND NUTRIENTS THEY CONTAIN.

ACID SOIL

This type of soil can be free draining and sandy, heavy and sticky, or even organic with a high peat content. Clay soils are often acid, and peaty soils, where the organic matter has not decomposed, are almost always acid.

Some soils, even if originally alkaline, can gradually become more acid as a result of the lime being washed out of the upper layers close to the soil

Above: Spectacular camellias prefer acid soil, where they can grow to the size of a small tree.

Above: Azaleas are a form of rhododendron, and like them they require an acid soil to survive.

surface. This is because rainwater is slightly acidic, and it dissolves the lime in the soil and washes (leaches) it down through the soil. As a result, soils in high rainfall areas are more likely to be acid than alkaline.

Plants that Depend on Acid Soil

Most plants that grow naturally on acid soils (known as calcifuge) usually struggle when grown in anything else. This is because they are unable to take up enough iron from an alkaline soil.

24

Some excellent garden plants grow only in acid soil, so if your garden has this condition, you can look forward to growing some real treasures.

Acid soils are generally not a problem to plant because in addition to those plants that prefer them, many plants also tolerate them. If your soil is not very acid and your climate isn't too wet, there is little restriction on what you can grow, although it may be wise to avoid Mediterranean plants such as *Cistus* and lavender which thrive in dry alkaline conditions.

Many evergreen shrubs will grow on acid soil. The glossy ovate green leaves of rhododendrons, azaleas, camellias and skimmias provide

Above: Pieris thrive on acid soil. They are grown for their red-flushed young leaves and cascades of white bell-like flowers.

wonderful backdrops for their often startlingly bright blooms that provide colour from mid-spring through the early summer. Pieris has the added attraction of red-flushed young leaves.

Permanent foliage plants also include ground covers and creeping plants like gaultherias, heathers and heaths.

Deciduous trees growing on acid soils produce some stunning autumn foliage colour. Outstanding among these are the maples (*Acer*). Many of the spring- and summer-flowering deciduous shrubs also have good autumn colour.

Plenty of perennials and annuals that grow on a wide range of soils can be used to provide seasonal highlights for the border. Wake robin, Himalayan blue poppies and lupins, however, require a slightly acid soil.

Above: Lupins come in many lovely shades and have a distinctive peppery scent. They require a slightly acid soil.

25

Year-round Interest

Acid-loving shrubs are often associated with their stunning spring flowers. The showy white, pink, red or yellow flowers of camellias, rhododendrons and azaleas bloom in abundance and are deservedly much admired. The waxy beauty of magnolia blooms, in cream or blush, is breathtaking. Witch hazels produce their surprisingly frost-resistant and fragrant, spidery blooms, in yellow to dark red, from midwinter to early spring.

Many deciduous shrubs, including maples and witch hazels, are prized for their autumn foliage colour. And there are berries, too. Several species of

Above: Heather (Calluna vulgaris) *needs acid soil to surive. Most varieties flower in late summer and autumn.*

Gaultheria produce white or purple-red fruit at this time. Some shrubs also have attractive bark.

For colour through spring and summer try Wake robin, Himalayan blue poppies and lupins.

Heathers form stunning carpets of flower colour in late summer and autumn. Many varieties are grown for their foliage, which changes colour during the year.

Above: Magnolias make splendid specimen shrubs. Many species need an acid soil.

Above: Spring- and summer-flowering Wake robin (Trillium grandiflorum) *grows well in moist, shaded soil.*

Neutralizing Acid Soil

Adding lime to the soil is an easy and effective way to reduce the acidity. However, it needs to be applied to ground that is bare of plants, dug in and left to break down for several weeks at least, or preferably longer. This is only really practical on vegetable plots, which can be left bare during the winter.

Lime should never be applied at the same time as fertilizer, as the lime will cause the fertilizer to break down too quickly. It can be used when renovating or making a new border, but most ornamental plants tolerate moderately acid soil, so it is not generally worthwhile trying to neutralize acid soil in order to grow acid-hating ornamentals in your garden.

An alternative to liming is to incorporate spent mushroom compost, which is rich in lime. You may even have the benefit of a small crop of mushrooms, as there are often spores in the compost.

PLANTS FOR ACID SOIL

Acer
Amelanchier
Azalea
Calluna vulgaris
Camellia
Erica cultivars
Gaultheria procumbens
Hamamelis
Lupinus
Magnolia
Meconopsis betonicifolia
Pieris
Rhododendron
Skimmia
Trillium grandiflorum

Above: An ornamental border should not need any application of lime for the plants to do well, even on acid soil. This colourful display of established fuchsias and dahlias will tolerate moderately acid conditions.

27

Left: Many silver-leaved plants, such as Artemisia *and* Stachys, *enjoy the free-draining conditions of an alkaline soil.*

unavailable to lime-hating plants, which then grow poorly as a result and often have yellowing leaves.

Plants that Depend on Alkaline Soil

Some plants can only grow in an alkaline soil, and these are known as calcicole, or lime-loving. They have adapted to cope with the high alkalinity and cannot survive on other types of soil.

Most plants are more tolerant, but many still enjoy alkaline conditions. Among them are many Mediterranean plants, including *Santolina*, *Artemisia*, *Helianthemum*, *Cistus* and herbs, which benefit from the good drainage.

ALKALINE SOIL

These soils are predominantly found in chalky or limestone areas or where there is builder's rubble in the soil. They are free draining with only moderate fertility.

In some areas a shallow layer of soil overlies solid chalk or limestone rock, which can make gardening problematic. The plant roots will have great difficulty penetrating the soft rock, which can lead to poor anchorage, particularly in trees. Also, during dry periods a thin soil can hold only limited reserves of water and the upper levels of the rock become extremely dry.

Once established, however, many plants will produce an extensive, deep root system that penetrates fissures, so that when rain does fall, they can absorb the maximum amount before it drains away.

High alkalinity in soil can cause various nutrient and trace elements to become locked in a form that is

Above: Mediterranean plants, such as Cistus, *thyme and sage, cope well with alkaline conditions.*

28

Planning Displays

Warm and well-drained chalk and limestone soils play host to a diverse mix of plants, some with more delicate floral attributes than others, but all repaying close inspection.

A host of attractive flowering shrubs tolerate alkaline conditions, such as *Berberis*, *Buddleja davidii*, *Choisya ternata*, *Deutzia*, *Philadelphus*, *Sorbus* and viburnums. Many members of the pea family, including brooms, *Gleditsia* and *Robinia*, often excel on these soils.

Clematis and honeysuckle are useful climbers, the former for their long flowering period and the latter for their intoxicating scent.

Tough perennials like *Acanthus*, *Achillea*, *Eryngium* carnations, *Hypericum* and *Verbascum* are all

Above: Free-flowering mallows (Lavatera) *are tolerant of a wide range of soil conditions. They bloom throughout summer.*

useful for the middle to back of a border. Wild flowers such as cornflowers and foxgloves can be included. Smaller perennials for the foreground include *Bergenia*, *Doronicum*, scabious and drought-resistant thymes.

Plants with silvery-grey foliage like pinks, saxifrage and *Gypsophila* seem to have a softening effect on a sunny border, and they contribute their own attractive flowers. In shady spots you can plant stinking hellebore, wild orchids, *Iris foetidissima*, *Colchicum* and *Campanula*.

For filling in gaps, there are numerous annuals and biennials, including *Lavatera*, *Matthiola*, *Tagetes* and many everlasting flowers that can be dried in the autumn.

Above: Berberis is a versatile shrub that will tolerate many soil types, including alkaline ones.

Year-round Interest

With so many lovely plants thriving on alkaline soil, maintaining interest through the year is not a problem.

There are bulbs that flower in every season, but spring is when most of them produce their jewel-like colour. Spring flowers also come from plants as diverse as *Helleborus orientalis*, peonies, *Doronicum* and lilac. In summer *Helianthemum*, pinks, carnations, *Gypsophila*, *Verbascum* and clematis take over. Lavender and scabious continue well into autumn, when cotoneasters and firethorn flash their red, orange or yellow berries.

The Christmas rose (*Helleborus niger*) reveals its graceful white flowers through winter.

Some deciduous trees grown for autumn foliage are often described as lime-tolerant (typically *Acer davidii* and *A. rubrum*). Yet they do not always produce their foliage display on soils with a high alkaline content.

Above: French lavender (Lavandula stoechas) *thrives in the free-draining conditions of alkaline soil.*

Instead, the leaves shrivel and fall, so to avoid disappointment it is better not to plant them in alkaline soil. However, *Sorbus sargentiana*, *Euonymus alatus* and *E. europaeus* will produce brilliant autumnal colour, even on poor soils over chalk.

Above: Bulbs are useful for spring colour. Here, massed tulips fill a border in late spring.

PLANTS THAT THRIVE IN
ALKALINE SOIL
Buddleja davidii
Clematis
Cotoneaster
Dianthus
Doronicum
Gypsophyla paniculata
Helianthemum nummularium
Helleborus
Lavandula
Paeonia
Pyracantha
Scabiosa
Syringa
Verbascum

Correcting Alkaline Conditions

Even though there is a wide range of plants that will tolerate high alkalinity, if you want an even richer diversity of species it will be necessary to improve the organic content of the soil. Adding copious quantities of bulky organic material, such as well-rotted farmyard manure, leaf mould, garden compost and turf, will improve moisture retention and the humus content of the soil. Incorporating organic matter is best done soon after a period of rain.

Adding dried blood and balanced artificial fertilizers can also help to improve the nutrient levels. Chalk soils tend to be lacking in potash, which must be applied for non-lime-loving plants to do well.

Sometimes, breaking up the top 60cm (24in) layer of underlying chalk with a fork or spade will help roots to develop more easily and give plants a good start.

Above: Adding well-rotted manure, garden compost or leaf mould will improve the soil structure and nutrient content.

Above: A prolific clematis scrambles over a wall. It thrives in alkaline conditions as long as its roots are protected from the sun.

31

SANDY SOIL

The low clay content in sandy soils (less than 8 per cent) makes them much less water-retentive than clay soils. Their particles are also larger than those of clay, making the soils light, free-draining and relatively infertile.

Sandy soils warm up quickly in spring, so planting out can start early, but they also cool down quickly.

Making the Best of a Sandy Soil

The easiest solution for coping with a sandy soil is to grow only drought-resistant plants that require few nutrients. Many of these originate in dry areas of low fertility, and you will find enough plants to create interesting displays without having to resort to wholesale enrichment of the soil.

Above: Brachyglottis *grows in sites that are too dry for many other plants, but it needs plenty of sunshine.*

Most plants that can cope with a sandy soil are deep-rooted, so that they can seek out moisture at low levels. Cacti and other succulents have fleshy leaves, stems or roots which can store water when it is available for use during dry periods.

Other plants have silvery-grey foliage to reflect sunlight or sparse, small, leathery or spiny leaves to reduce moisture loss through evaporation from the plant. Many of these plants are Mediterranean in origin.

Above: Drought-resistant plants such as thyme are perfect for growing in light sandy soil.

> ### MEDITERRANEAN PLANTS FOR SANDY SOIL
>
> *Brachyglottis*
> *Cistus*
> *Helianthemum*
> Lavender
> *Origanum*
> Rosemary
> Sage
> *Santolina*
> Thyme

Planning Displays

With foliage ranging from spiny yuccas to the soft feathery fronds of tamarisk, you can use all the different foliage shapes, textures and colours to good effect. Many spiny plants have architectural stature around which you can base your planting. Among these are the giant thistle (*Onopordum acanthium*) and the spiky-leaved, metallic-blue flowered *Eryngium*. *Echinops ritro* 'Veitch's Blue' has stunning blue, globular thistle flowers. Silver foliage perfectly sets off the mauve and soft hazy blue flowers that many of these plants produce. Red valerian (*Centranthus ruber*) also combines well with silvers and greys. Or you could try the yellow-green of spurges for an interesting effect.

Above: Black-eyed Susan (Rudbeckia) *enjoys free-draining conditions, but do not let the soil dry out completely.*

Above: Yellow-green spurges make an interesting contrast with the silver of Elaeagnus *'Quicksilver' and a deadnettle.*

Grasses such as blue fescue (*Festuca glauca*) will add shape and movement. Allow sun-loving ground-covering plants such as *Nepeta* and rock roses to spill over from a border onto paths. In more shaded border edges encourage woodland plants.

Cornfield annuals, which grow on a wide range of soils, are useful for filling in blocks of colour. To create a meadow-like planting, which can be left semi-wild, sow seed in spring or autumn with a good mix of other wild flowers and grasses.

> **SUMMER ANNUALS FOR SANDY SOIL**
>
> *Calendula officinalis*
> *Centaurea cyanus*
> *Eschscholzia californica*
> *Gypsophila*
> *Lobularia maritima*
> *Papaver rheas* Shirley Series
> *Rudbeckia hirta*
> *Silene alpestris*

Year-round Interest

Sea buckthorn provides year-round value. It has narrow silvery leaves and tiny yellow spring flowers, which on female plants are followed in autumn by abundant orange berries. In winter, when many other plants have died, the buckthorn's shapely stems continue to provide interest.

From spring to autumn, silvery foliage provides a perfect backcloth for the bright colours of nearly all the popular summer annuals. Among the perennials, the tall spires of *Acanthus spinosus* carry white flowers and purple bracts from late spring to midsummer, red valerian blooms from late spring to the end of summer and yellow, pink or white achilleas last all summer long.

Spiny herbaceous plants like thistles, *Eryngium* and *Echinops* can be left standing after they have finished flowering, so that their intricate outlines will continue adding interest.

Above: Eryngium giganteum *thrives in the poorest of soils, as long as they are well drained and in full sun.*

On acid soils, heather flowers in pinks and white from midsummer to autumn. Its foliage comes in many shades of green or golden yellow and often changes colour in winter quite dramatically. Some varieties of heather flower in winter or spring, and these can tolerate alkaline soils.

Above: Like other heathers, crimson-flowered Calluna vulgaris *'Darkness' enjoys sandy soil as long as it is acid.*

PLANTS THAT PREFER SANDY SOIL

Acanthus spinosus
Achillea
Calluna vulgaris
Centranthus ruber
Cistus
Echinops ritro 'Veitch's Blue'
Erica
Eryngium giganteum
Euphorbia
Festuca glauca
Lavatera
Nepeta x *faassenii*
Onopordum acanthium
Papaver orientale
Phormium
Tamarix
Yucca gloriosa

Improving Sandy Soil

Adding plenty of organic matter, such as well-rotted manure, garden compost or leaf mould, will improve sandy soil. Many ornamental garden plants, however, will still need frequent and thorough watering during dry periods, and regular applications of fertilizer to increase the nutrient levels.

Creating Sandy Conditions

You may wish to grow some plants that thrive on sandy soil but find that your soil is too wet, heavy and fertile. In this case, you can create a dry sandy or gravelly garden. It does not need to be very large, but would provide the ideal spot for displaying some attractive plants.

> **GARDENER'S TIP**
>
> Heather (*Calluna vulgaris*) makes an excellent ground cover for sandy soil that is also acid. The many cultivars allow you to create a permanent carpet in a choice of shades that change according to the season.

Creating an arid-planting area will involve scraping away some of the topsoil to reduce fertility. Mix in enough sharp sand and gravel to improve drainage and create the sort of conditions you need. Adding areas of gravel or pebbles on the surface will add to the impression of a dry landscape.

If drainage is very poor, consider introducing some drainage channels filled with gravel to take away excess water fast.

Above: Potentillas are perfect plants for poor, free-draining soils. Alpine types prefer a gritty, sharply draining soil.

Above: Evening primrose and daisy-like feverfew both enjoy a sunny position on sandy soil.

35

Left: Yellow-flowering Berberis linearifolia *will thrive in most soils, but will benefit from improved drainage on very heavy ones.*

growth, making them very fertile. Plants growing in clay soil suffer less from the effects of drought in all but the driest of summers.

Clay soils can be acid, neutral or alkaline, which will also affect your choice of plants. Generally, however, the clay content of soil is a more important factor than its acidity or alkalinity in determining which plants will do well.

CLAY SOIL

This type of soil will consist of more than 25 per cent clay particles, which makes it moisture-retentive, heavy and sticky. It may become waterlogged in wet weather, is slow to warm up in spring, and may bake hard in summer.

Really heavy, sticky clay soils are unworkable when wet and easily compacted and must not be walked on.

Due to their moisture retention, however, clay soils also hold on to nutrients that plants need for healthy

Making the Best of Clay Soil

Grow plants with a vigorous constitution, as those are the ones likely to do best. Plants need to be resilient enough to withstand wet soil in winter

Above: Pyracantha makes an impenetrable barrier when grown as an informal garden hedge.

GARDENER'S TIP

Physically working clay soil is largely a matter of timing. If you try to do it when it is too wet it will form an impenetrable layer at the depth you dig down to, for plant roots and draining water alike. Leave it until it is too dry and you will be working with what feels like lumps of rock.

Left: The delightfully scented Rosa *'Zéphirine Drouhin' is thornless and is an excellent climber.*

without rotting. But in the summer, they can take advantage of the soil's moisture-retaining properties, even when the surface is baked hard.

Planning Displays

Several resilient shrubs grow well on clay. Choose those that offer spring or summer flowers, autumn foliage or berries, or attractive coloured stems for the winter months.

Roses, too, are more tolerant of clay than many plants, and in a border that has been well prepared and enriched you can achieve a more or less traditional scheme with roses and herbaceous underplanting.

Generally, those reliable herbaceous perennials that tolerate a heavy clay soil are also plants that grow well in moist marginal, waterside plantings, such as *Astilbe, Mimulus, Phormium, Hosta, Houttuynia, Lysimachia, Gunnera* and *Rodgersia*. These provide plenty of striking architectural foliage and some arresting blooms.

It is possible to grow some bulbs in clay soil, but they will not survive if the soil becomes waterlogged during wet periods. Planting them on a layer of grit will help.

SHRUBS FOR CLAY SOIL

Berberis
Cornus
Cotoneaster
Crataegus
Philadelphus
Pyracantha
Viburnum opulus

Above: Hostas thrive in moist soils, and in time they will spread to form a large, domed clump.

Left: Berberis is a good shrub to plant if you have a small garden and want year-round colour.

mock orange. *Berberis* produces bright yellow flowers in spring, and berries in autumn, adding to the colourful yellow, orange or red berries of *Cotoneaster* and *Pyracantha*. Guelder rose also has fleshy red berries and crabs have their apples.

In winter the coloured stems of dogwood and the contorted twigs of *Salix babylonica* var. *pekinensis* 'Tortuosa' are visually arresting. Small willows are covered with silver catkins if you cut them back hard each spring to produce masses of new growth.

Year-round Interest

As there is such a variety of plants that you can grow on all but the heaviest of clay soils, planting for interest through the year should not be a problem.

Small trees and shrubs have much to offer. The blossom of cherries, crab apples and hawthorn in spring is followed by that of guelder rose and

Above: The white flowers of Crambe cordifolia *create an ethereal haze when planted in a large group.*

PLANTS THAT THRIVE ON
CLAY SOIL

Astilbe
Caltha palustris
Crambe cordifolia
Gunnera manicata
Hosta
Papaver somniferum
Philadelphus
Primula vulgaris
Rheum
Rodgersia
Rosa
Trollius

Large-growing leafy perennials like *Gunnera*, *Rheum*, the giant thistles and *Crambe cordifolia* grow especially well on clay, usually to dramatic proportions.

Among flowering perennials yellow primroses and cowslips are soon followed by meadow flowers such as burnets and cranesbills. A host of summer flowers includes hollyhocks, *Mimulus*, *Phlox* and foxgloves.

Improving Clay Soil

The best way to improve clay soil is to add plenty of organic matter in early autumn or late spring, when the soil is workable. This will open up the soil and make it more balanced, allowing

Above: Roses like the moist fertility of clay soils, particularly when plenty of organic matter is added.

nutrients and moisture to be readily absorbed by plant roots. It will also improve drainage and make the soil more workable when digging is required. Applications of fertilizer will also be more effective.

Where waterlogged soil is a problem, you can try growing bog-loving plants, or improve the drainage – either by digging in grit or, more expensively, installing drainage channels filled with shingle.

Clay soils can be quite acid, especially when they are waterlogged and moss grows on the surface. If you are making a new border it may be worth altering the pH level. You can do this by adding lime as described in the section on Acid Soils.

Above: Primroses (Primula vulgaris) *are ideal for a cottage garden or mossy bank, as long as the soil remains moist.*

Planting in Different Locations

THE ASPECT OF A PLOT, THE AMOUNT OF SHELTER IT HAS, THE DEGREE OF SHADE OR SUN IT RECEIVES AND THE MOISTURE CONTENT OF THE SOIL ARE ALL RELEVANT WHEN CHOOSING PLANTS THAT WILL THRIVE OVER A LONG PERIOD.

ASPECT

The direction your garden or border faces and its relationship to your house or adjacent buildings will influence the environment your plants will be growing in. As the sun moves around the house, different areas of the garden can be thrown into shade or receive the full glare of the sun for various amounts of time. Shade can be full, partial or dappled. In winter a deeply shaded position can be very damp and cold, whereas in summer it can be pleasant. The sun can at times be far too hot in summer, but of great benefit during short cold days. And as the seasons change, your garden may be subjected to frost and bitter winds.

Above: Clematis montana *will grow happily on an east-facing wall which gives it some protection.*

All these factors should be considered before planting, as they will have a bearing on which plants will do well in different parts of the garden.

Heavily Shaded Gardens

Some gardens may have shade from the house for long stretches of the day. In winter deep shade will make the garden cold and damp. The winter cold will be aggravated if the garden is also exposed to strong, cold winds, so a sheltering hedge may help, but in spite of these disadvantages, there are plants that not only tolerate these conditions but actually prefer them.

Above: Sweet-smelling Mexican orange-blossom (Choisya ternata) *can survive conditions in a shaded, cold garden.*

East-facing Gardens

An east wind in winter is the cruellest and when combined with a frost can spell instant death to plants that are less than hardy, and will nip tender buds. As with a shaded garden, a fence or hedge on the boundary will give some protection. However, a garden with a predominantly easterly aspect has the benefit of morning and early afternoon sun.

Gardens in Full Sun

The most sought-after aspect for most gardeners is a sunny one. With a house providing shelter against cold winds and a garden that takes full advantage of the sun's warming rays throughout the year it seems like an ideal location. At the height of summer, however, the sun can be relentlessly hot and glaring and will quickly dry out thin soil.

Some form of shading, perhaps attractive fences, screens of climbers, tall shrubs or small trees will be welcomed by many plants, as well as humans.

Sunny gardens are ideal for growing hot-climate and sun-loving plants, and exotic tender and half-hardy plants will thrive and even last well into the autumn if the garden is protected from wind.

West-facing Gardens

These gardens are likely to have some shade through the mornings, until the sun swings round at its highest point. But they then benefit for the rest of the day and in summer this can be quite late, when the low rays intensify colours. These are also warm gardens, unless they catch some of the colder winds, so you will need to assess whether some protection is needed.

Above: Blue Agapanthus *share a sunny border with vibrantly coloured summer bulbs such as lilies and* Crocosmia.

PLANTS FOR HEAVILY SHADED POSITIONS

Berberis x *stenophylla*
Camellia japonica
Clematis alpina
Choisya ternata
Garrya elliptica
Hydrangea petiolaris
Ilex corallina
Jasminum nudiflorum
Mahonia japonica

PLANTS FOR EAST-FACING POSITIONS

Bergenia cordifolia
Chaenomeles x *superba*
Cotoneaster horizontalis
Euphorbia griffithii
Hamamelis mollis
Helleborus feotidus
Lonicera periclymenum
Rosa rugosa
Vinca major

PLANTS FOR SUNNY POSITIONS

Agapanthus
Canna indica
Eccremocarpus scaber
Echinacea purpurea
Echinops ritro
Helenium
Kniphofia
Lilium lancifolium
Osteospermum
Yucca filamentosa
Zauschneria californica

PLANTS FOR WEST-FACING POSITIONS

Ceanothus
Crocosmia cultivars
Geranium 'Johnson's Blue'
Humulus lupulus 'Aureus'
Papaver orientale
Penstemon cultivars
Vitis coignetiae

Selecting Suitable Plants for Different Aspects

Before growing any new plants in your garden it is wise to establish that they will be suitable for the situation you intend them to occupy. A good local nursery will give advice on the best plants for your locality and particular situation.

Make sure, also, that you select a few plants to give some colour or interest for each season. Even if your garden faces predominantly east or is shady and cold, there should be several plants that will give pleasure even in the depths of winter.

Above: *A smoke bush* (Cotinus) *has been planted so that the evening sun shines through its purple foliage.*

WINDY SITES

Gusting wind can spoil plants in exposed areas. Light plants are at risk of being blown over. Plants with soft, tender foliage are likely to be scorched by the wind resulting in brown, withered leaves and poor growth.

Creating a windbreak will minimize the problem. One that is partly permeable to the wind is much more effective than a solid one, which can cause localized turbulence where the wind is deflected. Black windbreak netting is efficient but unsightly; depending on where you want to put it you could disguise it with trellis. A trellis clothed with climbers would slow down much of the wind, even without netting. Where there is sufficient room, a

Above: Spiraea japonica *is a tough shrub that can withstand strong wind. This one is 'Goldflame'.*

screen of tall, wind-tolerant shrubs planted along the most vulnerable side will be very effective. Many plants will tolerate this kind of exposure while providing colour and interest throughout the year. A broken windbreak would allow a good view to continue to be appreciated.

Staking vulnerable plants will also help protect them in windy areas.

Above: Helleborus orientalis *tolerates most conditions but needs shelter from strong, cold winds.*

WIND-TOLERANT PLANTS

Cornus alba 'Aurea'
Cotinus coggygria
Euonymus fortunei cultivars
Hamamelis virginiana
Hippophäe rhamnoides
Hydrangea paniculata
'Grandiflora'
Lavatera olbia
Lonicera pileata
Mahonia aquifolium
Philadelphus 'Belle Etoile'
Spiraea japonica
Tamarix tetrandra
Taxus baccata
Thuja occidentalis

SHADY MOIST SITES

Some people might regard the presence of a permanently shaded damp patch in their garden as a real problem, because many plants cannot cope with dark, wet conditions. Most bulbs, for instance, dislike very wet soil and will simply rot if waterlogged. Many ordinary garden plants will also die in persistently wet conditions.

It is these very conditions, however, that account for the lush and often large foliage of moisture-loving plants. Big leaves are nature's way of ensuring that the maximum amount of chlorophyll is exposed to the limited light to help photosynthesis (food manufacture) by the plant.

Above: Many plants and shrub thrive in shady gardens – choose appropriately for your soil type.

Above: Grow lily-of-the-valley (Convallaria majalis) *in full or partial shade in a moist location.*

Making the Best of a Shady Moist Site

The best way of coping with the area is to stop regarding it as a problem and see it as a wonderful opportunity for growing some lovely plants that would be unhappy in a drier situation.

Wetland plants have distinct preferences for the different types of wet site, so you need to match the plants to the conditions of your site. Most simply prefer permanently moist soil. Some plants can cope with particularly wet sites that are virtually permanently boggy and occasionally waterlogged. Similarly, some plants can grow in dappled or deep shade. Some, of course, can cope with all types of shade.

Above: A dense planting of different types of hosta keeps weeds at bay in a moist shady border.

Planning Displays

Make the most of the great variety of luxuriant foliage produced by shade- and moisture-loving plants. You can contrast the different types, colours and forms of foliage to make an interesting green tapestry of leaves. For example, place tall, strappy irises next to soft feathery ferns or the big pleated leaves of *Veratrum*.

If you work with a wide selection of different foliage forms and colours, you can create a planting that has as much interest as a colourful sunny flower border. And if you include a few evergreen shrubs as well, such as aucubas, skimmias, mahonias and fatsias, the display will last throughout the growing season, and into winter. All these shrubs have the added bonus of beautiful spring flowers, many of which are followed by colourful fruits. For foliage at ground level be sure to include hostas, bergenias and ivies.

Make the most of those perennial plants that flower in moist shade by placing them as occasional colourful highlights against the lush green foliage. The yellow spires of *Ligularia*, for instance, show up splendidly against a green backdrop. Where the planting edges are in dappled or partial shade, you have the opportunity to include more brightly coloured woodland plants than would grow in the darker shade.

Above: Delicate yellow flowers of Alchemilla mollis *contrast with lacy fern fronds in a shady damp corner.*

45

Left: Winter aconites (Eranthis hyemalis) *come through the soil before much else is stirring on the woodland floor.*

Woodland plants provide some real treasures in spring: winter aconites, primroses, snowdrops, snake's-head fritillaries and wake robin followed by lily-of-the-valley and wood anemones. Dicentras produce arching sprays of pendulous pink or white flowers.

Summer highlights are provided by many shade-loving perennials such as delicate *Astilbe, Astrantia major* and *Ligularia. Meconopsis cambrica, Impatiens* and pansies have long-flowering seasons. Rodgersia flowers in pinks, reds and white. The blues of monkshood (*Aconitum*) are useful from midsummer to autumn.

Helleborus niger and *H. orientale* produce white or greenish cream blooms through winter to spring. Witch hazels and sarcococcas also produce fragrant flowers in winter, in yellow and white respectively.

Year-round Interest

Even in a shady, damp spot you can guarantee some colour and interest for every season.

Aucubas have glossy green leaves and bear small red-purple flowers in mid-spring, which on female plants are followed by bright red berries in autumn. Variegated leaf forms are better in dappled shade. The scented spring flowers of skimmias are pink in bud opening to creamy white and followed by green berries usually ripening to red. The yellowish-green autumn flowers of mature ivies are followed by small black fruit, which are a good source of food for birds.

For dappled shade *Fatsia japonica* has big, glossy hand-shaped leaves. In partial shade evergreen mahonias have scented yellow spring flowers followed by blue to black berries. Rhododendrons and camellias both have showy spring blooms. *Viburnum davidii* bears tiny white flowers at this time, and on female plants these give way to turquoise fruits.

Above: The delightful flowers of Astrantia major *brighten up lightly shaded corners in summer.*

Creating Shady Damp Conditions

Even if your garden is not naturally wet, you can take advantage of a shady area to create a damp spot. Dig out a hollow, line it with black butyl liner with some drainage holes punched through, then return the soil, mixed with plenty of organic matter.

The liner will act like a layer of natural clay, helping to hold the moisture in the soil and reducing the need for watering.

However, if you do create an artificially moist site, you will have to be prepared to keep the soil moist by watering in periods of drought.

Above: *The delicate flowers of* Dicentra *thrive in a partially shaded border. They prefer neutral to alkaline soil.*

PLANTS THAT THRIVE IN
MOIST SHADE

Astilbe hybrids
Astrantia
Dicentra
Eranthis hyemalis
Fatsia japonica
Hamamelis mollis
Helleborus
Hosta
Rhododendron
Rodgersia
Sarcococca
Viburnum davidii

Above: *Rodgersias enjoy a waterside location. They grow in full sun as well as partial shade, rather than full shade.*

SUNNY MOIST SITES

Areas around natural ponds and streams can be damp or wet, and they tend to be open and sunny. The margins of a pond are waterlogged, which means that only plants adapted to have their roots permanently or seasonally in water will survive there. The dampness of the soil decreases the further away from the pond it is. A different range of plants are adapted to each level of dampness, and there is no shortage of plants that love these type of conditions.

Making the Best of a Sunny Moist Site

The moist areas around a pond or along a stream are the ideal place to create a lush garden. Wetland foliage plants tend to be vigorous, often

PLANTS FOR SUNNY
MOIST SITES

Caltha palustris
Cornus alba
Darmera peltata
Filipendula
Gunnera
Iris sibirica
Ligularia
Lysimachia nummularia 'Aurea'
Lysichiton
Primula bullyeana
Primula denticulata
Rheum
Ranunculus ficaria
Rodgersia
Trollius
Salix
Zantedeschia aethiopica

growing to giant proportions in summer. Even in lower temperatures all the foliage plants seem to double in size daily. This is splendid for large areas, but if you only have a small site you may have to forgo the large plants and use smaller ones instead.

The water's edge provides the opportunity for growing some exquisitely flowered marginal plants. The plants must be able to cope with extremely wet conditions, and at certain times of the year to grow in water. Marginal plants create a perfect transition between the exuberant foliage on firm land and the special qualities of water.

Left: Gunnera manicata *produces some of the largest leaves seen in gardens, up to 2m (6ft) long on stalks that can be 2.5m (8ft) long.*

Planning Displays

A sunny damp garden or area is an excellent opportunity to grow some exciting large perennial foliage plants such as gunneras, rodgersias and rheums, which also thrive in more shady conditions, but they need plenty of space. In a small area, you can still create an impressive effect with the lush foliage of hostas, with the added bonus of their delicate flowers in summer. Ligularias, irises and astilbes also flower well in these conditions.

Position the tallest plants either at the rear or in the centre of a moist plot, where they will not hide smaller plants. Smaller growing plants can then be planted in front of them.

Plenty of smaller perennials bear delicate, exquisitely coloured blooms above their lush, spreading foliage.

Above: The red, jagged foliage of the ornamental rhubarb, Rheum *'Ace of Hearts', is spectacular.*

The bright yellows of marsh marigolds, lesser celandines and globe-flowers are counter-balanced by the hazy blues of water forget-me-nots, purple loosestrife and creamy meadowsweet creating a country cottage effect. Many primulas come in an exciting range of colours and are invaluable for smaller settings. Once established they will spread quickly.

For permanent structure, dwarf Japanese maples and small weeping willows work well. Many have stunning autumn foliage, and some also have colourful bark that looks good in winter. Avoid larger willows as these would soon grow to a huge size, and their roots are extensive.

*Above: Creeping Jenny (*Lysimachia nummularia *'Aurea') works well as a ground cover, as long as all perennial weeds have been removed first.*

49

Year-round Interest

With large lush foliage and flower stems reaching for the sky, plants that thrive in the damp, sunny site make a dense and luxuriant effect from spring through to late autumn. Spring and early summer are perhaps the very best seasons, but careful inclusion of certain plants will guarantee colour later on as well.

Flower colour is available from spring to autumn, starting with the golden-yellow flowers of the marsh marigolds. *Lysichiton americanum* produces bright yellow flowers in spring. Purple drumstick primulas (*Primula denticulata*) flower in late spring, and *P. bulleyana* contributes hot colours in early summer, followed by the arum lily with its elegant white blooms.

Above: In a moist corner under dappled shade, primulas, forget-me-nots, columbines and bluebells celebrate the arrival of spring.

Above: The arum lily (Zantedeschia aethiopica) *is perfect for a waterside planting. It will also grow in shallow water.*

Perennial foliage plants last from spring to summer, but the giant leaves of *Darmera peltata* will turn red in autumn before they disappear. This plant also bears white to bright pink flowers on 2m (6ft) long stems in late spring. Do include rodgersias: their leaves turn bronze and red in autumn and their white or pink fluffy flowers are followed by dark red fruits.

Evergreen foliage plants provide year-round interest. Include *Bergenia* for edging and enjoy the added bonus of their pink blooms early in the year.

For a splash of winter colour, the bare red stems of *Cornus alba* cannot be beaten. Cut these hard back every spring to guarantee plenty of new stems. Different cultivars have variously coloured autumn leaves.

Maintaining Sunny Moist Conditions

The foliage of the vigorous plants makes excellent ground cover, which helps to conserve moisture. But even a naturally moist area may dry out during hot dry summers, as do many natural watercourses. You may need to water the area to maintain the moistness that the plants require.

Avoid planting tall trees that could eventually overshadow the site. If nearby plants threaten to encroach the area, you will have to prune them carefully to maintain their distance.

Creating a Moist Area

If you want to grow moisture-loving plants but you don't have a suitable site, you can create a damp patch quite easily by digging out soil to make a

Above: This lush summer border has been planted with a delightful combination of fresh yellows and greens.

hollow and lining it with butyl pond liner. Mix plenty of organic matter into the soil and return it to the hollow.

If you are making a pond, it is a good idea to run the liner under the soil some way from the margin of the pond in order to create a damp area. Garden ponds do not have to be large, and even a 1 x 1m (3 x 3ft) pond, with a butyl liner, will provide the correct environment for a good selection of water-loving plants. If you make the pond with more than one level, with a gradual slope towards the edge, you can grow a wide range of aquatic and marginal plants, as well as attracting a host of wildlife.

Left: The fresh, bright colours of these marginal plants create an attractive naturalistic arrangement.

SUNNY DRY SITES

Most gardens have patches where there is less moisture than elsewhere. "Rain shadows" caused by buildings or other structures, shallow or rocky soil, or disturbed sandy or gravelly subsoil can all cause dry conditions. Any of these situations combined with full sun will render any attempts to wet the soil artificially unsuccessful. Sunny gardens or borders set against a wall or next to a patio are particularly likely to be hot and dry.

On the positive side, dry soils are quick to warm up in spring, allowing you to plant out earlier than in many other sites. But you will need to keep young plants well watered.

Above: Rosemary does particularly well in a dry, sunny location as it is native to the Mediterranean.

Making the Best of a Sunny Site

A sunny dry site does not need to be a problem if you select plants that appreciate such an environment. Mediterranean plants are an obvious choice. Lavender, rosemary, sage, salvia, santolina, rock roses (*Cistus*), helichrysum and marigolds are just some of the plants that like a position in full sun and dry soil.

These plants have evolved and adapted to cope with high temperatures, low rainfall and often with poor soil. These adaptations, which include silvery, downy and sometimes succulent foliage, are often what make the plants so attractive and useful in displays for the inside as well as outside.

Above: The evergreen leaves of sage provide fragrance all year round, and they are useful in the kitchen.

Above: Geranium *'Johnson's Blue'* produces masses of veined purple-blue flowers during the summer.

Planning Displays

A dry planting in full sun works particularly well if it is planned with a feel for a naturally dry landscape. You can even create a dry-gravel river bed effect that will set off the drought-resistant plants beautifully. Group the plants together to make islands of flowing colour rising out of the gravel. Decide where the architectural plants will go first, then fill in with smaller plants, to make pleasing associations.

Try to blend or contrast flower colours with the foliage. Silver and grey associate well with the purples, blues and mauves that are so common among Mediterranean plants. For contrast with the silvers try the darker green foliage of rock roses. Or use the very hot colours sparingly as eye-catchers.

Be sure to include some aromatic plants that will release their fragrances in hot sun. Mediterranean herbs are highly fragrant. Plant them where you will brush against the leaves as you walk past to release their heady aromas.

You can include grasses, too. They grow in mounds, create interesting backgrounds for borders and add movement and sound as their leaves rustle in a breeze. If you combine a variety of species you can create a stunning effect of shape, texture and colour.

Above: Grasses add form, colour and movement to a display, and they are easy to manage.

53

Year-round Interest

When deciding which plants to use, plan for a succession of interest, with foliage, flowers and then seedheads. Grasses are invaluable, providing interest for most of the year; from summer onwards their tall flowerheads will move gently in the wind.

Year-round foliage plants include spurges, especially *Euphorbia characias* and *E. myrsinites*, which have succulent grey-green or blue-green leaves respectively and flowers with yellow-green bracts from spring to early or midsummer. Rosemary can be grown through mild winters.

Spring is something of a famine for arid-area flowers, but some crocuses, especially the hybrids, prefer well-drained and poor soil conditions, so are worth trying, as are tulips later in the season. *Convulvus cneorum*, a leafy silvery-green evergreen, bears its funnel-shaped white flowers from late spring to summer.

For summer colour there is a wide choice. Cranesbills flower prolifically. *Lavatera* 'Barnsley' has masses of funnel-shaped white flowers ageing to soft pink throughout summer, up to 2m (6ft) high. Some types of allium do well in dry areas, and they flower profusely in summer in shades of pink, purple and white.

From late summer to early autumn, the blue and purple-blue flowers of the shrub *Caryopteris clandonensis* show prettily against its grey-green leaves. Sedums flower at this time, too, in bright pinks and ruby-reds, and are irresistible to bees.

Leave interesting seedheads after flowering to prolong the plant's features. Grey cardoons for instance develop large heads after their thistle-like, purple summer flowers are faded.

Left: The graceful plumes of Cortaderia selloana *last through the winter. The plant looks best in a prime position where it can be seen in its full glory. Cut down completely when the fronds are past their best in early spring to encourage fresh growth.*

Improving a Sunny Dry Site

Although it is usually best to accept the existing conditions and grow drought-tolerant plants, you can take some measures to increase moisture and nutrient levels in the soil. Adding garden compost or leaf mould in the autumn will help.

A mulch such as composted bark in summer will reduce evaporation and suppress weeds, or you can use a permanent mulch of gravel or pebbles, which also provide a beautiful backdrop for the plants.

Creating a Dry Planting Area

It is possible to create a dry area where you can display and enjoy plants from hot, arid areas. Choose a site that receives plenty of sunlight, and preferably one that is sheltered. You will need to scrape away some of the topsoil and use it elsewhere. In wet

Above: Massing plants together can create a lush effect in a hot, dry courtyard.

climates, digging in channels of grit will improve the drainage, allowing the soil to dry out more quickly than it normally would.

A sunny patio with planting spaces between the paving stones is an ideal setting as the area will retain heat well, especially if close to the house. Or you could build a raised bed and fill it with a fast-draining mix that could include gravel or grit.

Above: The round heads of Allium christophii *appear in early summer. Here, they are accompanied by longer flowering* Linaria purpurea.

PLANTS THAT THRIVE IN
A SUNNY DRY SITE

Brachyglottis (syn. *Senecio*)
Calendula
Caryopteris clandonensis
Echinops ritro
Eryngium bourgatii
Euphorbia
Geranium
Helichrysum
Iris germanica hybrids
Kniphofia hybrids
Lavandula
Lavatera
Santolina chamaecyparissus
Sedum

Above: Ivy grows well in dry shady sites, particularly against a wall, but the variegated types do like some sun.

SHADY DRY SITES

Areas beneath a tree canopy or under a wall, fence or hedge often lack moisture. Trees take up an enormous amount of water from the soil, often leaving it dry. Walls and fences can interrupt driving rain, making one side drier than the other. Hedges combine both these drawbacks by interrupting rainfall and taking up moisture from the surrounding ground.

Shade can be deep, with no sun at all, or it can be partial, with some sunlight falling on the site at certain times of day. Dappled shade occurs when sunlight is filtered by leaves and branches. Some shade plants prefer particular types of shade, others can cope with a range.

Making the Best of a Shady Dry Site

This is one of the most difficult sites to contend with, but a few well chosen plants can transform even the most unpromising of areas. Most plants that cope well with dry shade are those that naturally grow in the shadow of other vegetation.

Busy Lizzies are among the very few flowering annuals that will survive in shade, but they do prefer to be kept moist if possible. Many plants that are more naturally found growing in moist shade will tolerate dry shade conditions. These include foxgloves, *Aquilegia*, hellebores and the tall *Acanthus mollis*.

Ivies cope extremely well with dry shade, including deep shade. There are many varieties, with a whole range of different leaf formations that will grow in even the deepest shade. Variegated ivies require some light to colour well.

Above: The spurred violet, blue, pink or white flowers of granny's bonnet (Aquilegia) *will tolerate a dry shady site.*

Planning Displays

Heavily shaded areas will not support a bright array of flowering plants, so dry shade plantings have to rely heavily on structure and foliage. Various evergreen shrubs, such as skimmias, hollies and mahonias, can cope with a certain amount of dryness in the soil. Aucubas are invaluable for deep shade, but the variegated varieties, with beautifully yellow-mottled leaves, prefer partial shade.

Above: Geranium macrorrhizum *produces abundant flowers even in shade, and will spread to cover a large area.*

Try to create contrasts in leaf colour, texture and shape. The glossy prickly leaves of hollies and mahonias, for instance, can be placed against the smooth-edged leaves of other plants. *Iris foetidissima* has long strappy leaves and seems happy in the darkest of spots.

Ivies are unbeatable for clothing fences and walls in a variety of leaf shapes and colours. They can also be used for ground cover, as can periwinkles. Epimediums can also be grown as ground cover under trees and shrubs, where their dainty yellow, white, pink, red or purple flowers provide welcome colour.

In lightly shaded areas, resilient perennials such as monkshood, sweet violet, and some of the cranesbills are good for providing patches of colour against the green foliage.

Above: A shady area with dappled light is the romantic setting for this combination of foliage plants.

> **GARDENER'S TIP**
>
> Dry shady sites are the most difficult to bring bright colour into. One solution is to introduce containers of seasonal plants in flower. These will have benefited from growing in better conditions and will be able to survive a few weeks of gloom. When they finish flowering return them to a brighter situation to recover.

57

Year-round Interest

Plantings in shade rely heavily on ever-green foliage plants for interest, but a number of these also produce flowers, as do many of the foliage perennials.

The yellow spring flowers of mahonias make a wonderful contrast with their glossy green foliage, and some have the bonus of being scented. Many perennials also flower in spring providing earlier colour. Pink flowers brighten up bergenias, and *Brunnera macrophylla* has blue forget-me-not-like flowers. Where it is not too dry epimediums provide a wide range of colour from spring to early summer. Periwinkles will be scattered with a carpet of violet-blue from spring to autumn.

As summer approaches, more perennial flowers appear. *Anemone x*

Above: Helleborus foetidus *prefers a site with dappled shade and a neutral to alkaline soil.*

Above: The bright berries of a small skimmia planted among bluebells create a startling contrast.

hybrida has pink or white flowers in late summer and autumn, which is when *Liriope muscari* produces spikes packed with blue, bead-like flowers, while monkshood supports spires of blue flowers.

Autumn is the time for a superb display of berries, which can appear on aucuba and hollies, both bright red. Some skimmias bear red, black or white berries after their dainty white flowers. The large seed capsules of *Iris foetidissima* split open at this time of year to display yellow seeds. Through winter and early spring hardy cyclamen planted under trees produce their bright pink flowers and often patterned leaves. *Helleborus foetidus* has nodding bell-shaped green flowers. The scented blue or white flowers of sweet violet see winter out.

Above: Carpet-forming Anemone blanda *will tolerate partial shade. Its flowers appear in spring.*

Improving Shady Dry Conditions

You can alter the level of shade in parts of the garden. If you have a large tree, for example, removing the lower branches allows more light to reach the ground beneath. The branches in the main canopy can also be thinned to create a dappled light. In a dark, sunless area, a fence or wall opposite the site can be painted white to reflect the available light towards the shaded bed or border.

Artificially watering a dry site will help to moisten it, but to maximize the effect, improve the soil by mixing in plenty of organic matter. Adding a mulch to the surface will impede evaporation. Many shade-loving perennials are naturally woodland plants, and so need a woodland-like soil. This should be high in organic matter.

An alternative approach, easier than trying to change the conditions, is to bring in containers temporarily, with flowering or brightly variegated plants to add interest and colour.

PLANTS THAT TOLERATE DRY SHADE

Aconitum
Anemone x hybrida
Aquilegia
Aucuba japonica
Bergenia
Digitalis purpurea
Helleborus foetidus
Epimedium
Euphorbia
Hedera
Iris foetidissima
Liriope muscari
Mahonia
Skimmia
Vinca

Above: Imported potted plants can bring temporary colour to dry and shady parts of the garden. They can be returned to more suitable areas to recover.

AIRBORNE POLLUTION

Pollution can be a problem for plants in busy urban areas, especially in small front gardens. Deposits from vehicle exhausts settle on foliage throughout the year, and if the road is salted in winter the salt is splashed by cars on to the nearest plants as the traffic passes. Some plants are more tolerant of airborne pollution than others so it is worth knowing which these are if you live near a road, where traffic is constantly streaming past or snarled up in slow-moving jams.

The solution may be as simple as a hedge of plants that can tolerate this kind of treatment along the most vulnerable part of the garden. Such a

Above: Olearia x haastii *will produce a mass of snowy white blossoms, even in a polluted atmosphere.*

Above: Privet *(*Ligustrum lucidum *'Excelsum Superbum') makes a colourful and useful hedge beside a busy road to act as a barrier that will protect the garden.*

barrier would protect more delicate species behind it. Good hedging plants are *Berberis, Cotoneaster,* holly and privet. But if a hedge is not practical, you may need to concentrate on growing plants that are tolerant of these unfavourable conditions.

Pollution-tolerant Plants with Year-round Interest

A number of pollution-resistant evergreen and deciduous shrubs provide flowers and interesting foliage for the whole year.

Many of the evergreen shrubs have handsome glossy, leathery, dark green leaves, but there are also variegated varieties such as the spotted laurel to

Above: *Silver-leaved* Elaeagnus *'Quicksilver' provides year-round colour and is a useful windbreak.*

PLANTS THAT TOLERATE
POLLUTED AIR

Aucuba japonica
Aquilegia vulgaris
Berberis
Bergenia cordifolia
Cotoneaster
Elaeagnus
Fatsia japonica
Forsythia
Garrya elliptica
Geranium endressii
Helleborus niger
Helleborus orientalis
Hemerocallis
Hosta
Ilex aquifolium
Iris
Lamium
Ligustrum
Olearia x *haastii*
Philadelphus
Pulmonaria
Rudbeckia
Symphytum
Viburnum
Weigela florida

provide extra interest. Some of the deciduous shrubs, including many of the viburnums, end their year with a flourish of vivid autumn colour. Many also produce beautiful spring, summer or even autumn flowers; the summer flowers of *Philadelphus* are delightfully fragrant. For autumn and winter, holly berries are hard to beat and from midwinter to early spring pretty catkins hang from the branches of garryas, which also make useful and effective windbreaks.

The great variety of cotoneasters makes them especially useful as ground cover, for growing up walls or hedging. Different types will bear white to deep pink flowers from spring to summer, most with autumn berries.

In addition to shrubs, there are some virtually indestructible perennials, such as *Bergenia* and *Pulmonaria*.

Above: *Perennial lungwort* (Pulmonaria) *makes good ground cover in shade and can withstand the effects of car fumes.*

61

Planning with Plants

USE THIS LIST OF PLANTS DESCRIBING THEIR IDEAL CONDITIONS AND SEASON OF INTEREST TO PLAN YOUR GARDEN DESIGN.

Plants	Sow	Plant Out	Season of Interest
Acanthus spinosus (s, d)	spring	autumn	spring to midsummer
Acer (s, m)	n/a	autumn	autumn foliage
Achillea (s, d, m)	spring, in situ	n/a	summer, autumn
Aconitum (ps, s, m)	spring	autumn, spring	summer
Alcea rosea (s, d)	summer, in situ	n/a	early to midsummer
Alchemilla (s, ps, d, m)	spring	early summer	summer
Allium (s, d)	n/a	autumn	summer
Amelanchier * (s, ps, m)	n/a	autumn	spring, autumn
Anemone x hybrida (s, ps, m)	n/a	divide in spring	late summer to mid-autumn
Anemone nemorosa (ps, m, d)	n/a	divide in spring	spring to early summer
Aquilegia (s, ps, d, m)	spring	autumn, spring	late spring, early summer
Aruncus (fs, ps, m)	autumn, spring	autumn, spring	summer
Astilbe (s, m)	n/a	divide in winter	summer
Astrantia major (s, ps, m)	autumn	spring	summer
Aucuba japonica (s, ps, fs)	n/a	autumn	year-round
Azalea * (ps)	n/a	autumn	spring
Berberis (s, ps)	n/a	autumn	spring, autumn
Bergenia (s, ps, m)	n/a	divide in autumn	spring
Brachyglottis (syn. Senecio) (s, d)	n/a	autumn, spring	year-round
Brunnera macrophylla (ps, m, d)	spring	autumn, spring	spring
Buddleja davidii (s)	n/a	autumn, spring	summer
Calendula officinalis (s, ps, d)	spring, in situ	n/a	summer to autumn
Calluna vulgaris * (s, d)	n/a	autumn, spring	summer, autumn
Caltha palustris (s, m)	n/a	spring	spring

Achillea

Anemone ranunculoides

Plants	Sow	Plant Out	Season of Interest
Camellia * (ps, m)	n/a	autumn	spring
Campanula 'G.F. Wilson' (s, ps, d)	spring	autumn	summer
Canna indica (s, m)	spring, autumn	early summer	summer, autumn
Caryopteris x clandonensis (s, d)	n/a	autumn, spring	summer. early autumn
Ceanothus (s, d)	n/a	autumn, spring	late spring
Centaurea cyanus (s, d)	spring, in situ	n/a	spring to midsummer
Centranthus ruber ^ (s, d)	spring	autumn	late spring, summer
Chaenomeles x superba (s, ps, d)	n/a	autumn, spring	spring
Choisya ternata (s, d)	n/a	autumn, spring	late spring, autumn
Cistus (s, d)	spring	autumn, spring	summer
Clematis (s, ps, d)	n/a	autumn	spring, summer or autumn
Colchicum autumnale (s, d, m)	n/a	summer	autumn
Convallaria majalis (ps, fs, m)	n/a	divide, autumn	late spring
Convolvulus cneorum (s, d)	spring	autumn	spring to summer
Cornus alba (s, ps)	n/a	autumn	year-round
Cotinus coggygria (s, ps, m, d)	n/a	autumn	year-round
Cotoneaster (s, ps, d)	n/a	autumn	year-round
Crambe cordifolia (s, ps, d)	spring, autumn	spring, autumn	spring, summer
Crocosmia cultivars (s, ps, m)	n/a	spring	summer
Cynara cardunculus (s, d)	spring	autumn, spring	summer, early autumn
Daphne (s, ps, d, m)	n/a	autumn, spring	late spring
Darmera peltata (s, ps, m)	spring, autumn	autumn, spring	autumn
Dianthus (pinks) (s, d)	n/a	autumn, spring	summer
Dicentra spectabilis ñ, ^ (ps, d)	spring	autumn, spring	late spring, early summer
Digitalis purpurea (ps)	late spring	autumn	early summer
Doronicum (ps, m)	spring	autumn	spring
Eccremocarpus scaber (s, d)	early spring	autumn	late spring to autumn
Echinacea purpurea (s, d)	spring	autumn	summer, early autumn

Camellia

Crocosmia

Plants	Sow	Plant Out	Season of Interest
Echinops ritro (s, ps, d)	mid-spring	autumn	summer
Elaeagnus (s, ps, d)	n/a	autumn, spring	year-round
Epimedium (ps, m, d)	n/a	autumn	spring
Eranthis hyemalis (s, m)	spring	autumn	winter, early spring
Erica cultivars * (s, d)	n/a	autumn	winter
Eryngium (s, some d, some m)	n/a	spring, autumn	summer, autumn
Eschscholzia californica (s, d)	spring, in situ	n/a	summer
Euonymus fortunei (s, d)	n/a	autumn	year-round
Euphorbia (s, some d, some m)	spring	autumn	year-round
Fatsia japonica (s, ps, m)	n/a	autumn, spring	year-round, autumn
Festuca glauca (s, d)	autumn, winter	spring, autumn	year-round
Filipendula (s, ps, m)	autumn, spring	spring, autumn	early summer
Forsythia (s, m)	n/a	autumn	spring
Fremontodendron ñ, ^ (s, d)	n/a	autumn, spring	spring to autumn
Fritillaria imperialis (s, d)	n/a	autumn	early summer
Fuchsia magellanica (s, ps, m)	n/a	autumn, spring	summer
Galanthus nivalis (ps, m)	n/a	autumn	winter
Garrya (s, d)	n/a	autumn	winter
Gaultheria procumbens *, ñ (ps, m)	n/a	autumn, spring	year-round
Geranium (s, ps)	spring	spring, autumn	early summer
Gunnera (s, ps, m)	spring, autumn	autumn	spring to autumn
Gypsophila ^ (s, d)	spring, in situ	autumn	summer
Hamamelis (s, ps, m)	n/a	autumn	winter
Hedera (s, ps, fs)	n/a	autumn	year-round
Helenium (s, m)	spring	autumn	summer
Helianthemum ñ, ^ (s, d)	spring	autumn	late spring, summer
Helichrysum ñ, ^ (s, d)	spring	autumn	late summer, autumn
Helleborus ñ, ^ (ps, s, m)	n/a	autumn	winter, spring
Hemerocallis (s, m)	autumn, spring	autumn	summer
Hippophäe rhamnoides ñ, ^ (s, m, d)	n/a	divide in spring	spring to autumn

Euonymus fortunei

Hedera

Plants	Sow	Plant Out	Season of Interest
Hosta (fs, ps, m)	n/a	autumn	spring to autumn
Houttuynia (s, m)	n/a	autumn, spring	spring
Humulus lupulus (s, ps, m)	summer	autumn, spring	spring to autumn
Hydrangea (s, ps, m)	n/a	autumn, spring	summer, early autumn
Hypericum (s, ps, some d, some m)	n/a	autumn, spring	summer
Ilex (s, m)	n/a	autumn, spring	year-round
Impatiens (ps, m, d)	spring	early summer	summer to autumn
Iris foetidissima (s, d)	n/a	late summer	early summer
Jasminum nudiflorum (s, ps, d)	n/a	autumn, spring	winter
Kerria japonica (s, ps, d)	n/a	autumn	spring
Kniphofia hybrids (s, ps, m, d)	n/a	spring, autumn	summer, early autumn
Lavandula (s, d)	spring	autumn	summer
Lavatera (s, d)	n/a	spring	summer
Leycesteria formosa (s, ps, d)	n/a	autumn, spring	summer to early autumn
Ligularia (s, midday shade, m)	autumn, spring	spring, autumn	summer
Ligustrum (s, ps)	n/a	autumn, spring	year-round
Lilium lancifolium *, ñ (s, ps, d)	n/a	autumn	late summer, early autumn
Liriope muscari (fs, m)	n/a	summer	autumn, winter
Lonicera (s, ps)	n/a	autumn, spring	summer
Lupinus slightly * (s, ps, d)	spring, autumn	autumn, spring	summer
Lysichiton (s, ps, m)	n/a	autumn	spring
Lysimachia (s, ps, m)	spring	autumn	summer
Magnolia (s, ps, m)	n/a	autumn	spring
Mahonia (fs, m)	n/a	autumn	winter, spring
Matthiola ñ, slightly ^ (s, m)	spring, summer	spring	late spring, summer
Meconopsis betonicifolia ñ, slightly * (ps, m)	spring, autumn	spring	summer
Mimulus (s, ps, m)	autumn, spring	spring	summer
Nepeta x *faassenii* (s, ps, d)	autumn	spring	summer
Olearia x *haastii* (s, d)	autumn, spring	spring	summer
Origanum ^ (s, d)	autumn, spring	autumn, spring	summer

Hydrangea

Lonicera

Planning with Plants

Plants	Sow	Plant Out	Season of Interest
Osmanthus x *burkwoodii* (s, ps, d)	n/a	spring	summer
Osteospermum (s, d)	spring	spring	summer
Paeonia (s, ps, m)	n/a	autumn, spring	late spring to autumn
Papaver (s, d)	spring, in situ	autumn, spring	early summer
Pelargonium (s, d)	late winter	spring	summer
Penstemon cultivars (s, ps, d)	spring	autumn, spring	summer
Philadelphus (s, ps, d)	n/a	autumn	summer
Phlox annuals (s, d)	early spring	early summer	early summer
Phormium (s, m)	n/a	spring, autumn	year-round
Pieris * (s, ps, m)	n/a	autumn, spring	year-round
Primula bullyeana (ps, m)	spring	autumn, spring	summer
Primula denticulata (ps, m)	spring	early summer	mid-spring, summer
Primula vulgaris (ps, m)	spring	spring, autumn	spring
Pulmonaria (fs, ps, m)	n/a	autumn, spring	spring
Pyracantha (s, ps, d)	n/a	autumn, spring	year-round, autumn
Ranunculus ficaria (ps, fs, m)	n/a	autumn	early spring
Rheum (s, ps, m)	autumn	autumn	spring to autumn
Rhododendron * (ps, m)	n/a	autumn	spring
Rodgersia (s, ps, m)	spring	autumn, spring	spring to autumn
Rosa (s, m)	n/a	autumn	summer
Rosmarinus officinalis (s, d)	spring	spring, autumn	year-round
Rudbeckia (s, m)	spring	autumn	summer, autumn
Salix (s, most m)	n/a	autumn	year-round
Salvia officinalis (s, d)	spring	autumn, spring	year-round
Santolina (s, d)	autumn, spring	spring, autumn	year-round, summer
Sarcococca (fs, ps, m)	n/a	autumn, spring	year-round
Scabiosa ñ, slightly ^ (s, d)	spring	autumn	summer
Sedum (s, d)	autumn	spring	summer, early autumn
Sempervivum (s, d)	spring	spring	year-round

Primula

Pyracantha

Plants	Sow	Plant Out	Season of Interest
Skimmia (ps, fs, m)	n/a	autumn, spring	year-round
Spiraea (s, m)	n/a	autumn, spring	summer
Symphytum (s, ps, m)	autumn, spring	autumn, spring	spring
Syringa ñ, ^ (s, d, m)	n/a	autumn, spring	spring
Tagetes (s, d)	spring	summer	summer
Tamarix tetrandra (s, d, m)	n/a	autumn, spring	year-round
Taxus baccata (s, ps, fs, d)	n/a	autumn, spring	year-round
Thuja occidentalis (s, m)	n/a	autumn, spring	year-round
Thymus ñ, ^ (s, d)	spring	autumn, spring	year-round
Trillium grandiflorum *, ñ (s, m)	n/a	autumn, spring	spring
Trollius (s, ps, m)	spring	autumn, spring	spring
Tropaeolum speciosum ñ, ^ (s, ps, m)	n/a	autumn, spring	summer to autumn
Typha latifolia (s, in water)	n/a	spring	summer
Verbascum ^ (s, d)	n/a	autumn, spring	summer
Viburnum (s, ps, m)	n/a	autumn, spring	winter
Vinca (s, ps, m)	n/a	autumn, spring	year-round
Viola odorata (s, ps, m)	spring	autumn, spring	late winter, early spring
Vitis coignetiae ñ, ^ (s, ps, d)	n/a	autumn, spring	autumn
Weigela florida (s, ps, d)	n/a	autumn, spring	late spring, early summer
Yucca gloriosa (s, d)	n/a	spring	year-round
Zantedeschia aethiopica (s, m)	n/a	spring	late spring to summer

Trillium

Vinca

KEY

Plants marked with * require acid soil;

Plants marked with ^ prefer alkaline soil;

Plants marked with ñ prefer neutral soil.

(s) = sun

(ps) = partial shade

(fs) = full shade

(d) = free-draining soil

(m) = moist ground

67

SHADE, TONE & HUE

Knowing how colour works and how to match hues to create visual harmony or eye-catching contrasts is fundamental to planning a successful scheme for any garden, no matter what its size. This chapter shows how colour can influence the atmosphere of the garden, and how you can blend colours to create just the effect you want.

Left: *Colour is the most immediately noticeable aspect of any garden.*

Visual Delight

WE EXPECT TO FIND COLOUR IN OUR GARDENS, BUT TO CREATE
STUNNING EFFECTS AND ENSURE A CONTINUOUS SHOW THROUGHOUT
THE YEAR WILL REQUIRE SOME UNDERSTANDING OF HOW COLOURS
WORK TOGETHER AS WELL AS A BASIC KNOWLEDGE OF WHEN PLANTS
ARE AT THEIR BEST. WITH CAREFUL PLANNING, EVEN THE SMALLEST
GARDENS CAN PROVIDE YEAR-ROUND COLOUR.

YEAR-ROUND COLOUR

As the year progresses, different types
of plant come into their own. Using the
right mix of plants and blends of colour
will ensure that a garden has plenty of
colour the year round. In mixed borders, shrubs provide the basis of any
planting, giving it structure as well as
colour. These can be in-filled with a
multitude of other types of plants,
mostly herbaceous perennials, bulbs,
and annuals, their seasonal time and

*Above: Yellows and creams blend to create
a restful feel to this summer border.*

colour chosen to complement the more
permanent plants. Beds devoted to particular types of plants can be planted up
on a rotation basis.

BORDERS

Spring-flowering bulbs can be planted
in borders used for summer bedding,
providing colour early in the year.
Herbaceous and mixed borders also
benefit from a generous scattering of
bulbs to help provide colour and
interest until the late spring, when the
early summer plants take over.

*Left: Irises and primulas dominate this
late-spring border for a striking effect.*

Certainly, the flowers of some bulbs are short-lived compared with summer flowers (often no more than a couple of weeks at their peak), but this shortcoming is easily rectified by inter-planting with spring bedding plants such as winter-flowering pansies, forget-me-nots and polyanthus. They ensure a superb display for more than a month, by which time the beds will probably have to be cleared when the ground is prepared for summer flowers. They also help to fill in around the base of tall bulbs such as tulips that can otherwise look rather stalky.

Make sure that mixed borders include shrubs that flower at different times of the year.

The planting schemes used by your local parks department can provide some useful ideas for successful colours and plants, especially if your plant knowledge is limited.

Above: *The colourful bark of* Salix *is at its best in the winter months.*

CONTAINERS

An ideal way to ensure a display of plants at their peak is to plant them in containers. This allows plants to be moved about as they come into flower and fade. Tubs, troughs, window boxes, and even hanging baskets can all be replanted for spring colour.

PERMANENT COLOUR

Annuals and perennials are wonderful for providing successional colour, but growing them does involve work – sowing, potting on, planting out, deadheading, dividing and clearing away dead matter. So some gardeners prefer to create most of their colour using more permanent plants such as heathers and evergreen shrubs, including conifers and ivies which require less maintenance.

Left: *Dahlias provide strong colours for the autumn border.*

71

THE EFFECTS OF COLOUR

Colour has a strong influence on mood and you can use it in your garden to create different effects. Reds are restless and passionate, blues can be calming, yellows are cheerful. Colours also affect the tones of other colours next to them, creating slight changes in their appearance. The way colours work is explored in more detail later in the chapter.

Nothing in a garden is static and whatever effect you create will undergo changes through the day and according to the season. The colour of a flower or leaf will change as it develops, from bud to fall.

LIGHT

Each season has a different type of light, and this affects the hues of plants. Light also changes throughout the

Above: The copper-tinted leaves of the Phormium *make an interesting contrast with small, vivid geranium flowers.*

day. Pale flowers stand out in shade and at dusk, while bright ones seem to bleach out in the midday sun.

USING FOLIAGE

Most foliage is green, but the number of different greens is almost infinite. Careful arrangement of these various greens will enhance the display, but even more can be achieved by incorporating into the garden the large number of plants, especially shrubs, that have foliage in other colours, including yellow, gold, silver, white, purple and blue.

To enjoy coloured foliage at its best, remember that purple and silver-leaved plants need the sun to retain their colour; golden and yellow foliage, however, often need a dappled shade

*Left: The various smoke bushes (*Cotinus*) mostly have excellent purple foliage. They look especially effective when they are planted so that the evening sun shines through the leaves.*

Above: The variegated Hosta 'Golden Tiara', *with its creamy-edged leaves, brightens a shaded corner.*

as too much sun can scorch the leaves and too much shade causes them to turn greener.

VARIEGATED FOLIAGE

Some plants have leaves in two or more colours, known as "variegated" foliage. There are many different types of variegation. In shrubs most variagations are gold, followed closely by cream and white. These have the effect of lightening any group of plants they are near. Green-on-green variegations also have a lightening effect, but variegations involving purples often introduce a more sombre mood.

Variegated plants should be used with discretion. They can become too "busy", and if several are planted together they tend to clash. Reserve them for use as accent plants, to draw the eye. They are useful in shade or in

Right: The purple foliage of Canna 'Roi Humber' *is eyecatching against red, yellow and green.*

a dark corner because they shine out and create interest in an otherwise unpromising or dull situation.

Although many variegated shrubs will tolerate full sun, many prefer a light, dappled shade, out of hot sun.

HOW TO USE THIS CHAPTER

Choosing a Colour Scheme outlines the basic principles of using and blending colours in an artistic way, and explains what is meant by the description of "hot" and "cool" colours. In *Colour in the Garden*, the effects of different colours are explored, showing how you can create the mood and atmosphere you want. For example, a garden that is restful to be in requires calm colours such as pinks, white, lilac and blue that blend together well without jarring. A garden that is full of bold and strong contrasting colours and shapes will have the opposite effect but may be visually stunning.

Choosing a Colour Scheme

PLANTS ARE AVAILABLE IN A WONDERFUL RANGE OF COLOURS, WHICH GIVES GARDENERS TREMENDOUS SCOPE WHEN DESIGNING AN AREA. START BY PLANNING YOUR COLOUR SCHEME ON GRAPH PAPER USING COLOURED PENCILS, TO GIVE YOU A BETTER IDEA OF THE END RESULT.

USING COLOUR

There is such vast choice of colour in plants, that with a little imagination it is possible to paint any picture you like and create any mood you desire.

Not all colours mix well, so rather than randomly scattering colours, it is better to use them in drifts, placing plants so that each has a harmonious relationship with its neighbour. When this is done, the eye can move effortlessly along a border, enjoying inherent subtleties as it passes over a thoughtfully blended whole.

If in doubt about colour combinations, bear in mind that white or blue will go with almost any other colour, and look good. Pastel shades are forgiving colours. The ones to be careful with are brilliant orange and strong magenta, which could look disconcerting when placed together.

BLENDING COLOURS

Unless you want a monochromatic scheme, the basic principle is to blend colours. If you want to use two different colours that oppose each other on the colour wheel in close proximity, you can sometimes find another colour that will link them. Blue and red are in stark contrast to each other, and you may prefer to keep them apart by placing a purple plant between them, which will greatly improve the appearance of the flower border. Incorporating areas of interesting foliage in suitable colours is often an excellent way of linking and separating blocks of colour.

Left: Silver leaves, a dusty pink and the magenta flowers of Digitalis *are unified by the purple* Aquilegia *and* Ajuga *which both stimulate and please the eye.*

Above: The hot yellow and reds of the primulas contrast perfectly with the blue Myosotis.

LEAF COLOUR

Foliage plays an important part in any colour scheme and wonderful effects can be created by placing a stunningly different coloured flower against an interesting leaf colour. For instance the delicate pink of an opium poppy *(Papaver somniferum)* is beautifully set off against silver-grey leaves.

HOT AND COOL COLOURS

When you are decorating the whole mood of a room can change depending on whether you are using hot or cool colours. It is exactly the same when you are designing and planning a garden.

Hot colours – the flame reds and oranges – are lively and will bring a dash of excitement to a border. Intense blues will definitely cool things down,

and white imparts a general sense of purity and tranquillity. Each colour has many tones and shades and all of these can be found in flowers and the many varieties of foliage.

Pastel colours have a romantic quality, and are often suitable for a dull, grey climate. However, a garden devoted entirely to pale colours such as these can be rather boring.

THE COLOUR WHEEL

Artists and designers use what is known as a colour wheel, in which colours that are situated next to each other on the wheel have a sympathetic bond and will work well together. Purple and blue as well as blue and green, for example, look good together. Colours on opposite sides of the wheel are contrasting and may clash with each other. Orange, for instance, will stand out quite starkly against blue.

There are occasions, however, when combining opposing colours can be used to create a focal point or to add life in an otherwise bland scheme.

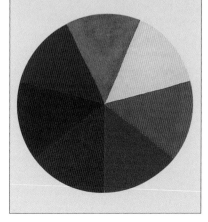

Colour in the Garden

As you plan for colour in the garden, decide which effect you wish to achieve. You can use calming, soft colours or include a bright, vibrant focal point or a hot border. You may even choose to create peace and tranquillity with a completely white border.

Using Hot Colours

Confine hot colours to one border, possibly as a centrepiece, but use softer colours in the other beds to ring in

Above: Kniphofias have several alternative names, of which "red-hot poker" aptly describes the colour of many of them. These shafts of hot colours are useful not only for their brightness, but also for their shape.

the changes and to provide a more tranquil planting area. It is possible to create a border containing nothing but red flowers, but it is always more interesting to have one that incorporates other hot colours as well. However, many people prefer to use a limited number of hot-coloured perennials in a cooler-coloured border, where they will act as a strong focal point and make a dramatic statement. Red or yellow flowers are the strongest colours for impact.

Hot colours have a tendency to "advance" – that is, they seem much closer than they really are – so if you want to make a long border appear shorter than it is, plant the hot colours at the far end.

Use the different hues of foliage to link the hot colours with cool colours in the border.

Above: The glorious ruby-red flowers of Rhododendron 'Dopey'.

Using Cool Colours

Although blues are, in theory, cool colours, those blues that are tinged with red are warm. Combined with the warm pinks, the overall effect is

Above: The cool colours of Nemophilia menziesii *(Californian bluebell).*

one of cool calm. Use blues, purples and pinks, including many of the pastel shades, to achieve this effect.

Pastel colours create a misty effect, which means that they can be mixed together or dotted around. An even better effect can be achieved by using drifts of colour, merging the drifts.

Above: Use bright-red plants, such as Dahlia *'Bishop of Llandaff', as a bold focal point.*

RED FLOWERS

Amaranthus caudatus
Antirrhinum 'Scarlet Giant'
Begonia semperflorens 'Volcano'
Canna
Cleome hassleriana 'Cherry Queen'
Crocosmia 'Lucifer'
Dahlia
Geum "Mrs. J. Bradshaw'
Impatiens (various varieties)
Kniphofia (red hot poker)
Lobelia erinus 'Red Cascade'
Monarda 'Cambridge Scarlet'
Paeonia
Papaver rhoeas
Pelargonium (various varieties)
Penstemon barbatus
Petunia 'Red Star'; P. 'Scarlet'
Tropaeolum majus 'Empress of India'
Verbena (various varieties)

RED

The fiery reds are hot, exciting colours. They combine well with oranges, and golden and orange-yellows, but don't generally mix well with blue-reds, which are more sub-dued. Use them wherever you want to inject some vibrancy into your garden designs – in beds and borders or in hanging baskets and other containers. But remember that too much of a good thing can become monotonous, so use these strong colours sparingly.

Hot reds can be found in many perennials, but are especially well rep-resented in summer annuals, which are so useful for adding dramatic patches of colour between other plants.

77

Above: This brilliant bright orange Osteospermum *makes a strong contrast against green foliage.*

ORANGE FLOWERS

Antirrhinum
Canna 'Orange Perfection'
Crocosmia
Dahlia
Eccremocarpus scaber
Erysimum
Euphorbia griffithii
Geum 'Borisii'
Hemerocallis
Kniphofia
Ligularia
Papaver orientale
Potentilla 'William Robinson'
Primula bulleyana
Rudbeckia hirta
Tagetes erecta
Tropaeolum
Trollius
Zauschneria californica

ORANGE

A warm, friendly colour, orange has quite a wide range of shades. At the deeper end of the spectrum it is quite definitely a hot colour, exciting and vibrant, but at the golden end it is warm rather than hot and can be used more freely.

Orange mixes well with most colours although the redder shades are not so complementary with the bluer reds, including purple and pink, unless you like to combine colours that clash. It shows up well against green foliage and can be picked out at a distance.

Autumn gardens often display orange tones, not only in flowers, such as chrysanthemums, but in trees and shrubs with coloured foliage and brightly coloured berries.

Above: This Calceolaria, *with its flame-orange flowers, is a striking annual to use in the border.*

Many annuals and biennials can add a vibrant orange note throughout the year, including winter-flowering pansies followed by wallflowers (*Erysimum*), snapdragons (*Antirrhinum*) and pot marigolds (*Calendula*). During summer, nasturtiums (*Tropaeolum*) and African marigolds (*Tagetes erecta*) will follow.

YELLOW

There are three distinct yellows within this part of the spectrum, all exhibiting different qualities in a planting scheme. One side is tinged with green and may be described as a cool colour, while the other side is tinged with orange, making it very much a hot colour. These hot yellows have a warm, cosy feeling about them, and go well with flame-reds, oranges and creams. In

Above: The yellow heads of Achillea *'Coronation Gold' float above its delicate foliage.*

between the two yellows are pure clear yellows. These will blend happily with most other colours.

The green or lemon yellows look much better when associated with greens blues and white. They can be bright, but create a fresher effect than the warmer yellows.

Above: The stately yellow spires of Verbascum *add height to a traditional summer border.*

YELLOW FLOWERS

Achillea
Aurinia saxatilis
(syn. *Alyssum saxatile*)
Canna
Centaurea macrocephala
Chrysanthemum
Coreopsis verticillata
Dahlia
Erysimum 'Jubilee Gold'
Geum 'Lady Statheden'
Helianthus
Heliopsis
Hemerocallis
Inula
Ligularia
Primula
Rudbeckia

79

GREEN

Foliage can provide an effective link in borders and beds. Dark green is good used with hot colours, whereas soft green and silver suit cool colours, especially pink, pale blue and pale, greeny yellow. Blue foliage, which can be found in some grasses and hostas, can also be useful in linking or separating blocks of colour.

BLUE

The different shades of blue can be bright, clean-cut colours with a great intensity, or softened to such an extent that they only have a whisper of colour left, creating a very soft, hazy image. Intense blues can be used in a bold way in the garden, but the softer blues are good for romantic container arrangements, especially those in large stone pots or urns.

Above: *Use the delicate* Nigella damascena, *with its blue flowers and feathery fronds, in a cool border.*

BLUE FLOWERS

Agapanthus praecoc x subsp *orientalis*
Ageratum houstonianum
Brachyscome iberidifolia
Campanula medium
Centaurea cyanus
Consolida ambigua
Eryngium x *oliverianum*
Felicia bergeriana
Lathyrus odoratus
Limonium sinuatum 'Blue Bonnet'
Lobelia erinus
Myosotis
Nigella damascena
Nolana paradoxa 'Blue Bird'
Salvia farinacea 'Victoria'

Blues are versatile and can be combined with most colours. They create a rather rich, luxurious combination with purple-reds, but avoid mixing them with orange-reds. With orange, however, the effects can be startling, so use this combination sparingly.

Blue and yellow is another exciting combination, giving a fresh, clean-looking contrast. The pale blues and yellows, however, are more hazy and have a soft, romantic image, but still retain a distinctive, fresh quality.

Blues set against silver or grey foliage create an interesting combination that is distinct yet soft.

PURPLE AND VIOLET

Even a patch of purple appears as a strong block of colour, never as a misty haze. Over-use of this solid colour can have a deadening effect. As purple

Above: Digitalis *creates wonderfully elegant spires of flowers, bringing height to a planting scheme. These flowers vary in colour from a light pink to purple.*

too much, creating a leaden effect. Lime-green flowers such as lime zinnias and the lime foliage of *Helychrysum petiolare* 'Limelight' make excellent border companions.

Lavenders combined with pinks are a delightfully romantic combination and have the bonus of a delightful scent. When used with creamy-yellow they have a soothing effect.

PINK

This colour can be quite bright, even startling and brash, particularly when tinged with purple and moving towards cerise and magenta shades. On the other hand it can be very soft and romantic. You have to be careful

tends to sink back into green foliage, it is better to contrast it with foliage that is silver or grey.

Violet is a more lively colour, and has still more vibrancy when on the dark side. Nonetheless, it should still be used with care and discretion.

Both purple and violet can be used more extensively if they are mixed with other colours. Lighter colours, such as yellows and whites, contrast with and stand out against purple. Purple also harmonizes well with purple-reds and purple-blues, but if these are too dark, the colours tend to blend

Above: The delicate pink flowers of Oenothera speciosa rosea *have creamy white centres.*

81

PINK FLOWERS

Anemone hupehensis
Astilbe x *arendsii* 'Venus'
Centaurea Cyanus
Cleome hasslerianna 'Colour Fountain'
Cosmos bipinnatus 'Sensation'
Dicentra spectabilis
Geranium x *oxonianum*
'Wargrave Pink'
Impatiens
Lathyrus odoratus
Matthiola, Brompton Series
Penstemon
Petunia, Resisto Series

Above: Cream blended with soft mauve and gently variegated foliage creates a soothing effect.

in choosing the right colour for the effect you want to achieve. Pinks tend to mix best with lavenders and soft blues. But they can be used with reds to tone them down slightly. Pinks do not mix harmoniously with bright yellows and oranges.

CREAM

White mixed with a little yellow makes the sensuous and luxurious shade of cream. It goes well with most colours, adding a slightly mellow hue and often blending in sympathetically with hot colours.

WHITE

Long associated with purity, peace and tranquillity, white flowers add sophistication to a scheme. White goes well with most other colours, and it can be used to lighten a colour scheme. Used with hot oranges and reds, pure white can create a dramatic effect. White and blue is always a popular combination and it can be particularly effective to combine different shades of white with a mixture of pastel colours.

White is visible until well after dark, and so it is a good colour to plant where you eat evening meals. It also can be used to illuminate dark

Left: The large pompom heads of creamy yellow Marigold 'French Vanilla'.

corners of the garden. White busy Lizzies (*Impatiens*), for example, in a hanging basket against a dark background or in shade, will shine out.

A disadvantage with white flowers is that they often look unsightly when they die. To keep such displays at their best, deadhead once a day.

Some gardeners devote whole borders, even whole gardens, to white flowers. Although these are referred to as white gardens, there are usually at least two colours present, because most white-flowered plants have green leaves. A third colour, in the form of grey or silver foliage, is also often added.

There are many different shades of white, and they do not always mix sympathetically. On the whole, therefore, it is better to plant pure whites since the creamier ones tend to "muddy" the picture. Many white and cream flowers have bright yellow centres, and it is best to avoid these if you are planning a white border.

Above: *The tiny flowers of* Gypsophila elegans *make a delicate display in any summer border.*

WHITE FLOWERS

Alcea rosea
Anaphalis margaritacea
Clarkia pulchella 'Snowflake'
Cosmos bipinnatus 'Purity'
Gypsophila elegans 'Giant White'
Impatiens 'Super Elfin White'
Lathyrus odoratus
Lobelia erinus 'Snowball'
Lobularia maritima
(syn. Alyssum maritimum)
Matthiola (white varieties)
Nicotiana alata
Osteospermum 'Glistening White'
Pelargonium (various white forms)
Petunia (various white forms)
Viola x *wittrockiana* (white varieties)

Left: *This white* Osteospermum *will lighten any scheme, from hot oranges to misty blues.*

83

PERFECT
PATIOS

At its simplest a patio or terrace
provides a level seating area for
enjoying the garden, but to make it
visually link the house and garden as
well as cater for all the activities you
might need it for requires a little
thought and planning. Whether you
are contemplating a new patio or
wishing to enhance the one you
already have, this chapter is packed
with helpful information on style,
construction materials, screening and
lighting as well as effective planting
ideas for year-round display.

Left: *A perfectly sited patio adds a new dimension
to your outdoor space.*

The Garden Floor

If garden beds and borders exist for plants, a patio or terrace is conceived with people in mind. This is a dynamic part of the garden, and the style we set here is a reflection of our lifestyle as much as of our skill as gardeners.

Above: A charming, well-furnished terrace invites you to step out of the house for morning coffee, afternoon tea or alfresco meals on summer evenings.

What Is a Patio?

A garden designer might refer to the patio or terrace as an interface. Traditionally, it is the area that links the house with the garden, though in an urban setting the patio may constitute the whole of the outdoor space.

Whatever the size of the garden, a patio shares some aspects of both the indoor and the outdoor environment. Increasingly people think of such an area as an extension of the house. Paving or decking, tables and chairs, awnings and even heaters mean that it can function like an additional room,

an extra living space that is especially suitable for entertaining, eating and relaxing. But it can also be the setting for the garden's most spectacular and precious plants.

The patio now merits (and receives) as much care and thought when it comes to selecting materials and furnishings – its style, in other words – as we give to sitting rooms, bedrooms, kitchens and bathrooms.

FROM HOUSE TO GARDEN

Ideally, there should be a smooth transition from house to garden. Many people harbour the image of a beautiful house with full-length windows flung wide open and leading on to a spacious terrace which, in turn, overlooks a manicured lawn and an immaculate garden.

Something of that feeling of escape can be created in every garden, even where space is at a premium, but many gardeners have to balance the wish to have a patio or terrace with a desire for a lawn, for a herb or vegetable garden, for beds and borders for flowers and shrubs or for a greenhouse or shed. Except for the smallest courtyards, deciding how much space can be allocated to any or all of the different functions of a garden is part of the planning process, and designing and building the patio must take into account the style of the remainder of the garden, just as its surface and decoration must reflect the interior and exterior style of the house.

Patios and terraces are usually understood as adjoining the house, keeping them warm and sheltered, and within easy reach of the kitchen and other living areas. However, there is no reason why a paved area or deck cannot be created at a distance from the house, linked to it by a path. A large garden might accommodate a second patio, on which could be built a summerhouse or arbour, providing a sheltered place to sit in summer, when you can feel you are in the heart of the country rather than a mere stone's throw from your back door.

Above: A secluded corner is made more appealing by the climbers that clothe and soften the vertical surfaces.

The Garden Floor

Enjoying Your Patio

Increasingly the patio or terrace has become associated with relaxation, and it should be a peaceful place to unwind and forget the strains of modern living. Food always seems to taste better in the open air, and summer cooking outside is a pleasure even for those who show little enthusiasm in the kitchen. Nowadays, barbecues can be fitted into the smallest spaces and the patio has become a place for dining and entertaining.

Making this space a pleasant, sheltered outdoor room can be achieved by the addition of permanent structures, such as pergolas and screens, or by thoughtful planting, to create shade, colour and fragrance in summer

Above: Choose garden furniture that is in keeping with the style of your terrace. Smart enamelled metal suits the look and scale of a small urban courtyard.

but to allow all the available natural light to reach the windows of the house in winter. A sympathetic choice of materials, and furniture that is both

Above: In a small garden, a simple bench in a sheltered corner will provide a welcome sitting area, especially when it is surrounded by fragrant flowers.

comfortable and appropriate to the patio in size and scale, will increase your enjoyment. Such is the lure of the outdoors that, once you have created your perfect patio, it will be the centre of your home all summer long.

HOW TO USE THIS CHAPTER

This chapter is intended to inspire you with fresh ideas and possibilities, but whether you design and build the patio yourself or employ a garden designer and a building contractor, you will still have to define its basic function. The first section, *Planning Considerations*, explores some of the issues you need to consider when you are preparing the design. *Structural Elements* evaluates the relative merits of the materials that are likely to be at your disposal and the impact they will make, as well as offering hints on how to shelter the area from the elements and to enhance security and privacy. *Patio Planting* describes some suitable plants for the patio.

Choosing a Style discusses some of the styles that are popular in garden design today and suggests how they can be achieved, both through the materials used in construction and through planting. Finally, *Special Features* focuses on those finishing touches that make a patio personal to its owner and that will increase your pleasure in it: choosing the appropriate furniture, lighting and heating the patio, and creating focal points.

Above: Dense planting gives this tiny patio a jungle-like lushness, while the mixed floor materials add an air of informality.

Planning Considerations

THERE ARE SEVERAL ISSUES TO CONSIDER WHEN YOU ARE PLANNING A PATIO OR TERRACE. TIME SPENT AT THE EARLY STAGES IS NEVER WASTED AND WILL ENABLE YOU TO DEVELOP A SPACE YOU WILL WANT TO RETURN TO AGAIN AND AGAIN.

SITE AND ACCESS

Consider where the patio is to be sited. Easy access from the house is important, and the position of doors leading into the garden may determine your choice. If the patio will be adjacent to the house, will it run the full length of the building? Will it be the same depth throughout or will it have a curved or angled edge to reflect other features in the garden or house?

A patio can also be sited some distance from the house, with a path leading to it, or you might prefer two

Above: Wooden decking is an ideal material for a patio or terrace where the site is not level.

or more linked spaces. A concealed area can be especially successful. Imagine a path that disappears among trees or shrubs, leading to a simple, open, paved circle with a single architectural plant or statue at the centre. This kind of feature can make for dynamic contrast and bring an element of surprise into the garden.

A level site poses few problems, but if the ground slopes you need to consider whether you want to construct retaining walls or raised beds so that the patio itself is level and whether you will have to build steps or a ramp so that you can easily and safely get from the patio to the garden.

Make sure that a patio that adjoins the house slopes slightly away from it toward a drain or a border, so that rainwater cannot accumulate near the house wall and cause damp problems.

SIZE MATTERS

Unless it occupies the whole of a small plot, the patio needs to be in scale with the rest of the garden. If it is too small, you are unlikely to make good use of it, but if it is too large, it might look exposed and unwelcoming. If the

Above: A zigzag path prevents the eye from leaping to the far edge of the patio, tricking you into believing that the space is larger than it is.

Above: Plants growing around the patio will soon spill over the edges of paving and steps, but at first you can use containers to soften their hard lines.

patio has to be large to link two buildings, try breaking up the expanse with changes of level or materials, a raised bed or even a small tree or fountain.

If you are using paving, make sure that the scale of the materials is in proportion to the overall area. This aspect of the design is often overlooked but will have a significant effect on the success of the area. Big patios are best paved with large slabs, and small with small. In a small area, granite setts are easier on the eye than large slabs, which seem to accentuate the restricted dimensions.

At the planning stage, be sure to allow adequate room for tables and chairs; as well as using them, you will want to walk around them, perhaps serving your guests who are sitting around the table. Make sure there is space for chairs to be pushed back – the last thing you want is for chairs to topple backward into the neighbouring plants. Leave room for containers and remember that plants in surrounding borders will billow out in summer, further reducing the ground space.

Steps and paths must be wide enough to be safe, and if you need to include handrails or a balustrade, remember to allow for these in your ground plan. The ideal path should be wide enough to allow two people to walk along side by side in comfort, and a width of 2m (6ft) will not seem excessive once plants in adjacent borders have flopped over and softened the edges. If space is really limited, make sure that you will, at least, be able to manoeuvre a lawnmower between the borders or push a wheelbarrow through the garden with ease.

SUN OR SHADE?

Whether the patio is to be in sun or shade may already be determined by the lie of the house and elements beyond the garden, such as nearby buildings and trees. This is especially likely to be the case in town gardens.

Where you can exercise choice, your future use of the patio may well be influenced by whether it is predominantly in sun or shade and how this varies according to the season and time of day. If the far end of your garden catches the evening sun, you might use and enjoy the spot more if you created a paved area and furnished it with a table and chairs.

Above: If the patio is hot and sunny, there is nothing more refreshing than the sound of bubbling water, as the designer of this feature realized.

The idea of breakfasting on a sunny terrace is particularly appealing, and if you have a patio near the house that gets the morning sun, it is sure to get plenty of use at this time of day. By lunchtime, however, when the sun is much stronger, the same spot may be too hot for comfortable eating.

Often, it is only when the weather is really hot that we remember the need for shade, and although most of us probably dream of long days basking in the sunshine, we are continually reminded about the dangers of over-exposure to ultraviolet light. If the site you have chosen has no natural shade, consider building a pergola over which you could grow deciduous climbers or think about erecting an awning, which can be removed and stored from autumn to spring.

The solid shade cast by a building can make an area too chilly except on the warmest days, but a patio that is overhung by a deciduous tree can be enjoyed on sunny days in spring yet will offer some protection from the sun in summer when the tree is in full leaf. It is pleasant to relax with a drink on a patio or deck that is warmed by the evening sun, even if this was in shade during most of the day.

WINDY SITES

One of the worst problems to beset gardeners is swirling wind. Most small, enclosed gardens are unaffected by this problem, but if the site is relatively open, strong gusts can mar your enjoyment at any time of year. A long, narrow garden flanked by tall walls or fences may suffer from the wind-tunnel effect. You can shelter a patio with a fence, or with trees and shrubs. If you choose the latter, plant deciduous species, because they tend to filter the wind; dense evergreens can help to create even stronger currents.

On the other hand, if the patio is to do double duty as a utility space for drying washing, a certain amount of wind can only be an advantage.

Above: Planting up to the edge of the paved area is the best way of linking this shady patio with the rest of the garden.

Above: A well-maintained hedge is not only attractive but also affords maximum privacy and shelter from gusting wind.

Planning Considerations

CHILDREN

If there are children in the family, they will enjoy having a smooth, level patio to play on, but safety issues are paramount. Although bumps and falls are part of growing up, concrete surfaces and raised areas with no guard rails pose particular hazards. Instead of concrete or paving slabs, consider using softer materials, such as decking, bark chippings or even the rubberized tiles that are used in public play areas.

Open water should be avoided altogether in gardens where small children play. If you must have a water feature, install a small bubble fountain over cobbles, or a wall-mounted spout, and sink the reservoir into the ground.

ELDERLY AND DISABLED GARDENERS

Ease of access is a vital consideration for anyone with restricted mobility. If the garden falls steeply away from the house, rather than terracing the patio, create instead a gentle slope that can be navigated from level to level by wheelchair users. If you can install a raised bed, perhaps with a hand rail, along one side of the slope, so much the better: it will help to prevent falls and other mishaps, besides bringing any plants within reach of the gardener.

Surface materials require special consideration, too. If you opt for paving, it should be laid smoothly, with no proud edges that can trip any

Above: A well-built sandpit in a warm corner can make for hours of creative play.

Above: Raised beds surrounding a perfectly even paved surface make this patio the ideal outdoor space for a disabled or elderly gardener.

Above: Decking squares are easy to lay, and are available with a ridged surface that gives a safer footing for the very young and old than plain, smooth wood.

gardeners who are not absolutely stable on their feet. Some smooth concrete surfaces can be slippery when wet, so either roughen the surface with aggregate to prevent slips and falls or use some other material that is already rough. Grooved or ridged decking provides a better grip underfoot than plain wood and can also be laid in attractive patterns.

Older gardeners will want to avoid surfaces that are going to require constant attention and maintenance. Even paving slabs will attract moss and lichens in time (the first sign is a greenish tinge, usually around the edges) and will need to be treated. Special products are available that have to be sprayed or watered on; alternatively, the lichen has to be removed the hard way, with water and a wire brush. Softwood decking is easy to lay, but unless it is tanalized (pressure treated) it will require regular applications of preservative.

FAMILY PETS

Cats and dogs will adore basking in the sun on smooth, warm paving stones. Extensive areas of fine gravel are best avoided if you or your neighbours have cats, which are likely to see it as a large and convenient litter tray. Chemical deterrents are available, but their effect is temporary. If you are troubled by visiting cats, it may be worth investing in sound- or motion-activated deterrents, which either emit a high-pitched whistle or spray intruders with water.

Male dogs regard almost anything as a potential urinal, and even the best-trained and exercised animals have accidents sometimes, so keep some disinfectant handy.

SPRINGING A SURPRISE

Although most patios and terraces will be fairly open spaces in the garden you can still introduce an element of surprise. If you have a large garden, with a patio adjoining the house, you may wish to close up the far side by means of a fence or wall so that the rest of the garden is virtually hidden, and perhaps accessible only through a gate. In this way, the patio itself becomes almost literally an outdoor room. A less extreme feeling of separation can be created by dense planting to either side of a path leading away from the patio. If the path turns a corner and disappears out of sight, the invitation to explore the garden will be well-nigh irresistible.

In a large garden, an alternative effect can be achieved by siting a patio some distance from the house and screening it, either by tall planting or by a wall or fence, so that you seem to alight on it as if by accident; the presence of a seat will encourage you to linger there. Ideally, to increase the illusion that you have really made an escape, the house should not be visible from the patio, but if this is not possible, arrange any seating to face away from the house – instead directing the eye to a pool, a statue or an especially fine architectural plant.

RELAXING AND ENTERTAINING

If you like to entertain a lot and to dine alfresco, you need to allow ample room for a table and chairs. Bear in mind that people will want to push their chairs back from the table without falling into the borders, and to be able to walk around behind them. If the table is in a sunny position, you'll

Above: Use paint to alter the atmosphere of a corner of your patio. You can easily change the colour if you tire of the effect.

Above: In a large garden you can create an element of surprise with winding paths and gateways to secret enclosed areas.

96

Above: If your table is sited in the middle of a sunny terrace, a large parasol is an essential accessory in summer.

need to provide shade in the middle of the day. Choose a large parasol, or one that you can set at an angle, so that it shades your guests as well as the food on the table.

You might want to consider building an integral barbecue into the patio wall, but these days transportable models, which can be stored in a utility room or garage when not in use, are widely available and are not too costly. Whichever type of barbecue you prefer, safety considerations should make sure it can be used well away from any potentially flammable materials, including overhanging plants. You'll also need a level surface nearby where you can rest plates.

Privacy will be an issue for most people, especially town-dwellers. If you use the patio for sunbathing, you will probably welcome shelter from prying eyes, possibly in the form of a fence or trees, but make sure that the shadow is not cast on the patio itself or you will be defeating the object.

Above: Colourful balls signpost the path to a second paved area, tucked away out of sight of the rest of the garden.

97

Structural Elements

THERE IS A WIDE RANGE OF MATERIALS THAT CAN BE USED TO CREATE
A PATIO OR TERRACE, AND SOME OF THE MOST POPULAR ARE
DISCUSSED HERE, TOGETHER WITH SOME SUGGESTIONS ON HOW TO
SCREEN THE AREA AND WHICH PLANTS ARE MOST SUITABLE.

CHOOSING THE SURFACE

The siting and size of your patio will
both influence your choice of surface
material, but there are several other
factors to consider, including cost,
ease of laying, maintenance and appearance. The style needs to be appropriate to its setting, and if you have an
old property, reclamation yards are a
good source of suitable materials.

*Above: Restraint is the keynote of this
modern, elegant decked area.*

Decking

As an alternative to paving, the use of
wooden decking is now well established. It is a natural choice in areas
where wood is in abundance and the
climate is relatively dry and sunny. Its
nature makes it ideal for strong, geometric designs and it ages sympathetically. Decks are ideal if you need to
make a raised platform over sloping
ground, and a rail around the deck
will enhance the colonial feel.

Decking is laid on a framework of
timber joists, in the same way as a traditional interior wooden floor. The
joists are themselves supported on pil-
lars, and the sides of the decking are
usually covered with facing boards to
conceal the space beneath.

You can customize decking by
painting or staining it, but whatever
finish you choose will fade with age so
you may need to repeat the treatment
every year or so. The better quality the
wood, the better it ages. Hardwood is
more resistant to decay than softwood, but if economy dictates that
you must use softwood, make sure it
has been tanalized (pressure treated)
for longer life.

Above: Slabs and gravel are common enough building materials but can still have distinction if used with discretion.

Apart from traditional boards, decking is widely available in the form of square wooden tiles, which can be laid in geometric patterns to add interest to the surface. A grooved finish will provide a safer walking surface than smooth wood in damp weather.

Stone

Natural stone is beautiful to look at but is expensive and usually heavy to handle and difficult to lay, especially if the individual stones are of different thicknesses. Some stones break up easily and cannot be recommended for paving. Make sure you find a good match with the local stone, especially where this has been used as a building material.

Concrete and Artificial Stone

One of the most versatile of all building materials, concrete has become a fashionable alternative to paving, as new laying and colouring techniques give it a fresh style. You can either accept it for what it is and opt for a great sweep of unadorned concrete – perfect in a high-tech or minimalist garden – or you can use it in one of its less immediately obvious forms, as slabs, which look to all intents and purposes like natural stone and are available in a variety of shapes, colours and textures. Good-quality concrete slabs are a good imitation of real stone and are much cheaper and easy to lay.

You can make your own paving slabs from concrete, which you can tint to the exact colour you want. Either make individual slabs in a mould or just lay the concrete and groove the surface before it is fully set to suggest paving slabs (for this you will need a keen eye and a steady hand).

PATIO PLANNING AND BUILDING BASICS

• When a patio is built to adjoin the house, make sure that the final surface of the patio is not higher than the damp-proof (water-proof) course.

• Lay paving stones or concrete so that the patio slopes very slightly away from the house wall toward a drain or border, to prevent puddles forming. The drop should be about 16mm per metre (5/8in per yard).

• If you have to include steps in your design to cope with changes of level, define the edges clearly with contrasting materials.

COMBINING ELEMENTS

While you might initially decide it is a good idea to stick to a single building material to keep a patio or terrace looking smart and uncluttered, it can be effective to combine different elements. In fact, it makes sense to do so. Think about how you decorate indoors: a sitting room, for instance, combines a number of textures – carpets, heavy-duty furnishing fabrics, sheer curtains – and a bathroom can unite chrome with ceramic tiling and mirrors or warm cork tiles.

If your patio is a large one, using more than one material for the surface can help to break up an expanse that

Above: A mixture of large stones and cobbles creates a natural-looking area, enhanced by informal planting and the trickle of water from a bubble fountain.

might otherwise start to seem bleak. It can also help to define different parts of the patio, such as the area around the table, or the children's play area.

Combining materials is also a good way of introducing small quantities of desirable but expensive elements into the design. A small mosaic motif or an edging strip of expensive tiles can be incorporated with more workaday materials to provide interest and focus. Alternatively, introduce areas of cobbles set in concrete. Decking

Above: This clever use of different materials, textures and colours helps define discrete areas of the patio. The gravel softens the hard edges of the bricks.

shade might be appropriate on a large patio or a specimen shrub on a smaller one. This can also be an excellent way of creating a herb garden close to the house, so that you do not need to walk far from the kitchen every time you want to pick a handful of fresh herbs for garnish or flavour. The paving will also help to contain rampant herbs such as mint.

If you have opted for gravel laid over a membrane spread directly on garden soil, a few judiciously pierced holes will allow for planting. You need to choose the plants carefully, however, because some species will actually seed themselves in the gravel and can push their roots through the membrane if this is water-permeable.

Above: In spring, brilliant blue grape hyacinths (Muscari) will happily push their way through gravel.

works surprisingly well with gravel, but you should be careful when combining decking squares with concrete slabs. If they are of roughly the same size, the eye gets confused and will "jump" from one to the other, which can be unsettling and discomfiting.

Water and decking work well together to create a seaside feel. An expanse of water is cooling, but where space is limited or the presence of young children rules out a pool, a vertical water feature incorporating a spout or a small bubble fountain might be considered.

In a paved area you could miss out a few slabs here and there to allow for planting – a tree that will cast light

101

Above: Brick (block) paving weathers gracefully and looks wonderful when colonized by small plants and mosses.

Brick

If your house is built of bricks (blocks), it is usually easy to find a good match for use on the patio. House bricks, whether new or reclaimed, are, however, not the best type to use as paving: they are not frostproof and tend to crack and crumble in extreme weather. For durability, look for the highest specification. Facing and engineering bricks are frost-resistant.

Bricks are eminently suitable for patterned paving. They can be laid in a variety of bonds, much as walls are built, and are also suitable for herringbone or basketweave effects.

Tiles

Terracotta tiles are beautiful, and make it possible to use the same style of flooring outdoors as you have used in the kitchen, but they are less durable than other types so are best used under cover, perhaps for a covered loggia or summerhouse. Pottery roofing tiles can be used laid on edge, either on their own or in conjunction with other materials, as a large quantity is needed to cover the ground.

Cobbles and Setts

If you can find a source – usually a reclamation yard – old street cobbles and setts are attractive, but they are not always easy to walk on, and any seating placed on cobbles will be distinctly unstable. They are best used to break up larger areas of paving, either in the form of a strip to demarcate separate areas or to highlight an edge or as decoration, in the form of swirls and spirals.

Above: Bright tiles in a formal pool are elegantly set off by a terracotta edging.

Gravel

Easy to lay and to maintain, gravel is an ideal surface material. It can be laid direct on compacted earth, ideally over a weed-suppressing membrane, or on top of another hard surface. It is available in a range of grades and colours, and it has the additional advantage of combining well with other hard surfaces. It is very useful for filling awkward corners and curved areas. The main drawbacks are that it must be contained by edging if it is not to travel, both around the garden and into the house on the soles of shoes, and it is irresistible to cats.

Railway Sleepers

Available from reclamation yards and some specialist garden suppliers, railway sleepers (ties) are usually used for edging raised beds, as low walls or as steps. Sleepers are heavy and when they are used in a single row they usually need no fixing. However, if they are used as steps or to create a raised bed several sleepers high, when there will be a considerable weight of soil behind them, they should be held together with brackets.

Sleepers can be laid directly on the ground, but if they are impregnated with preservative, lay them on plastic sheeting and line the inside with plastic to prevent the tar from leaching into the soil and harming the plants. If possible, buy untreated sleepers.

Above: Smooth stones and pea shingle look attractive but are best used as decorative details as they may not be easy to walk on.

Mosaics

If you are naturally creative – or have a good friend who is – you can enliven any outdoor space with a mosaic that will give pleasure throughout the year. Mosaics work especially well near water – a reminder of the Islamic concept of the paradise garden, even though your principal source of inspiration may lie elsewhere.

Experiment with patterns of broken tiles or coloured stones, even sea shells, in a dry mix of sand and cement. Once you are satisfied with the design, sprinkle with water to set the mortar or simply allow soil moisture to be drawn up by capillary action, which will do the job for you. Mosaics tend to be less durable than other forms of paving, so restrict their use to areas that will not be subjected to heavy traffic or use them to make small patterns or decorative motifs.

103

WALLS AND FENCES

At the most basic level, walls and fences mark the boundaries between neighbouring gardens. The need for privacy is often important, particularly in a small town garden, and a solid wall or fence will provide maximum security and privacy.

Within the garden, however, these structures may have different functions. They can be used to divide separate areas and levels or to provide shelter, and when a new patio is being designed, you may want to erect additional fences or walls at the same time.

If a windbreak is required, for example, a trellis fence will filter the strongest winds better than a solid wall. A compromise can be achieved by

Above: Use wall-baskets and hanging baskets to bring colour to plain walls.

topping a low fence or wall with trellis panels. If you want to preserve a lovely view from the terrace, a low fence may be adequate shelter for small plants.

Walls

A new garden wall is a luxury few can afford these days owing to high labour costs, and there are, in any case, often local regulations governing the height of solid boundaries, so if you already have a wall, make the most of it.

Within a garden, however, as long as you have space to dig out the footings, walls can be used either to enhance the privacy of a patio or to create secret places and hidden corners. A wall up to 1m (3ft) tall can be built by anyone with the relevant skills, but seek professional help with anything higher.

A wall to edge a patio can be built of a material that matches the house and patio floor itself. Brick and stone are obvious choices, but concrete can be incredibly stylish, especially if the house is a modern one, and the material lends itself to abstract and innovative designs. Glass blocks are excellent in a contemporary design, and are extremely attractive in association with water features.

Brick, glass and concrete can also be used to make curved structures, but the weight and the techniques involved suggest that their construction is best left in the hands of professional contractors.

Above: Unusually patterned stones make an idiosyncratic boundary wall. Planting softens the effect, preventing it from becoming overpowering.

Above: Basketweave fencing is a sympathetic background for plants and is easy to erect. It requires regular varnishing to lengthen its life.

Fences

Most fencing is made of softwood, and ready-made panel fences are easy to erect, popular and effective. As a rule, the more expensive the fencing, the better the quality and the longer it is likely to last. Wherever possible, use tanalized (pressure-treated) wood to ensure a long life.

When you are using a fence within the garden to create a shelter around a patio, consider it from both points of view. For example, a fence around the edge of a sitting area might prevent you from seeing the compost heap, but if the patio is next to the house it might also pose a security problem: you might not be able to see the back of your house when you are working elsewhere in the garden.

When you are choosing fence panels, look at how they have been made. Close-board fences, made of upright timbers, look good in a woodland garden and anywhere where you want to emphasize verticals. Interwoven fences tend to stress horizontal lines and are useful when you want to exaggerate the depth of the garden. In an Oriental-style setting, a bamboo fence is entirely appropriate, but it can be too lightweight for use anywhere other than in a sheltered corner. Trellis has the advantage that it functions well as a windbreak but can be clothed with dense climbers in summer to provide maximum privacy.

All fences can be painted or stained, either to soften their impact or to help them blend in with their surroundings. Alternatively, you might want to make a strong colour statement by painting them so that they really stand out. Whatever you do, make sure that any preservative or paint you use on the fences is plant friendly.

HEDGES

A hedge can be planted either to give privacy or to mark off one part of the garden from another. Thorny hedges, such as pyracantha, can also offer increased security if they are used around the boundary, but they are not ideal near children's play areas or beside paths and sitting areas.

Deciduous or Evergreen?

If you just want a windbreak, a deciduous hedge would be a good choice, because the bare branches will filter strong winter winds but in summer the leaf cover will provide shade and help to minimize noise. For an evergreen barrier, conifers such as yew (*Taxus*), box (*Buxus*) and *Thuja* are

*Above: Traditional and still best, tightly clipped box (*Buxus*) is a splendid choice for low hedging to surround beds in a formal garden.*

traditional choices, but they need regular clipping for a sheer surface and to restrict the height.

Do not plant Leyland cypress (x *Cuprocyparis leylandii*) within the garden: it will take the nutrients from other plants and will need to be clipped three or four times a year to prevent it from taking over completely.

Bear in mind that evergreens tend to be less tolerant of urban pollution. This is an important factor in a town garden, hence the popularity of privet (*Ligustrum*), which shows outstanding resistance.

Informal Hedges

In a town or Oriental-style garden, bamboos can make an elegant screen, and the light rustle of their leaves in summer is an added delight. Make sure you choose carefully: some species are invasive, and it is a sensible precaution to restrict the root system wherever they are planted. Plant them in large tubs and sink these into the ground or surround the roots with paving slabs buried vertically.

Climbing and rambling roses make good barriers and have the bonus of summer flowers and fragrance. Alternatively, an informal evergreen hedge can be created with spotted laurel (*Aucuba japonica* 'Crotonifolia') or

HEDGING PLANTS FOR PATIOS
Aucuba
Berberis
Buxus
Cotoneaster
Escallonia
Euonymus
Fagus
Fuchsia
Griselinia
Ilex
Laurus
Lonicera nitida
*Prunus (*evergreen*)*
*Rosa (*some*)*
Rosmarinus
Santolina

Portugal laurel (*Prunus lusitanica*), while a mixed hedge of hawthorn (*Crataegus*) and holly (*Ilex*) will suit a country or cottage garden.

Above: Hollies make good hedges, and berrying forms provide food for birds in winter. Ilex aquifolium 'J.C. van Tol' has the advantage of almost spineless leaves.

*Above: The cherry laurel (*Prunus laurocerasus*) makes an excellent informal evergreen hedge. This is the attractive cultivar 'Castlewellan'.*

107

Patio Planting

IN A LARGE GARDEN, THE PLANTING IS DESIGNED TO CONTRIBUTE TO THE OVERALL PICTURE, AND IS OFTEN SEEN FROM A DISTANCE. THE PATIO IS THE PLACE TO GROW SPECIES THAT ARE REWARDING AT CLOSE QUARTERS, SUCH AS THOSE WITH LAVISH FLOWERS OR A HEADY SCENT.

BRINGING THE PATIO TO LIFE

A beautifully designed patio or terrace with pleasing proportions may need only the minimum of plant material to decorate it. The focus of interest may be a beautiful specimen tree, or a pair of elegant containers. Most people who have a garden, however, eventually become hooked on plants, often in spite of themselves, and want to grow more unusual species. It is worth knowing which plants lend themselves especially well to this area of the garden and how they should be grown.

Above: Raised beds, generously planted with miniature roses, will be a source of colour all summer long.

Raised Beds

If you are constructing a completely new patio, you may decide to incorporate raised beds to edge the patio, in place of a balustrade or low wall. On a hard surface they must have in-built weep holes for drainage. Make sure the beds are not so wide that you cannot reach the centre (assuming there is access from both sides); this usually means limiting the width to 1.2m (4ft).

A raised bed has several advantages. It is effectively a large container, which makes it possible to grow plants that would not thrive elsewhere in the garden. Bringing in acid soil, for example, will create a suitable medium for rhododendrons and heathers, which you would not otherwise be able to grow if your soil is alkaline. If the garden soil is poor, raised beds give you the opportunity of importing new soil. Adding grit to improve drainage will open the door to a whole range of alpines and dwarf bulbs.

Combining raised beds with other borders and beds at ground level can bring a certain dynamism to the design, which is especially important if space is restricted.

Above: Ballerina apple trees are ideal patio plants. They can be trained to arch over to make a fruiting bower.

FLOWERS FOR SUNNY PATIOS
(a = annual or biennial; p = perennial)
Argyranthemum p
Bergenia p
Felicia p
Fuchsia p
Iris stylosa p
Pelargonium p
Tropaeolum a
Verbena a and p
Viola a and p

SELECTING PLANTS

What you grow in the ground adjoining the patio is obviously a matter of personal choice. The patio is often quite sheltered and if it is near the house it may benefit from the residual warmth of the walls, allowing you to grow less-hardy species.

If the patio is bounded by walls or fences on one or more sides, the rainfall will be restricted. Either be prepared to water the plants during dry weather or restrict your choice to drought-tolerant species, including bulbs and many herbs.

Planting in Sun

If your patio is sunny, you'll be spoiled for choice when planting up containers for spring and summer colour. Many fruits and vegetables are also extremely decorative, and a surprising number can be grown in containers on the patio. Ballerina apple trees were specially bred for this purpose, but almost any cultivar is suitable provided it has been grafted on to a dwarfing rootstock. Figs thrive in containers against a warm wall, and the root restriction helps produce bigger crops earlier in the plant's life. Luscious strawberries and tomatoes also make attractive plants for a sunny corner, with the bonus that you can pick the ripe fruit from your garden chair.

Above: Well-filled borders and containers soften the severe lines of this simple paved area and create a lush feel.

109

Planting for Shade

If you want the patio to be a shady area for summer relaxation you may have to plant to create shade. Among the many widely available and reliable deciduous trees are ornamental cherries (*Prunus*) and crab apples (*Malus*), which have delightful spring flowers. The best of all shade trees are, perhaps, catalpas and paulownias, both of which have large leaves. Both respond well to pruning so can be planted even where space is limited.

Your patio may already be shaded by walls and trees, but there are plenty of plants that will flourish in cool conditions, and it is easy to create a lush, jungle-like effect with luxurious foliage plants such as hostas and hardy ferns.

Above: This small area has been designed as a cool retreat, with a pool shaded by cleverly supported ivy and a thick wall of luxuriant foliage to create a screen.

Climbers and Ramblers

House walls or fences that abut a patio cry out for the softening effect of climbers. If possible, allow space for small beds between the patio and the wall or fence. Because they are largely woodland plants, most climbers appreciate the cool root run that the paving or decking over their roots will

---

FLOWERS FOR SHADY PATIOS
(a = annual or biennial; p = perennial)
Convallaria majalis p
Dicentra p
Impatiens a
Lobelia a
Pulmonaria p

---

provide. Make sure that such plants receive plenty of water. Your choice of climber will depend on the aspect of the wall: some species revel in the reflected heat; others are happier in shade. Some large-flowered clematis varieties, for instance, will produce flowers of a richer colour when shielded from intense sunlight.

Climbers can also be grown in containers, either placed against a wall or trained on a support that is incorporated in the pot. Some of the weaker-growing or annual climbers are best for containers. Rampant plants, such as wisteria and bougainvillea, can be grown in pots but will need hard pruning to keep them within bounds.

If you want flowering climbers for a confined space, good choices are to be found among the large-flowered hybrid clematis and miniature climb-

> CLIMBERS FOR PATIOS
> (* = shade tolerant)
> *Bougainvillea (*not hardy*)*
> *Campsis radicans*
> *Clematis* *
> *Hedera* *
> *Humulus lupulus*
> *Hydrangea petiolaris* *
> *Jasminum officinale*
> *Plumbago auriculata (*not hardy*)*
> *Rosa* (miniature climbers*)*
> *Trachelospermum jasminoides*
> *Tropaeolum speciosum*
> *Wisteria*

ing roses. The so-called patio roses and miniature climbers have been specially bred with present needs in mind: they are compact plants that produce an abundance of flowers over a long period. They are ideal for planting in beds, borders and containers. Some of the roses bred for groundcover can also be trained upward, to cover walls and trellises.

Above: Hedera helix '*Buttercup*', *smaller growing than many ivies, produces its best leaf colour in a sunny position.*

Above: The annual Ipomoea tricolor *has vivid blue flowers and is perfect for guiding over a trellis.*

111

Above: The poached-egg plant (Limnanthes douglasii) *is a modest annual that will obligingly seed itself in the cracks of paving and in gravel.*

Perennials and Annuals

Flowering herbaceous plants put the flesh on the bones of the garden, as it were, producing an abundance of greenery and, in most cases, a spectacular show of flowers over a long period. The more compact, sturdy forms are best suited to the patio whereas tall, floppy plants, such as delphiniums and some peonies, which need to be staked, look more effective when planted in the herbaceous border.

Most valuable of all for the patio are the tender perennials, such as felicias, verbenas, pelargoniums and osteospermums, which you can grow from seed or buy as small plants in late spring. These showy plants produce a seemingly unending succession of flowers from the start of summer until the first frosts. They are ideal for all kinds of patio containers, from hanging baskets to large troughs. If you have a greenhouse, plant tender perennials in pots and tubs that can be moved under glass for the winter.

Annuals will also produce flowers all summer, although many varieties should be sown successively for the maximum flowering period. Deadhead the plants regularly to encourage them to produce further blooms, and feed them well to maintain their flower power. While perennials and shrubs will give structure to your planting plan, growing annuals allows you to transform the look of your patio with a fresh colour scheme each year.

Above: The succulent-looking evergreen Sedum aizoon *will thrive in the heat reflected by paving.*

Low-growing Shrubs

Compact, tightly growing shrubs are ideal for patios because they are easy to control and naturally stay within bounds. Evergreens that have a pleasing shape, such as Mexican orange blossom (*Choisya ternata*), are obviously desirable, but there are others, such as box (*Buxus*), that can be clipped to shape and some, such as *Phillyrea*, that can be allowed to grow more freely. Small shrubs such as camellia, fuchsia and skimmia can be grown as specimens in containers.

Patio and groundcover roses are recently bred varieties that are quite unlike the often gangly hybrid teas and cluster-flowered roses: they are low-growing, tough and disease-resistant. They smother themselves in flowers and repeat well throughout the summer, making them perfect plants in every way for a sunny patio.

Bulbs and Corms

Many bulbs are ideal patio plants, and not just in containers. Early spring bulbs, such as crocuses and dwarf narcissi, look delightful pushing up through gravel. If you have a hot spot near a sheltering wall, include some of the late-flowering South African species, such as crinums, nerines and *Amaryllis belladonna* (the true amaryllis, not the hippeastrums sold under this name for growing indoors in winter).

SHRUBS FOR PATIOS
Buxus
Calluna
Camellia
Choisya ternata
Conifers *(dwarf forms)*
Erica
Fuchsia
Hebe
Ilex
Phillyrea
Rhododendron (dwarf forms)
Rosa (patio, miniature and groundcover forms)
Skimmia

BULBS FOR PATIOS
Agapanthus
Amaryllis belladonna
Crinum
Crocus
Dahlia (dwarf forms)
Iris
Lilium
Nerine

*Above: The aptly named pineapple lily (*Eucomis bicolor*) is not quite hardy but will thrive in sheltered conditions.*

113

Foliage Plants

Delightful as flowers are, they are present for a much shorter period in the plant's annual life cycle than leaves. Leaves are the backdrop to any planting, and once you learn to appreciate their variety of shape, colour and texture, you will come to value them as much as flowers.

Some plants are grown primarily for their foliage. In fact, some of the best – ferns – do not flower at all in the conventional sense. Mainly shade lovers, these are ideal for bringing life to cool, shady, moist corners, perhaps adjoining a basement flat. Team them with hostas for contrast, but watch out for slugs and snails, which also like shady, moist conditions.

Grasses are increasingly popular, and with good reason. They are easy to maintain, and even those that are not evergreen provide a long period of interest, since the old foliage is retained by the plant over winter. A riming of frost on a cold winter's morning only adds to their beauty. They are useful for softening a vivid planting of flowers and work surprisingly well with conifers.

Above: *A cool, shady patio with a bubble fountain to provide a moist atmosphere is the perfect environment for potted hostas and tree ferns (*Dicksonia antarctica*).*

PLANTS WITH GOOD FOLIAGE

Ajuga reptans
Aloe
Aucuba
Conifers
Eriobotrya japonica
Ferns
Grasses
Hebe
Hedera
Hosta
Ophiopogon nigrescens
Pulmonaria
Stachys olympica

Architectural Plants

Some plants are grown for their overall impact – usually termed their habit – and they make striking shapes in the garden. If you intend to use the patio mainly in the evening and at night, it is worth including some of these in the planting: they are supremely effective

Above: Melianthus major, *with its luxuriant leaves, stately yuccas and steely blue oat grass add contrasting colour and form to a striking group of foliage plants.*

with subtle lighting, which will highlight large glossy leaves or distinctive silhouettes. Fatsias are usually grown as houseplants, but they are more or less hardy and take kindly to life outdoors in a sheltered spot. Their palm-like, evergreen leaves bring a touch of the exotic to the garden.

Above: Plant Ophiopogon planiscapus *'Nigrescens' against a light backdrop.*

ARCHITECTURAL PLANTS FOR PATIOS

Cordyline
Cycas revoluta
Eriobotrya japonica
Fatsia japonica
Mahonia x media
Phormium
Trachycarpus fortunei
Yucca

Choosing a Style

THERE ARE AS MANY STYLES OF PATIO AS THERE ARE STYLES OF
INDOOR DÉCOR. THIS SECTION EXPLORES JUST A FEW OF THE DESIGN
TRENDS THAT ARE POPULAR TODAY AND SUGGESTS WAYS IN WHICH
THEY CAN BE INTERPRETED ON A PATIO OR TERRACE.

DEFINING STYLE

The decorative aspects of a patio –
from the plants in the borders to the
cushions you place on the garden
chairs – are personal, and what repre-
sents good taste to one gardener may
well be anathema to another.
However, factors such as proportion
and scale are universals. No matter
how you decorate your outdoor space,
a successful patio will be in proportion to the rest of the garden and to
the house, and it should be sympathetic in overall appearance to the
style and materials used for the other
buildings against which it is set.

*Above: Foliage plants clothe the fences
and screen a seat in a restful corner of the
garden, providing dappled shade and
shelter from the breeze.*

Other aspects of design depend on
your approach to life, and it is these
that we tend to think of as embodying
a particular "style". Fashion plays a
part too, and even if you think you are
not a slave to the latest trends, some
become so commonplace that you
can hardly avoid them. Wooden decking is now so widespread and easily
available that it has become the first
choice of many people who would
previously have considered only

Above: Neat metal containers, filled with a phormium, ferns and clipped evergreens, give the garden an orderly air.

Above: These exuberant climbing roses ensure a private and fragrant retreat, even in a town garden.

paving. With a trend as popular as this, however, you need to consider carefully whether it is really the most appropriate material for your garden.

Some people like to give order to their spaces. Others have a more relaxed attitude and may tolerate, even prefer, a certain dishevelment. The two are not mutually exclusive, but a tendency one way or the other may well be evident in how you design and create your garden.

Like the rest of your home, the garden allows you to express your personality. It also reflects the way you choose to spend your time. If you think of the patio as a quiet retreat, you'll plan for privacy and comfort. If your garden is often the setting for parties, your priorities will be space, seating and dramatic lighting effects. If the house opens on to the patio, it is a good idea to relate the two, perhaps

using furniture in similar styles or matching colours. You could extend a tiled floor outside, or echo a wooden floor with decking.

Remember that no scheme need be for ever, and you can change the look with new planting and furniture. Many people update their gardens as often as they change their interiors.

Above: A variety of natural materials can be laid in clean, geometric designs to suit a modern setting.

COUNTRY CASUAL

Many town-dwellers would like to bring something of the countryside into their garden, so that it becomes a kind of green lung, with the same function as a park in the middle of a city. The fact that the garden (or a proportion of it) is paved does not prevent this from happening, but a bit more effort may be required to create the desired effect.

Creating the Look

The choice of materials can be critical. Instead of municipal-looking, smooth concrete slabs, look for riven paving in different sizes to create a slightly haphazard look. Decking often looks a little cosmopolitan, especially when the boards are new, but old railway sleepers (ties) have a weathered charm. As far as possible, make sure that the edges of any paved area or raised bed are softened by planting.

When it comes to garden furniture, keep an eye out for wicker or cane chairs, which will have the appropriate rustic character. Weathered pieces of wooden or metal garden furniture can often be found second-hand, and some antique dealers specialize in old garden furniture of high quality – though this can be expensive. For a seaside look, use deck chairs or steamer chairs. A hammock slung between two trees (or possibly between a tree

Above: A simple arbour made from painted wooden trellis makes a pretty backdrop for plants and an inviting place to sit a while to enjoy the garden.

Above: Billowing plants in the borders and containers create an exuberant casual effect, disguising the formal shape of a small courtyard garden.

Above: A profusion of lush plants, like Zantedeschia aethiopica 'Crowborough', creates a relaxed, unstructured cottage-garden feel.

and a house wall) makes an idyllic picture in summer and is ideal for a nap on a warm afternoon.

An eclectic mix is appropriate, and *objets trouvés* can provide just the right note. An old metal watering can or that cartwheel will give a hint of rusticity. If you cannot find old terracotta pots, paint new ones with sour milk or yoghurt to encourage mosses and lichens to take a hold.

Planting

A cottage garden is primarily one of early and high summer. Typical flowers include all kinds of roses, especially the scented ones, old-fashioned pinks (*Dianthus*) and a host of annuals. Pelargoniums are cheerful and bright and will flower for months. Lavender (*Lavandula*) is an excellent low-grow-

ing hedging plant and will provide a romantic haze of colour when in flower (as well as attracting swarms of bees).

Aim for a riotous mix of colour and don't forget the fruit and vegetables without which no true cottage gardener could survive for long.

Above: A pot overflowing with herbs epitomizes the cottage garden style.

MODERN

If you have a beautiful, architect-designed house and are a naturally neat and tidy person with an uncluttered lifestyle, this may well be the look for you.

Creating the Look

Absolutely up-to-date materials are *de rigueur* for high-tech designers, and metals and plastics are likely to be used as often as more traditional materials. Inventive finishes are important: marble and granite, for instance – surely the most desirable of all traditional building materials – can be polished to a glass-like surface or given a more frosted appearance. Crushed CDs, a recent innovation to be used in place of gravel and crushed shells, have a real sparkle.

A smart urban look can be created using a limited colour palette, in both materials and plants. While natural materials are generally left to speak for themselves, artificial ones are often dyed to shades that would never occur in nature. You can find manmade pebbles in bright blues and reds and plastic pots in a range of colours.

If you have a keen design sense (or are able to employ a designer), you might like to experiment with asymmetric shapes, but make sure that the design is not too dominant. Look beyond gardening for your inspiration: architectural magazines and the world of industry and product design may well ignite your creative fire.

A possible drawback is that a garden in this style can date quickly as new trends emerge.

Above: Smooth tiles and mirrors create an illusion of space on a small modern terrace.

Above: Top-dressing pots with some of the cobbles that have been used for the patio surface will help give coherence to the overall design.

Above: Colour can be used on both boundaries and containers to create a sense of unity. Even the spiral plant supports are blue.

Planting

On the green front, stick to plants that have a strong outline and architectural form. Spiky succulents, such as agaves, are perfect but will not tolerate extremes of cold and wet. Phormiums and the Chusan palm (*Trachycarpus fortunei*) are hardier and just as dramatic.

Low-growing plants with metallic-looking leaves include *Houttuynia cordata* and *Ajuga reptans* 'Burgundy Glow'. Selected forms of *Pulmonaria saccharata* Argentea Group have interestingly marbled leaves, and *Heuchera* 'Pewter Moon' makes satisfying clumps of silver-grey foliage. Many grasses are perfect for the modern look,

and they can be used on their own, either planted *en masse* or displayed for effect in matching containers.

Most flowers do not really belong in a garden of this type, but they need not be eliminated entirely, and those with a sculptural form are best. Spring-flowering hyacinths have a stiff habit and their thick, glossy leaves look positively unreal. Planted in quantity, they look (and smell) sensational. For summer interest, grow lilies, with their trumpet-like flowers. *Zantedeschia aethiopica* is a plant of unsurpassed elegance, with cool-looking, heart-shaped leaves and smooth-textured, white, arum-type flowers. It is perfect near (or even in) water.

121

Choosing a Style

MEDITERRANEAN

Memories of Mediterranean summers make many of us long for lazy days of outdoor living, soaking up the sun or relaxing in leafy shade, surrounded by the scents of aromatic herbs, pines and citrus. A real Mediterranean garden is usually a shady place, often a court-yard, brightened with pots of vivid flowers and sheltered by a pergola draped with fruiting vines. Walls and woodwork, often bleached and cracked by the sun, are painted in the Mediterranean palette of clear blues, dusky pinks, terracotta or white.

Above: Pale decking reflects the available light and large terracotta containers give a strongly Mediterranean feel.

Creating the Look

In cooler climates, a Mediterranean-style patio can maximize the available sunshine by using white or pale paving to reflect heat on to the plants. Another way to achieve this is through the use of gravel or, if your budget will stretch to it, dolomite chippings. If you can lay out the garden as a series of terraces that face the sun, so much the better. A brick or stone wall that faces the sun will retain the day's heat and radiate it at dusk, appreciably raising the ambient temperature. To a lesser degree, so will stone and terra-cotta pots and paving.

Your Mediterranean patio should include a shaded area to offer relief from the sun on the hottest days. Erect a simple pergola over a seat or table, and plant climbers to scramble over it.

A positive aspect of this style is that you will feel as if you are always on holiday – at least as long as the sun is shining. As soon as wet weather arrives, you may notice that gravel starts to turn green as moss and lichens take hold. Either chemical treatments or a blast with a pressure washer will solve this problem for you.

Planting

Typical plants of the Mediterranean include most of the woody herbs, including thyme, rosemary and laven-der, which thrive in gritty, well-drained soil in your sunniest spot. These,

together with rock roses (*Cistus* and *Helianthemum*), with gummy, aromatic stems, will fill the patio with evocative scents as well as attracting bees and butterflies. Oleanders (*Nerium oleander*) are also characteristic of the region, with their leathery leaves and richly coloured flowers (but they are poisonous, so treat them with care). Pelargoniums flower all summer, giving bold splashes of white, pink and red. If you need an accent plant, a fig, olive or citrus tree would be perfect.

Most of these plants respond well to being grown in containers or raised beds, making them ideal patio plants.

Mediterranean plants do not take kindly to long periods of cold, wet weather, though they will survive lower temperatures if planted in open, gritty soil. You can move delicate subjects in pots under cover in winter.

Above: Brightly painted furniture and accessories, with flowers in strong, warm colours, create a Mediterranean feel in a sunny corner of this patio.

*Above: Evergreen bay (*Laurus nobilis*) grows readily in a container and the leaves are invaluable in cooking.*

123

Above: A sheltered corner of the patio takes on a jungly character when lavishly filled with foliage plants. Although they look exotic, they are all quite hardy.

HOT AND EXOTIC

Surprisingly, it is not actually necessary to live in a hot climate to create a tropical look in your garden, and the enclosed, sheltered conditions found on many patios, which may have protecting walls on two and even three sides, often provide the ideal micro-climate for many exotic plants that would not otherwise survive.

Creating the Look

The keynote to success is to include lots of foliage plants, preferably the large-leaved kind. If you have enough greenery you will actually increase the humidity level of the garden, creating the jungle-like environment in which these plants will thrive. Bearing in mind that a lot of tropical plants have

adapted to low light levels, this style can be an effective design solution to a predominantly shady site.

A timber deck creates the appropriate colonial atmosphere, and the furnishings might be either huge wicker chairs or teak recliners. A mosquito net would provide a witty reference to the tropics, especially if there were a pool nearby.

Planting

Huge bamboos actually look extremely effective in a confined space and are hardy. Try also banana palms (*Musa basjoo*), which will require some winter protection. If the patio is shaded, you may prefer a tree fern (*Dicksonia antarctica*). Buy the biggest you can afford, because they grow at a rate of only 2.5cm (1in) a year, so if you buy

Above: Small pans of succulents will enjoy the warmth reflected from the paving.

a youngster you will have to be prepared for a long wait. Large specimens are expensive but worth the outlay when you consider the drama they bring to a garden.

An interesting and less often seen alternative is the loquat (*Eriobotrya japonica*). In a cold climate it is hardly likely to fruit, but you can enjoy it for its exotic-looking, long, pleated leaves.

Remember that if you have a lot of houseplants you can move them outdoors in summer (when there is no risk of night frosts) to enhance the tropical atmosphere.

A Desert Patio

If your patio is really hot and exposed, a desert-style planting scheme might be appropriate, concentrating on cacti and succulents. Some cacti are surprisingly tolerant of cold. What they hate is damp, muggy weather, which causes rotting, so good drainage is vital.

Above: Succulents in pots, which do duty as houseplants, will benefit from being moved outside in summer.

They will thrive in gravel beds, which can be given extra structure by the addition of rocks or pebbles.

In this kind of garden you need to avoid any suspicion of lushness. Smooth-rendered walls will enhance the desert feel and reflect sunlight and heat on to the plants, staying warm even as the temperature drops in the evening. Leave gaps for the plants among paving stones, or make larger beds by laying a weed-suppressing membrane over the soil and planting through it before topping with gravel or cobbles. On a smaller scale, fill troughs or planters with succulents.

It is possible to replicate this look even in a cold climate if you keep your exotic plants in pots for enjoying indoors in winter. Plunge them into their beds in the summer.

ORIENTAL

The Zen principles on which the classic gardens of Japan and China are laid out probably baffle most Westerners, but this is no reason why we should not borrow some of the ideas to create Oriental-style gardens that are places of peace and tranquillity and conducive to contemplation.

Creating the Look

The true Japanese garden usually contains only a few plants. Everything depends on the balance of a few elements: rocks, raked gravel, water and maybe a conifer or Japanese maple (*Acer*). Any tree with an interesting outline will do, however. In essence,

Above: Low, clean lines using natural materials, and the restrained use of foliage plants, create an elegant, structured look that echoes Japanese garden design.

Above: Topiarized box, trained into the traditional cloud form, is a feature of Oriental-style gardens.

the style is rather akin to the minimalist garden and will suit anyone who does not have a great deal of time on their hands, since what plants there are need little maintenance. The style also lends itself to a shady site.

Alternatively, you might like to borrow some elements of feng shui. Although this philosophy is more often thought of in relation to interior design, the principles are equally applicable outdoors. You may want to incorporate wind chimes (but think of your neighbours, who might be profoundly irritated by the tinkling sound that you find so charming) and a water feature, but it is how you place them in relation to each other that counts. Any paths should be winding, to symbolize the winding route of life.

126

Planting

China is often referred to as the mother of all gardens, because a huge number of the plants that are now most prized in cultivation originated there. There is therefore no shortage of plant material available to help you create an Oriental look: whether you prefer blowsy peonies or delicate grasses, you will be able to find the appropriate species.

The classic Japanese garden is predominantly green, imitating a natural landscape. Japanese maples (*Acer japonicum* and *A. palmatum*) have an elegant habit that you can enhance by wiring the stems as they grow to create an authentic gnarled appearance.

Velvety, vivid green moss is essential to the look. You can encourage it to colonize rocks by painting their shady sides with sour milk or yoghurt, but keep walkways and steps clear of moss as it can be very slippery.

If you must have flowers, some of the China roses, such as *Rosa* 'Cécile Brünner', are delightfully dainty, and many of the so-called patio roses seem to owe much to their Chinese forebears, making them ideal for an Oriental garden. Oriental lilies and chrysanthemums, such as 'Emperor of China', could complete the picture.

On a tiny patio, you might like to include some bonsai in Oriental pots.

Above: This serene Buddha would make the perfect finishing touch to an Oriental-style patio.

Above: Dainty but floriferous, Rosa 'Cécile Brünner' is ideal for a large container in a Chinese-style garden.

Special Features

ONCE THE PATIO IS BUILT, FINISHING TOUCHES WILL HELP TO BRING IT TO LIFE. A CAREFULLY PLACED POT, AN UNUSUAL SCULPTURE OR INTRIGUING ITEMS OF FURNITURE CAN PROVIDE THE ACCENTS OF COLOUR AND SHAPE NEEDED TO TIE THE WHOLE SCHEME TOGETHER.

FURNITURE

The range of garden furniture available today is wide, and you can choose the type best suited to your needs. You need to consider, for instance, if the furniture is to stand outdoors all year round or if you are going to store it under cover when not in use.

Different furniture fulfils different purposes. A steamer chair is perfect for lolling in the sun with a refreshing drink and the Sunday newspaper but is less than ideal if you are eating a formal meal. If you are planning a barbecue, you might like to dispense with seating altogether, to encourage guests to mingle more freely.

Heavy furniture, such as cast iron and stone, is attractive but difficult to move once it is in place. If your patio is small and has to accommodate different activities at different times, lightweight, and folding, alternatives are more convenient.

Above: A simple garden bench and fragrant flowers are all that is needed to make a delightful sanctuary.

Above: These dainty metal chairs are surprisingly comfortable and make an ideal choice for a small area, as they are in keeping with its scale.

Above: These two throne-like chairs on a raised terrace echo the curves of the patio design and have been used as its most dominant feature.

Types of Furniture

Top of the range is cast-iron furniture, which is expensive and heavy and is, in consequence, no longer made in great quantities. Antique pieces are extremely sought after and are usually highly decorative. Aluminium reproductions are much cheaper and lighter but are not always entirely convincing. Wire furniture, often painted white but more often these days coated in plastic, is highly ornate and perhaps best suited to a Victorian-style conservatory, although it is light enough to carry on to the patio in warm weather.

Wooden furniture is also expensive, especially if it is made of teak (the best wood for the purpose), but it is a sound investment and ages sympathetically. It will need treating with teak oil from time to time to stop the wood drying out and cracking. You should make sure that any teak furniture you buy is certified as having been made of wood from a sustainable source.

Deck chairs and director's chairs are convenient because they can be folded up and stored flat when they are not in use. They are also light enough to be moved from place to place as needed.

Bamboo, cane and rattan furniture is ideal for creating a colonial look, but it is not especially weatherproof. A coat of varnish can help prevent cracking, but this type of furniture is seldom long-lived.

Plastic furniture is usually cheap and readily available, but you may need to shop around to find a range that is really sympathetic. On the plus side, it is lightweight and can be painted or otherwise customized with cushions made to fit. Pre-formed plastic chairs are often stackable, which makes winter storage easy.

129

WATER FEATURES

A pool or fountain will add life to the patio, in more ways than one. Not only is the sound of water reviving – most people find it soothing, particularly in the evening – but water will attract a range of fauna into the garden: frogs, toads and newts as well as a host of insects.

Types of Water Feature

A patio or deck that meets or overhangs a pool looks dramatic, while even a small pool set into the paving or decking brings all the pleasures of a pool in the open garden. Formal, geometric pools work best close to a house, and they should ideally be based on the proportions of the house windows or doors and built with the same type of materials as the house.

Remember that it will be difficult (if not impossible) to excavate for a sunken pool on an existing patio. If you are building your patio from scratch and would like to include a pool, allow for the depth of the water in the height of the patio. The alternative is to build a raised pool surrounded by paving, a wooden framework or railway sleepers (ties).

If you favour an expanse of still water, try to site the pool away from trees, as leaves will rot and pollute the water. Most surface-growing water plants do best in sun, but if the pool is purely ornamental a shaded site is permissible, and you can keep the water clear with a chemical cleansing agent.

On a large patio a fountain would be the ultimate luxury, especially in a hot, dry climate. Cascades can be

Above: A well-planted raised pool is ideal on a patio because it does not involve excavating below the hard surface.

Above: When running, the wall-mounted spout will be a focal point and provide the refreshing sound of trickling water.

impressive, but for a really imposing fall of water a large reservoir and powerful submersible pump are needed. If you have a small pool in a sunny position and would like a fountain, look for one that is solar-powered. These are becoming more widely available and more attractive. Some models have separate solar panels, but increasingly they are manufactured with integral panels.

If you have small children most kinds of water feature are best avoided altogether: it is possible to drown in even the shallowest water. Installing a bubble fountain can be a good compromise because no deep water is accessible, but remember that the reservoir and pump must be housed below ground level and hidden by cobbles that sit on top of a mesh. Such

Above: A keen sense of humour is evident in the design of this water spout in a wooden half-barrel. Small raised features like this are quite simple to install.

features involve excavating below the level of the patio, so this must be taken into account during the planning process.

Many styles of ready-made water feature are available from garden suppliers, and these are simple to install. Designs such as a brimming urn or village pump are popular, and if ground space is really restricted, a wall spout that feeds into a basin just below can be delightful. Wall-mounted water features should never be fitted directly to a house wall, and it may be necessary to erect a double wall to house the pipe and pump.

Introducing the electricity needed to power a submersible pump should be considered during the planning stages. Because water and electricity are a lethal combination, seek professional advice about the appropriate switches and cables.

Above: If you choose a water feature that relies on a circulating pump, make sure you can excavate below ground for the sump.

LIGHTING

You will get the most use from your patio or terrace on summer evenings if you add some form of lighting. If the patio is some distance from the house but is visible from it, lighting it can bring an element of drama that you can also enjoy from the comfort of indoors at other seasons. Floodlighting can be spectacular when the ground is covered in snow.

All electrical lighting systems powered from the mains should be installed by a qualified electrician. Regulations stipulate how deep electric cables should be buried, and these should be adhered to. As with cabling for a pool, the lighting cables should be laid before the patio or terrace is built, but if this is not possible they should be buried where no digging that could damage the wires is likely to take place.

Remember that outdoor lighting should be designed to be seen only within your own garden. Your neighbours may prefer their gardens to be dark at night.

Types of Lighting

The simplest way to illuminate your patio is with candles or flares. Obviously, these are not permanent, and they must be supervised at all times. Both are best in still weather, but flares are much less likely to blow out than candles; you will need to

Above: This brass oil or paraffin lamp is easily portable and looks beautiful whether it is lit or not.

ensure that they can be properly supported in the ground or in stable containers. Candles can be housed in lanterns and distributed around the patio or suspended from trees.

Low-voltage lighting is cheap but is best used to edge a path, since the light shed will not be particularly strong. For safety, paths should always be lit at night if the garden is going to be used then, and solar-powered lights are now available that are ideal for this purpose.

Floodlights are much more powerful, and many dramatic effects can be achieved if they are sited with care. If

Above: Dramatic uplighting from the patio gives this delicate maple an added attraction at night.

of terracotta. These are designed as wood-burners, but you will need to substitute a non-smoking fuel if you live in a smokeless zone. They are made in a range of sizes. They need to be supervised at all times when lit and can pose a hazard if there are small children around.

Gas patio heaters are surprisingly stylish. They are usually fed by bottled gas rather than connected to the mains supply and are lit at the top, the heat being deflected downwards by a small canopy. They can look rather like municipal street lamps, but on a cool autumn evening the warmth they emit will be welcome.

there is a tree overhanging the patio, it is a charming idea to festoon it with fairy lights (coloured or not) or individual lanterns.

Underwater lamps can be used to light up a pond and will keep any fish active until well into the evening.

HEATING

Various forms of heating are available to bring a touch of warmth to those evenings when there is a chill in the air after sundown.

Perhaps the cosiest is the chiminea, a Mexican stove, which is open at the front and the top and is usually made

Above: Lighting a water feature brings drama to the patio after sundown.

SAFETY FIRST

Be sure to keep a fire extinguisher handy at all times if you are lighting or heating your patio with any form of naked flame.

133

MIRRORS

Not everyone appreciates the use of mirrors in a garden. There is no doubt that they increase the sense of size of a small space, but some people are unnerved by catching a glimpse of themselves. There is also the argument that birds will fly into them, although this is unlikely in an enclosed space such as a patio or terrace, since most birds prefer to keep to the trees if there is no clear runway for take-off.

If you include a mirror, site it with care for maximum impact, angling it slightly so that visitors to the garden do not merely see their own reflections. Placed at the end of a path, it will make the garden seem endless. If you have no paths, put a mirror where it will reflect a particular feature: a statue, a large container or even just a garden door. Mirrors are especially effective in association with water features, but they must be set perfectly upright if distorting effects are to be avoided. Disguise the mirror's presence by surrounding it with planting to hide the edges.

Use mirrors designed for outdoor use; those made for indoors are not particularly weatherproof and will soon begin to deteriorate.

ORNAMENTS

A well-chosen ornament can bring a touch of distinction to a patio, especially in winter when there may be a shortage of plant material to bring the

Above: An unusual metallic trellis functions as a mirror, creating the illusion that the garden is more colourful than it actually is.

Above: An arbour festooned with flowers makes a frame for a piece of classical statuary, creating a theatrical effect.

area to life. They can be given a position of some prominence or be hidden among plants or pots to make a personal or witty reference. Reflected in water or a mirror, their impact will be doubled. At best, they give a sense of permanence to the garden.

Make sure the ornament is in scale, but err on the large side if you are in doubt. Too small an ornament will look mean and lost, but one that is large will look grand and imposing and will make a considerable impact on a small patio.

Types of Ornament

Garden statuary is a matter of taste. Top of the list would be a work (possibly abstract) from a sculptor's studio, but this is likely to be beyond the purse and aspirations of most gardeners. Garden centres stock a wide range of mass-produced ornaments, and whether your preference is for stone animals or abstract designs such as obelisks or balls, you will probably find something to suit your patio.

For something a little more individual, go to a reclamation yard, where you can often find old statues and other ornaments. A rusted piece of agricultural equipment can make an appealing *objet trouvé*. Ceramics can be beautiful, though the production process limits their size. If you are naturally creative, you could try making your own abstract piece.

Above: A sombre-looking statue adds grand ornamentation to a garden. Once foliage starts to grow around it, its appearance will be less stark.

Materials

Bronze is beautiful and ages sympathetically, but the price is likely to be prohibitive. Nowadays, synthetic resins provide a convincing substitute at a much lower cost. Stone ornaments are heavy, and reconstituted stone pieces often have a tell-tale seam left from the mould that betrays their manufacture. However, they weather beautifully, acquiring an attractive covering of moss in time.

Plastic ornaments are light and tend to blow over, so they are perhaps best used among plants rather than as stand-alone features. Ceramics need to be securely placed, since they can crack or even break if they fall over.

135

Awnings and Shade

If the patio catches the midday sun you may find the glare and heat all but unbearable in summer. If there is no tree nearby, an awning or overhead screen can cast the necessary shade.

Types of Awning

Some awnings are designed to be attached to a house wall and are operated either manually or electronically. This restricts both their use and their design: they are an option only if the patio abuts a house wall; there must be a sufficient stretch of wall to accommodate them, and they must be rectangular or square in shape. If placed just above a sitting-room window or a pair of patio doors, they will

Above: A bespoke awning over a patio can make a bold design statement.

have the dual function of shading the room. This type of awning is traditionally made of striped fabric with a scalloped or fringed edge. If you want something a little more individual, you could have a bespoke canopy made of canvas or sailcloth, to sling between poles or the patio walls.

If the patio is some distance from a suitable wall, a stand-alone awning will be required. At its simplest, this could be a large parasol; these are often designed to be used in conjunction with a table, and they have the advantage that they can be moved around as the direction of the sun changes. A rectangular gazebo, like a tent with open sides, will keep sun or rain off a larger table and chairs.

No awning is fully weatherproof. If accidentally left in the rain, they should be allowed to dry out fully then stored dry under cover.

Pergolas and Arbours

If you are building a completely new patio that is likely to be in full sun for most of the day, consider building a pergola to provide shade over part of it. A pergola is simply a framework of wooden posts with cross-pieces, but when it is clothed with climbing plants in summer it can become a shady room. A free-standing pergola constructed some distance from the house and built over a paved area will be a private, shady place.

A well-built pergola will be strong enough to support a large wisteria or fruiting vine, but it is also a perfect structure over which honeysuckle, roses and clematis can be trained. The deciduous hop (*Humulus lupulus*) will provide reliable summer shade but disappear in winter to admit all the available light.

An arbour is smaller in scale than a pergola but also offers opportunities to create a hideaway covered with fragrant climbers. Even a simple rustic arch, set against a hedge, will provide sufficient shelter for a table and two chairs, and a larger area, perhaps with a gazebo or summerhouse, will be a delightful retreat on a hot day.

Above: On a small patio, a focal point can be created at ground level by using surface materials creatively.

CREATING A FOCAL POINT

A focal point is an important aspect of any garden design, providing a resting place for the eye in much the same way as a fireplace in a sitting room, even though there may be other objects of interest present.

It need not be a permanent fixture. If, for instance, your patio is some distance from the house but visible from it, a well-positioned chair might be used to draw your attention to it.

A more permanent focal point can be provided by an ornament, a large container or an imposing plant, and other elements on the patio can be arranged to lead the eye toward it. A series of linked focal points can be useful in a large garden to draw different elements together, but they should be positioned so that they are not all visible simultaneously. Only when you arrive at one focal point will you be aware of the presence of another. Conversely, a single object can do double duty at the axis of two paths, providing the focal point for both. There is no limit to the number of visual games you can play.

Mark out the position of focal points with string stretched between pegs, and move them around until you find the right spot for the object. If the intended focal point already exists – for instance a garden door or a tree – use the string to determine the lie of the paths.

137

LOW-MAINTENANCE GARDENING

If you want a lovely garden but don't have the time or energy to do a lot of work in it, help is at hand. There are countless ways you can minimize the amount of maintenance your garden requires, while still keeping it looking beautiful. This chapter offers suggestions for designing an easy-care garden, as well as tips on reducing routine tasks and a wide range of plants that can be happily left to take care of themselves.

Left: Large shrubs cover lots of ground and stop weeds growing in profusion, helping to create a low-maintenance garden.

Making Less Work

CREATING AND MAINTAINING A BEAUTIFUL GARDEN DOESN'T HAVE TO BE TIME-CONSUMING. THERE ARE DOZENS OF WAYS IN WHICH THE VARIOUS COMPONENTS OF THE GARDEN AND THE PLANTING METHODS CAN BE ADAPTED TO MAKE MAINTENANCE EASIER.

Gardens should give pleasure and be places to enjoy. If yours takes up so much of your time in routine maintenance that you have little left in which to really appreciate it, you need to think about how to reduce the labour, without losing out on its beauty.

WHAT IS LOW MAINTENANCE?

Low maintenance does not simply mean cutting down on the number of plants that you grow. The choice of specimens and how you use them is more important – many plants

Above: *Ground-cover plants like this prostrate cotoneaster look better than bare soil, and they won't give weeds a chance to grow once they are established.*

require hardly any attention from one year to the next. You can also greatly reduce your workload with imaginative design and landscaping.

THE BENEFITS

A modestly sized, low-maintenance garden may require only half an hour a week to keep it looking good. But a truly low-maintenance garden, in which many labour-intensive components such as the lawn or difficult plants have been dispensed with, could require so little work that even if you took several weeks' holiday, it would have little effect on the appearance.

Left: Heathers and dwarf conifers are attractive all year round and need only occasional attention.

Assessing Your Garden

You need to assess which jobs you enjoy and which you dislike, then set about modifying your garden in the order of your priorities and how much time you want to save. If you enjoy propagating but hate weeding, for instance, you need to eliminate the weeds, and if you don't have time to mow the lawn you need to install other surfaces.

Take into account the style of your house and the existing shape and design of the garden itself to make sure that any new feature will fit in and not look out of place.

Check that new plants will grow happily in the soil and position. Some low-maintenance plants such as heathers and conifers have distinct soil preferences for you to consider.

How to Use This Chapter

Take from this chapter those ideas that will combine the plants and features you like with the amount of time you want to spend maintaining your garden. In *Easy Garden Maintenance* find out how to make routine jobs less of a chore. *Easy-care Gardens* contains ideas on how different features can be combined to create an attractive garden design needing minimal attention. *Low-maintenance Landscaping* explains how hard and soft surfaces can be used to reduce your workload. *Low-maintenance Plants* provides information on easy-to-grow plants. There is also a section showing how special features, such as a kitchen garden, can be made less time-consuming, as well as a chart to help you select and grow easy-care plants.

Above: Containers with low-maintenance plants can be used to add interest to areas of paving which also require minimal attention.

141

Easy Garden Maintenance

No matter how well designed a garden is, a small amount of routine maintenance will always be necessary, but there are various ways of making many of the regular tasks much less time-consuming and easier to do.

Labour-saving Tools

Using the right tools can save you time and effort, and will make the difference between a job being a pleasure or a chore. Good tools, especially power tools, can be expensive and take up space, so decide which ones will really reduce the time you spend gardening.

Nylon Line Trimmers

These useful tools will cut down long grass around trees, against fences and along edges in no time at all. Many can also produce a trim edge for the lawn much more quickly than traditional shears.

Lawnmowers

If you want to retain a lawn but wish to reduce mowing time, consider buying a mower with a wider cutting width. Rotary mowers are light and easy to use, but unless you are happy to leave the clippings on the lawn, or rake them up, buy one with a clippings collector. The same applies to wheeled

rotaries, which many people prefer. For a striped effect a cylinder mower with a rear roller is the best choice, although some other types now have rollers fitted to create a similar effect.

Hedge Trimmers

A powered hedge trimmer will save a lot of time on what is a dusty and unpleasant job if your garden has a lot

of hedge. A mains electric trimmer is the best choice for most small gardens where the hedge is within easy reach of a power supply, but for a large garden a petrol model may be more practical. Battery-powered trimmers are useful for small hedges.

Compression Sprayers

A large-capacity compression sprayer with a long lance makes all kinds of

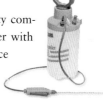

spraying work easy, whether you are applying foliar feeds, pesticides and fungicides, or growth inhibitors to reduce the frequency with which you have to cut your hedge. Keep a separate watering can fitted with a dribble bar and shield for weedkiller.

Basic Groundwork

Time spent preparing soil before planting will pay dividends in the long term in a low-maintenance garden. Soil that is in good condition provides the best start for new plants, which will then grow well and be better equipped to withstand pest and disease attacks.

Eliminating weeds

If your soil is light, weeds can easily be removed by digging. On heavier soil it may be easier to kill the weeds, which you can do by either covering the ground for several months with an impermeable mulch, such as a thick black polythene sheet, or applying a weedkiller.

After digging and hand weeding an area, leave the soil for a few weeks to allow seeds brought to the surface to germinate. You can then hoe off the weed seedlings before planting and so reduce the amount of weeding you will need to do later on.

Improving the soil

The best way to improve soil structure and fertility is to add plenty of organic matter such as homemade garden compost or well-rotted farmyard manure. When added to existing soil, it will improve drainage in heavy soils and water and nutrient retention in light ones. The traditional way to add it is by digging, but this is now widely regarded as unnecessary and even undesirable, except perhaps for initial preparation of very heavy soil. In most cases, simply applying a good layer of organic material to the surface is the best method, since worms will take it down into the soil.

Above: *Eliminating weeds before planting has long-term benefits for the garden.*

Above: *Digging in organic matter improves the quality of the soil.*

143

AUTOMATIC WATERING

A system that automatically delivers water when it is required will save hours of time every year, and it is better for plants, as they are less likely to suffer from water stress. There are many systems available, so you need to look at several to see which one will be best for your situation.

Most automatic watering systems are fitted with a suitable control system to reduce the pressure, and act as a filter.

Some systems are controlled by the moisture level in the soil, but most operate on a continuous drip basis. Drip feed systems are versatile enough to be used for plants in beds, borders or in containers. Use a T-joint to run branches or tubes for individual drip heads. A timing device will turn your watering system on and off automatically, yet can easily be deactivated if the weather is wet.

Above: Leaky pipe and perforated hose systems are suitable for beds and borders where they can be hidden.

Unless your garden is very small, it is best to install a pipeline buried just beneath the ground surface, then you can "plug in" various watering devices as necessary.

Leaky pipe and perforated hose systems are suitable for beds and borders or the kitchen garden. You can bury them beneath the surface or lay them on top of the soil.

Above: A pop-up sprinkler can be set into the lawn. The head is pushed up out of the ground by the water pressure when the tap is turned on.

Above: A drip feed system is ideal for hanging baskets and window boxes. It will eliminate the daily chore of watering by hand.

Above: Apply a slow- or controlled-release fertilizer to established plants in spring or early summer.

LOW-MAINTENANCE FEEDING

This really does pay dividends. If you see a garden with particularly lush and healthy-looking plants, the chances are they have been well fed.

Slow- and Controlled-release Fertilizers

If you use modern slow- or controlled-release fertilizers, you can feed your plants just a couple of times a year. Both allow the nutrients to seep out into the soil over a period of months but controlled-release fertilizers are affected by soil temperature. Nutrients are only released when the soil is warm enough for growth. Use a hose-end dilutor for applying a soluble fertilizer.

Feeding Beds and Borders

Most established plants, but especially demanding ones like roses, benefit from an annual feeding. Apply a slow- or controlled-release fertilizer in spring or early summer, sprinkling it around the bushes. Keep it away from the stem, sprinkling it further out where most of the active root growth occurs. Hoe it into the surface then water it in, unless rain is expected, to make the fertilizer active more quickly.

Feeding the Lawn

The quickest way to feed your lawn is with a wheeled spreader. Individual models vary, but you can usually adjust the delivery rate. Test the rate on a measured area of path first, then sweep up the fertilizer and weigh it to ensure the application rate is correct.

Feeding Container Plants

Plants grown in containers require supplementary nutrients to keep them healthy. You can mix controlled- or slow-release fertilizer granules into the potting soil when you plant, or slip sachets or pellets beneath individual plants as you plant them.

Above: Container plants need additional feeding such as this slow-release pellet.

REDUCE WEEDING

It is entirely possible to have a beautiful garden where weeds are seldom a problem. The trick is to not allow any space where they can gain a major hold. Reducing the amount of bare earth in your garden and introducing more hard landscaping will reduce the area that weeds can grow in.

In beds and borders dense planting and ground cover will blanket the ground so well that weeds are unlikely to gain a foothold. Where young plants have not yet reached their maximum spread, applying a mulch to patches of bare earth will ensure that weeds cannot grow.

Using Weedkillers

Pulling up perennial weeds by hand is time-consuming and often ineffective as they usually grow again unless you remove every piece of root. Digging

Above: A contact weedkiller applied through a dribble bar will be useful for clearing a large area that has been overrun by perennial weeds. You may need to shield adjacent plants from the spray.

Above: Difficult and perennial weeds, like this ground elder, can be killed by painting on a translocated weedkiller.

them up may not be possible in an established bed or border, and you may have to resort to a contact weedkiller. Beware, as most weedkillers will kill or damage whatever they come into contact with.

Deep-rooted perennial weeds, such as bindweed, can be very difficult to eradicate and are best treated by painting on a translocated weedkiller, such as one based on glyphosate. Other contact weedkillers may not kill all the roots, but this chemical moves to all parts of the plant.

GARDENER'S TIP
Paths can easily be kept weed-free for a season by using products sold for the purpose. A single application will quickly kill existing weeds and prevent the growth of new ones for many months. Use an improvised shield to prevent the weedkiller being blown on to the flowerbeds.

Above: Gravel makes an attractive surface, and can be weed-free with very little effort.

MULCHES FOR GROUND COVER

A mulch is a layer of material that will cover the ground completely to suppress weeds and conserve moisture in the soil by preventing loss of water through evaporation. It can be purely functional or it can be decorative, and it can be organic or not. Always prepare the ground thoroughly before applying a mulch, taking care to eliminate perennial weeds and work in plenty of organic material such as well rotted manure or garden compost. Make sure the ground is wet before applying a mulch; soak it first if necessary.

Loose Mulches

Most loose mulches, such as chipped bark, cocoa shells, gravel, garden compost and rotted manure, are more visually appealing than sheets, and the organic ones rot down to improve the soil's structure and fertility. They need to be applied about 5cm (2in) thick.

Sheet Mulches

Woven plastic mulching sheets are effective and economical, but unattractive. However, they can be used in combination with a decorative loose mulch, which can then be applied more thinly than the recommended depth. Sheet mulches are useful for low-maintenance shrub beds and newly planted trees, both of which can be left undisturbed for several years, and are best used when the bed or border is to be newly planted.

PLANTING THROUGH SHEET MULCH

1 Make a slit around the edge of the bed with a spade, and push the sheet into this.

2 At each planting position make a cross-shaped slit in the sheet. Fold the flaps open to plant, then fold back in place. Small plants can be planted using a trowel, but for shrubs you will need to use a spade.

147

Easy-care Gardens

SOME GARDEN STYLES LEND THEMSELVES PARTICULARLY WELL TO
LOW-MAINTENANCE GARDENING. THEY OFTEN RELY ON A VISUALLY
PLEASING USE OF HARD LANDSCAPING ELEMENTS COMBINED WITH A
MINIMUM OF WELL-CHOSEN PLANTING.

A MINIMALIST GARDEN

It is possible to create a striking garden using very little at all. The garden
elements can be pared down to the
absolute minimum and anything fussy,
distracting or unnecessary can be
excluded from the scheme.

A garden that relies on minimal
planting will be the most labour-
saving of all, but you need to choose
carefully. The few plants used must
work hard to earn their place there.

Using Space

Form and space are what matter in a
minimal design. Anyone embarking on
such a totally labour-saving design will
need an eye for shape and contrast, so
that the garden is pleasing to the eye,
yet uncluttered.

The design will rely on the clever
use of space, defined by a few strategically placed features, such as pots,
stones, statues or plants, or a bold
architectural feature such as a wall.

*Above: The painted wall and gravel act
as a foil to the carefully selected foliage
plants in this striking area.*

*Left: Strong architectural features, such as
the brick wall, unadorned pergola and
symmetrical oblong planter, are typical
elements of a modern garden.*

148

Simple dramatic juxtapositions can create sufficient interest. For instance, a paved or gravelled area can become a visually pleasing space with the addition of just a few carefully sited large pots containing some architectural plants, or perhaps a raised bed or pool. Pebbles or boulders can be used to add extra texture, and perhaps some flowering annuals will add a splash of summer colour.

Adding Colour

Colour in the form of painted surfaces can also be used for impact in a minimalist garden, perhaps on a large wall or the edges of a raised bed. It can be used to complement planted gravel or an expanse of paving.

Above: A striking individual plant such as this easy-care bamboo in a pot is complemented by the adjacent pebbles.

Positioning Plants and Pebbles

A few good plants can go a long way if they are carefully positioned to create form in an open space. They need to be dramatic in shape or colour so that they make an impact on the design. Architectural plants such as phormium, yucca, bamboo clumps or even small trees all work well, especially when used in isolation.

Pebbles are also a good way to introduce additional texture. They work particularly well in areas of paving or with potted plants.

Left: Form is paramount in this dramatic garden comprising a series of integrated islands.

149

GRAVEL AND PAVED GARDENS

Gardens that rely heavily on paving or gravel instead of lawn can be virtually maintenance-free. They need to be well planned, however, to avoid them looking oppressive and harsh. The solution is to include a variety of materials to create contrasting shapes and textures, and to complement this with the planting. Even the simplest of designs can be transformed into a garden full of charm and character.

Designing with Hard Materials

Different materials can be used effectively to divide a large area into smaller sections, creating interest through changes of texture, and even height if you introduce features such as raised beds.

Formal structures usually work best for paving, especially in a space bounded by walls. Bricks can be laid in attractive patterns, adding colour and warmth to a design. The small dimensions of bricks will create satisfying contrasts when juxtaposed with large paving slabs. Granite setts, cobbles and brick or clay pavers can also be laid in interesting patterns.

Gravel, which has a softer texture than hard paving, adds another type of contrast. It works with both formal lines and informal designs as it lends itself to curves. There are lots of different gravels available in many colours and grades. Choose one, or several, that will suit your design.

Above: Gravel is a sensible alternative to grass and will look good when used with the right plants and accessories.

Left: A raised central planting area and water features in this paved garden have been constructed from contrasting materials.

Additional Features

Including other features in paving or gravel gardens adds yet more interest. Ponds or fountains introduce the element of water. Statues, large containers and even benches all make excellent focal points.

Incorporating Plants

Beds and borders can easily be incorporated into gravel and paved gardens. If you do not want to be bothered with maintaining large planting areas, you can create small filled spaces within the gravel or paving.

Beds can be filled with some low-maintenance ground-cover plants, but focal plants may also be desirable to draw the eye, especially during winter. Architectural plants, such as

Above: Paving constructed in an interesting design becomes an extra feature in the garden.

Above: Even the tiniest area can become a gravel garden.

Cordyline australis (for warmer winters) or *Yucca gloriosa* (for cooler areas), work well as focal plants. Clipped box (*Buxus sempervirens*) is useful for formal designs. Two or three clips during the growing season are sufficient to keep it in shape.

Containers are another option, but they will require daily watering in summer unless you install an automatic watering system.

> **GARDENER'S TIP**
> The pattern to which bricks and pavers are laid alters the overall impression created when viewed en masse. The stretcher bond is most effective for smaller areas and for paths. Herringbone is suitable for both large and small areas. Basket weave needs a reasonably large expanse for the pattern to be appreciated.

151

A JAPANESE GARDEN

True Japanese gardens require very little maintenance as the components are mainly easy-care features such as gravel, pebbles, stones, wood, water and occasional, carefully-chosen and well-positioned shrubs or small trees.

Designing the Garden

A sense of tranquillity and areas for contemplation are important elements in a Japanese garden. The design must be kept simple and uncluttered, concentrating on outline, shape and contrasting surface textures, while the use of plants is restrained, resulting in a garden that satisfies the senses but requires mimimum aftercare.

Focal Points

Rocks and stones have a special importance in many Japanese gardens. They can be set in an area covered with fine pebbles, which are an ideal labour-saving ground cover. When wet, they change colour and catch the light.

Choose some special stones of varying size, colour and character, and arrange them asymmetrically in one or two areas, preferably in odd numbers. Traditionally, the pebbles are raked into variations of parallel lines and snaking spirals centralized on the main rock features. Gravel can be substituted for pebbles as a cheaper option.

Above: Strategically placed large stones are an intrinsic and symbolic feature of a traditional Japanese garden. They are said to focus the mind for contemplation.

Left: A classic Japanese-style garden is simple and uncluttered with various harmonious focal points.

PLANTS FOR A JAPANESE GARDEN

Acer palmatum
Azalea
bonsai trees
camellias
dwarf bamboos
Iris ensata
moss
small pines

You can inset a walkway of large paving slabs or sawn tree-trunk pieces in the gravel.

Minimal Planting

In an authentic Japanese stone garden the only plants might be mounds of green moss providing a softening contrast with the stones and rocks, but other types of Japanese-inspired garden include a few more plants, chosen for their interesting form or grace. These can be planted through the pebbles or in large simple containers.

If mosses, which thrive in moist conditions out of direct sun, cannot be encouraged to grow, try moss-like plants as an alternative, such as *Sagina subulata*, *S. procumbens*, or, in mild areas, the ground-hugging carpeter *Soleirolia soleirii*.

A Water Feature

Water, the essence of life, should always be present. In a real Japanese garden, it would be fresh running water, but for the low-maintenance gardener even a bowl filled with water

is calming in a garden and offers birds the opportunity to drink. A bubble fountain washing over pebbles or a running stream effect would be ideal.

Traditional Ornaments

In eastern philosophy, traditional garden features have their own significance within the strict rules and special meanings of the garden design. Bamboo wind chimes create soothing sounds, while a rounded lantern and a linear bridge are pretty, and useful for introducing contrasting shapes. You could introduce different ornamentation to suit your own preferences, with the purpose of providing contrasting shapes and colours.

Above: *Bamboo, smooth pebbles and rounded water features are ornamental and require little attention.*

A Hot and Colourful Garden

The kind of garden that is inspired by the Mediterranean countryside is packed with tough, self-sufficient plants that are colourful, attractive to bees and butterflies and wonderfully scented. It may also stock many aromatic edible plants that are useful for the kitchen. You might start off with a small patch or bed, but the benefits of this style of labour-saving garden are such that you may consider converting a larger area.

Mediterranean plants are resilient and drought-resistant. Their constant adaptations for survival in hot, arid areas – aromatic vapour, shimmering foliage, tough or spiny leaves and silvery hairs – also make them unappealing to pests, and their tough constitutions help them to resist disease.

Basic Groundwork

All the above make Mediterranean plants ideal candidates for a low-maintenance garden, as long as the ground is prepared so that they will thrive in temperate climates.

You will need to add plenty of grit or gravel to the soil to give it sharp drainage so that the plants do not have to struggle to survive in wet, compacted

Above: The graceful spring flowers of Tulipa sylvestris *and grape hyacinth grow amongst rosemary and lavender, just as they would in the wild.*

Left: Lavender, Cistus, Euphorbia *and asphodels make their distinctive mark on a gravel bed in summer.*

154

Left: This herb garden is full of leaf and vibrant colour a mere 15 months after planting.

ground, where they would inevitably rot as their roots need dry conditions.

A top layer of gravel or stones will work as moisture-retaining mulch that also keeps foliage crowns dry and absorbs heat for the benefit of the plants.

Designing the Garden

This kind of garden requires no planning to ensure the colours and textures complement one another. The plants naturally team well, forming a magical tapestry of wonderful partnerships.

The predominant shrubs and sub-shrubs are evergreen, with grey and silver tones, sustaining the garden through the quieter winter months. In spring, flowering bulbs pop up in bright reds and yellows. Summer explodes with foliage and flower.

Suitable Planting

Select only those types of plant that will survive with minimal attention and enjoy the sharp draining conditions of your garden.

Left: This herb garden is full of leaf and vibrant colour a mere 15 months after planting.

There is no need to add fertilizer or manure when planting. Most Mediterranean plants are adapted to grow in poor soil, and if it is too rich they will produce weak, sappy growth. In poor soil they will generally grow tougher and flower more freely.

Simply cover the surface of the soil with gravel and water the plants well until they establish themselves. After their first season, you will not need to water them. In severe summer drought, you can revive any stressed plants by dousing them with water; if watering is impractical, cut back the plants severely and they should revive.

Containers

Following the age-old Mediterranean tradition of growing special plants in pots you can grow a few brightly coloured geraniums against a white-washed wall, or perhaps a fig tree if you have a very sunny, sheltered corner in the garden.

MEDITERRANEAN PLANTS
Artemisia absinthium
Cistus
Cytisus
Eryngium
Euphorbia
Lavandula
Rosemarinus
Salvia officinalis
Thymus

A WILDFLOWER GARDEN

An established wildflower garden requires much less maintenance than a conventional one. Making one, however, can initially be quite demanding as there is some basic preparation of the soil required and the garden takes time to become established. Creating a large meadow will need much more effort, so it is advisable for the time-pressed gardener to concentrate on a small wildlife swathe.

Planting a Border

The simplest way to grow wildflowers is in an existing border, either on their own or with some other herbaceous plants and shrubs. This can work especially well if you combine wildflowers with the many garden plants that are forms of wild flowers, such as carpeting *Ajuga reptans* and self-seeding poppies and forget-me-nots.

Wildflowers can be sown or planted in the same way as other plants, but they will not thrive in ground that is fertilized.

PERENNIALS FOR WILD-
FLOWER PLANTINGS

Achillea millefolium
Ajuga reptans
Campanula rotundifolia
Cardamine pratensis
Centaurea scabiosa
Fritillaria meleagris
Geranium pratense
Monarda fistulosa
Primula veris
Ranunculus acris

Above: Once a threatened species, yellow cowslips (Primula veris) *are now quite widely seen in wild areas.*

On cultivated ground the ranker weeds tend to take over and smother the plants you want to encourage, so it is worth clearing the area of weeds first. Then you can sow the wildflower mixture or plant out perennials in the spring.

Colonizing a Lawn

You can scatter the wildflower seed directly over the area, but the competition from the grass will be intense. For better results, sow the seed in trays, prick out and grow the plants in pots first. Plant them out in spring, when the perennials are strong enough to compete with the existing grass.

Once the perennials are established, they will self-sow, which is always more successful than simply scattering seed yourself.

Converting a Field

If you are lucky enough to have a field and want to turn it into a wildflower meadow, your task is much harder. Before you can start sowing or planting wildflowers you will need to spend a whole year mowing the grass at regular intervals to keep it short. This will kill off most of the more invasive grasses, and leave only the finer ones. When the grass is under control, you can proceed as for a lawn.

Clearing New Ground

For those with a smaller area to convert, another effective method for establishing a wildflower area is to clear it completely, removing all traces of perennial weeds. Then sow a wildflower and grass seed mixture formulated for your area, as for a border. There are several suppliers for this type of seed.

Above: Cornflowers are a delightful addition to a wildflower garden with their intense lavender colouring.

Maintaining Wildflowers in Grass

Wildflowers growing in grass should be cut once or twice a year. The best time is in summer once the main flush of plants have seeded. Remove the cuttings to prevent feeding the soil.

Above: Create a tranquil summer haven within the informal splendour of a wildflower garden filled with colourful plants.

Low-maintenance Landscaping

YOU CAN ARRANGE YOUR GARDEN AND MODIFY THE WAY YOU PLANT BEDS AND BORDERS SO THAT VERY LITTLE REGULAR MAINTENANCE WILL BE REQUIRED. YOU CAN ALSO MAKE YOUR GARDEN MUCH MORE INTERESTING IN THE PROCESS.

Above: Mixing hard landscaping materials and plants makes an attractive alternative to a large area of lawn.

THE GARDEN FLOOR

The greater part of most traditional gardens is given over to a large expanse of lawn, which is often edged by a path or a small area of paving. Lawns are time-consuming and expensive to maintain in good condition, and they can be boring. There are ways of keeping mowing to a minimum, but anyone wishing to cut down drastically on the labour involved should consider alternative surfaces such as gravel or paving for at least part of the area normally covered by the lawn.

SIMPLER LAWN MAINTENANCE

If you want to keep a lawn there is a lot you can do to reduce mowing time to a minimum. Upgrading your lawnmower to a more powerful or wider cutting one is the most obvious, but

Above: This garden has been mainly planted with large shrubs that require miminal attention, leaving only a small central area of lawn that will not take long to mow.

158

Low-maintenance Landscaping

eliminating fussy beds and curved edges to borders might speed things up by allowing you to mow in straight lines. There are also other approaches to try. Alternatively, keep just a small area of lawn, and plant ornamental grasses, ground-cover plants or shrubs over the remaining area.

Trimming Edges

Unsightly untrimmed edges can make a garden look untidy, but trimming with shears, long-handled or ordinary, is tedious and time-consuming. If you have a lot of these to trim, invest in a powered lawn edge or nylon line trimmer with a swivel head, which can be

Above: Replacing lawn with low-maintenance plants will reduce mowing time.

used for this job as well as scything down persistent weeds. It is best to buy the sturdiest you can afford as the lighter versions can prove less economical in the long term.

Multi-level Mowing

Another way to reduce the amount of time spent mowing is to cut different parts of the lawn at different intervals, leaving some areas to grow longer. This involves cutting broad "pathways" regularly, and mowing other areas every second or third time with the mower blade set higher giving a more natural appearance. You can leave some grass uncut except for a couple of cuts a season, but it will probably need to be cut with a nylon line trimmer instead of a lawnmower.

Above: A nylon line trimmer will enable you to trim lawn edges with considerable speed.

159

MAKING A MOWING EDGE

Edging the lawn with brick or paving, so that the mower can run over it saving time and evergy, means that the only trimming you will need to do will be occasionally cutting back any long stems of grass that grow over the paving.

1 Lay paving slabs or bricks on the grass for positioning, and use a half-moon edger (edging iron) to cut an edge.

2 Slice off the grass with a spade and remove soil to the depth of the pavers, plus several centimetres (a couple of inches). Lay a sub-base of sand and gravel mix, and consolidate it using a piece of wood and a mallet.

3 For paving slabs, use five blobs of mortar for each slab, and lay them on top, then tap them hard, using a mallet. Bricks will just need a small blob of mortar under each.

4 Make sure the slabs are flush with the lawn, and use a spirit level to check that the slabs are laid evenly. Mortar the joints for a neat finish, otherwise unsightly weeds will grow in them.

> GARDENER'S TIP
>
> Choose a paving or brick colour that will blend well with the adjacent border. Creeping plants will soon extend over the surface to soften the effect.

ALTERNATIVES TO GRASS

If you like a green lawn, but don't enjoy or have time for regular mowing, you could consider a grass substitute. Those mentioned here are fine for occasional foot traffic and as a visual focal point, but they won't stand up to the hard wear of a children's play area like grass will.

There are other drawbacks to using grass substitutes for lawns. You won't be able to use selective lawn weed-killers on them, so you will have to hand weed as necessary for a season or two, until the plants have knitted together. Beware of common stonecrop (*Sedum acre*), an attractive yellow-flowered carpeter sometimes sold as a grass-substitute. It may become a serious weed in your garden.

Thyme

A quick spreader with attractive foliage and flowers, thyme makes a good grass substitute and is aromatic

Above: Romantic and unusual, chamomile is quite hardy and will last for many years.

when crushed. Culinary thyme (*Thymus vulgaris*) is too tall, so use a carpeter like *T. pseudolanuginosus* or *T. serpyllum*.

Chamomile

Another aromatic plant for lawns is chamomile (*Chamaemelum nobile*, syn. *Anthemis nobilis*). Look for the variety 'Treneague', which is compact and does not normally flower.

Clover

If clover is a problem in your lawn, it may make a good grass substitute. Once established it will keep green for most of the year and will tolerate dry soils. You'll only have to mow a couple of times a year, after the flowers appear, to keep it looking smart.

Above: Swathes of thyme make an eyecatching and fragrant alternative to a lawn.

161

GRAVEL

Decorative gravel is an excellent, inexpensive but practical garden surface. It is attractive, trouble-free, easy to lay and harmonizes well with plants. It will conform to irregular outlines, and it can be effective in a large or small area. Whole gardens can be turned over to gravel with some judicious use of complementary paving and attractive planting. An edging is a good idea, otherwise the gravel will become scattered into surrounding areas.

Many garden centres and stone or builders' merchants sell a wide range of gravels in different sizes and colours. You will find the appearance changes according to the light and whether the stones are wet or dry.

Above: Gravel makes an attractive background for plants and needs minimal maintenance.

Above: Curves present no problems for gravel. Using edging will keep the gravel in the right place.

Making a Gravel Bed

You can set a gravel bed in a lawn or within an area of paving. In a large lawn a winding ribbon of gravel, designed to imitate a dry river-bed, can look very effective. If the garden is smaller, a more compact shape, perhaps oval or kidney-shaped, may be more appropriate.

Cut out a shape using a half-moon edger (edging iron) and remove the turf about 10cm (4in) deep with a spade. If you want to grow drought-loving plants, dig in plenty of coarse grit. For growing more hungry plants, add well-rotted manure or compost. The gravel needs to be about 5cm (2in) deep. Keep the gravel well below the surface of the lawn, otherwise it will spill on to the surface of the lawn and damage the mower. Choose a size that will be noticeable if it does stray.

Large Gravel Areas

For anything larger than a small island bed, consider laying a plastic sheet over the area to suppress weed growth. If the gravel garden is low-lying or in a hollow, provide a sump for excess water to drain into. Ensure that the surface is quite smooth before laying the sheet, and overlap the joints. Tip gravel over the plastic sheet and rake it level to make a 5cm (2in) layer.

Planting in Gravel

Many plants will grow well in a gravel bed, but for a low-maintenance garden choose drought-resistant plants that won't need watering, even in dry spells. Scoop back the gravel and plant normally, but avoid planting too deeply and keep the gravel away from the immediate area around the stem.

If planting through a plastic sheet, scoop back the gravel then make cross-slits through the plastic. Enrich the soil with garden compost or fertilizer and plant normally. Fold back the sheet and replace the gravel, taking care not to cover the crown of the plant.

Above right: A recently planted gravel bed within a lawn is already showing plenty of colour. The plants will soon spread to cover much of the gravel.

Right: Soft mounds of thyme planted in a gravel area soften the effect, adding colour and con-trasting textures.

PAVING

A paved area needs practically no maintenance, just an occasional brush and every few years a blast with a high-pressure water jet. As well as being labour-saving it should contribute positively to your garden design, linking and complementing other elements of the garden.

Creating Effects

Builders' merchants and many garden centres stock a variety of attractive paving materials to suit most tastes and styles, and these can be laid to create all sorts of patterns, formal or informal. As well as different materials, surfaces can vary in texture. Big slabs are suitable for large areas, while bricks and pavers are better for small areas. A mixture of different paving materials will introduce variety and interest to a scheme.

Above: This crazy-paved area is softened by the addition of container-grown plants.

Above: Builders' merchants stock a variety of paving materials. Choose those that will complement other elements in the garden.

Concrete Paving Slabs

Large slabs made from concrete are a popular choice for patios, paths and drives. They come in a range of sizes, textures and colours, and are easy to lay once a solid foundation has been prepared. Slabs, especially circular ones, are suitable for use as stepping stones set in a lawn or in gravel.

Natural Stone

Although this looks splendid, it is very expensive and difficult to lay. It can be dressed, that is cut into regular shapes with smooth edges, or random, with irregular outline and thickness. The latter is suitable for crazy paving and looks much better than broken concrete fragments.

Bricks and Pavers

Concrete or clay pavers and bricks are very striking when they are laid in small areas. They are especially suitable for visually linking the garden to a brick house. They can be laid in

164

to be only 5–10cm (2–4in) thick for foot traffic but about 15cm (6in) if vehicles are to be driven over it. Concrete and brick paving slabs can be bedded on mortar, but clay pavers must be bedded on sharp sand using a plate compactor.

Plants and Paving

A few strategically placed plants will greatly improve the appearance of the paved garden without requiring too much extra work.

Plants in beds alongside the paving can be encouraged to fall on to the paving to soften the hard edges. Containers are useful, too, to break up a large expanse, or to introduce colour where there is no bed for planting in. But if you design the paving with integral planting areas or raised beds, the plants will need less watering than they would in containers.

intricate designs. Pavers come in a wide range of sizes, colours and thicknesses and have different finishes.

Laying Paving

Paving needs to be laid on to a firm base. The area will have to be excavated to a depth that allows for hardcore, mortar and paving. Hardcore needs

Above left: You can create planting spaces in paving by removing slabs to expose the soil below. A stone mulch disguises the soil and prevents it splashing on to the paving.

Left: Combining different types of paving will add considerably to the visual impact and interest.

165

BEDS AND BORDERS

Attractive, well-filled beds and borders bring a garden to life, but they are potentially time-consuming. You can reduce the amount of work involved simply by choosing low-maintenance plants and keeping them weed-free by mulching, perhaps with a decorative chipped bark, or with chemical controls. Whatever planting style you choose avoid using plants that grow rampantly, need constant cutting back or frequent pruning, and any with lots of seeds that germinate readily where you don't want them to.

Above: Foliage plants create colour and interest but require very little attention through the year.

Foliage

Interesting foliage often acts as a backdrop to flowers, but it can also be used on its own. The enormous range of

Above: Packed borders require little weeding once established.

greens as well as purples, bronzes, silvers and striking variegations makes it entirely possible to create unusual effects using foliage alone.

Evergreens are especially useful because they don't shed leaves like deciduous shrubs do or die down leaving dead matter to be cleared away as do perennials. However, deciduous shrubs produce some stunning autumn effects, which are particularly useful when the number of flowers is declining in your border.

Incorporating Flowers

However attractive foliage may be, for most people a garden would not be complete without flowers. Happily, many will perform well with little attention, and there are a number of different types of flowering plants to choose from.

With many different growth habits, sizes and flower shapes and colours, herbaceous perennials bring an extra dimension into a garden. Choose those that you can plant and forget, at least for a few years. They will flower year after year.

Shrubs are among the best plants for borders. Most will grow for years without any attention, but those that grow too vigorously (such as buddlejas and many roses) or that are tall and difficult to manage (such as lilacs) are best avoided. Fortunately, there are so many well-behaved shrubs, that a low-maintenance border is easy to achieve. Potentillas flower for months, as do hardy fuchsias, though these may be partly cut down in cold winter. Mahonia and hebe are also reliable.

Above: If you want to include summer bedding plants in your border choose a long-flowering type, such as geraniums.

Traditional seasonal borders are replanted twice a year with bedding plants to take full advantage of spring and summer flower colour. They are packed with colour but require most work and are best avoided if you have limited time. Using more permanent plants instead will involve less time.

Annuals are less work for the gardener as many can be sown in situ. They are invaluable for filling gaps with bright summer colour. You sow them in late spring and they flower in summer, and many will self-seed for years. Pot marigolds, nasturtiums, love-in-a-mist, and different types of poppy, including Californian and common field poppies, are all good self-seeders. Any seedlings that appear in the wrong place can simply be pulled up. When the plants have finished flowering they can be removed.

Above: Papaver somniferum *will self-seed on to any bare patches of soil in a border.*

167

Herbaceous Borders

Whole borders devoted to herbaceous perennials look stunning during the summer months and well into autumn. Plants like astilbes, dicentras and bergenias, which need no staking, spread relatively slowly and are easy to pull up when necessary, are ideal. If you are in doubt about a plant's suitability, always find out whether it needs staking, how fast it spreads and whether it is prone to pests and diseases. Phlox and perennial asters are prone to mildew, for example.

Mixed Borders

These contain a mixture of shrubs for structure and foliage and perennial plants, perhaps supplemented by annuals. Generally, they require less maintenance than herbaceous borders, especially if the emphasis is on low-maintenance shrubs, with some easy perennials to add colour.

When you plant the border, you will need to leave gaps to allow shrubs and perennials to grow. The gaps can be temporarily filled with annuals such as marigolds, poppies or nasturtiums, or bedding plants such as geraniums or begonias. This will keep down the weeds and look good.

Above: Self-sufficient spurge, purple sage, lavender and iris pack a mixed border with colour.

Left: Attractive, low-maintenance perennials in a border can provide years of interest with their colourful flowers and variety of foliage.

PLANTING A BORDER

After initial planting, you will need to water the border regularly in dry periods until the plants are established, but thereafer they should need little attention to keep them looking good over a long period.

1 Water the plants, then arrange the pots in their planting places. Try to visualize the plants at their final height and spread, then adjust their positions, allowing room for growth. Dig the first hole, and add some well-rotted compost, farmyard manure or slow-release fertilizer.

**RELIABLE AND EASY
HERBACEOUS PERENNIALS**
Anemone x *hybrida*
Anthemis tinctoria
Astilbe
Bergenia
Dianthus
Dicentra spectabilis
Echinops ritro
Erigeron
Hemerocallis
Kniphofia
Liriope muscari
Rudbeckia
Schizostylis coccinea
Sedum spectabile
Tradescantia
Veronica spicata

2 When you are ready to plant, knock a plant out of its pot and tease out some of the roots. Start at the back, or at one end of the border.

3 Return the soil and make sure the plant is at its original depth or just a little deeper. Firm it with your hands or a heel to expel large pockets of air in the soil and prevent wind rock. Water thoroughly unless the weather is wet.

Above: The several varieties of Sedum *provide pinks and reds in autumn. They require practically no attention and do not need staking.*

169

Low-maintenance Plants

PLANTS THAT REQUIRE LITTLE ATTENTION THROUGH THE YEAR AND ARE GENERALLY DISEASE- AND PEST-RESISTANT ARE THE ONES TO INCLUDE IN A LOW-MAINTENANCE GARDEN. THERE IS ENOUGH CHOICE TO ENSURE INTEREST AND PLENTY OF COLOUR AT ALL TIMES.

Left: Stipa tenuifolia *produces silky flowerheads that sway sensuously in summer breezes.*

reach 2.4m (8ft) or more. They can be used in beds, either on their own or in mixed plantings, to stunning effect.

Be cautious about mixing grasses among other plants, however, as some are difficult to control, and rampant species will soon take over a bed and become inextricably entwined with other plants, so clump-forming types are best. The more spreading grasses are better grown in an isolated spot, but the smaller ones will work in a border if you plant them in a large container sunk into the ground, with the rim flush with the surrounding soil. Annual grasses will self-seed unless you deadhead them after flowering.

GRACEFUL GRASSES FOR YEAR-ROUND INTEREST

Perennial grasses are easy plants. Once planted, they require very little attention, except occasional removal of dead foliage and old flower heads if they offend. Cutting back the dead foliage to ground level in early spring will encourage lots of new growth.

There are many types to grow, from compact dwarfs to huge plants that

GRASSES
Andropogon
Carex
Cortaderia selloana
Deschampsia
Festuca glauca
Hakonechloa
Miscanthus sinensis
Stipa arundinacea
Stipa tenuifolia

FERNS FOR MOIST SHADE

The intricate foliage of ferns makes these fascinating plants essential for moist, shady corners of any low-maintenance garden, where they will thrive without any intervention. Many die down in winter, but there are also plenty of evergreen species, and they are varied enough in shape and size to make an interesting planting despite the lack of flowers.

Above: Ferns can be used effectively in many areas of the garden. There are so many varieties, there will be plenty to suit the situation of any garden.

FERNS

Adiantum (some evergreen)
Asplenium ceterach (evergreen)
Asplenium scolopendrium
(evergreen)
Blechnum capense (evergreen)
Dryopteris affinis 'Cristata'
(evergreen)
Polypodium (some evergreen)
Polystichum setiferum (evergreen)

PLANTING FERNS

Most ferns prefer a moist, shady or partially shaded position, and will do especially well if you take time to prepare the soil by incorporating plenty of organic material. This is very important in an area shaded by a tree or wall, where soil is usually dry. If the soil is impoverished, rake a balanced fertilizer into the surface of the soil when you plant. If planting in late summer, autumn or winter do not use a quick-acting fertilizer.

1 Water the fern thoroughly about half an hour before planting. It is very important that ferns do not dry out, especially when newly planted.

2 Make a hole large enough to take the rootball. Firm the fern in carefully. Then water thoroughly so that the surrounding soil is moist down to the depth of the rootball.

3 To help conserve moisture and maintain a high level of organic material in the soil, mulch thickly. Top up the mulch each spring.

HEATHERS FOR CARPETS OF COLOUR

Robust heathers make excellent low-maintenance beds in open sunny positions. There are varieties to provide year-round colour and most have attractive foliage, which often changes colour according to the season.

If you have space, heathers look best planted in bold drifts. Depending on the size of the bed, plant them in groups of perhaps ten or twenty of each variety. If you make your selection with care, you can have some in flower in virtually every season of the year. They can also be used in combination with conifers to create striking effects.

Limited Maintenance

The only attention heathers need is an annual trim in mid-spring; cut out old flowerheads as well as any dead, diseased or damaged shoots. Apply a slow-release fertilizer after pruning.

Heathers can become woody with time and may require replacing after some years.

Above: A carpet of heathers is a glorious sight. Mix varieties that flower at different times for year-round interest.

PLANTING HEATHERS

Make sure you choose the correct type of heathers for your soil. Winter-flowering *Erica carnea* varieties, which are more correctly known as heaths, will grow on neutral or even slightly alkaline soil. True heathers, such as *Erica cinerea* and *Calluna vulgaris* varieties, need an acid soil. When planting, it is important to prepare the soil thoroughly, and adding peat to the planting area will benefit all types. Plant through a sheet of black plastic or a plastic mulching sheet to keep weeding down to the absolute minimum. Then you can mulch on top of the sheet with a more attractive material such as chipped bark or gravel.

1 Prepare the soil thoroughly before planting. Add plenty of organic material such as compost or well-rotted manure, especially if the soil is dry or impoverished of nutrients. If planting in spring or summer, rake in a balanced general fertilizer. If planting in autumn or winter, wait until spring to apply fertilizer to avoid scorching tender roots.

2 Start planting at one end or at the back of the bed. Space the plants about 30–45cm (12–18in) apart. The planting distance will vary according to the species and even variety, so check first. Plant with a trowel and press the soil down firmly with your hands to exclude any air pockets.

3 Use a mulch of peat or composted chipped bark to suppress weeds, conserve moisture, and improve the appearance of the soil while the plants are still young. Over time this will rot down and provide nutrients for the growing plants and may need topping up every few years.

HEATHERS

Calluna vulgaris
Daboecia cantabrica
Erica carnea
Erica ciliaris
Erica cinerea
Erica x *darleyensis*
Erica erigena
Erica mackaiana
Erica tetralix
Erica vagans

173

ARCHITECTURAL CONIFERS

Slow-growing conifers need little attention after their first year, as long as they are given a good start with careful site preparation and planting.

Dwarf and slow-growing conifers can be columnar, rounded, oval or prostrate in outline, and to look effective they are best grown as a group with contrasting shapes, sizes and colours. They are ideal for small beds or borders where they will soon provide year-round interest.

Planting Conifers

If you find it difficult to plan beds and borders on paper, stand the pots where you think the plants will look good and be prepared to shuffle them around until they look right. Bear in mind the eventual height and spread.

Dig a hole larger and deeper than the rootball, and fork in rotted manure, garden compost or planting mixture, especially on dry soils, then work in a controlled- or slow-release fertilizer. Mulch with a decorative material at least 5cm (2in) thick.

Above: Slow-growing conifers provide year-round colour.

Left: Dwarf conifers look good in a group. Before planting check how they will look together and make any necessary adjustments to their positions.

174

Above: Surround newly planted conifers and heathers with decorative organic mulch such as chipped bark.

HEATHER AND CONIFER BEDS

Dwarf conifers combine especially well with heathers, their foliage providing fascinating contrasts of texture and colour. There are hundreds of suitable heathers and conifers so you can design exactly what you want. Remember to choose varieties that are suitable for your soil type. The initial outlay may seem expensive, but the bed should last for a long time without the need for replanting and will require minimal maintenance.

DWARF CONIFERS

Abies cephalonica
'Meyer's Dwarf'
Chamaecyparis obtusa
'Nana Gracilis'
Picea abies 'Gregoryana'
Taxus baccata 'Standishii'
Thuja picata 'Irish Gold'

Planting a Mixed Bed

Arrange and plant all the conifers first, making sure they look pleasing from all angles. Space the heathers around the conifers, then plant them in groups or drifts of one variety at a time. Avoid planting the heathers too close to the conifers as all the plants will spread and merge into each other within a year or two. Meanwhile cover the bare soil with chipped bark or gravel.

Above: Conifers and heathers make a natural combination in this setting.

175

TIME-SAVING BEDDING PLANTS

Traditional summer bedding involves a lot of time and work. Even if you buy all the plants from a nursery to avoid the annual rituals of sowing, labelling and potting on, they still have to be planted out in the garden. However, if you like the instant cheerful brightness of seasonal bedding rather than the predictable show from shrubs and border plants, you can compromise by mixing a temporary selection of seasonal bedding with established planting. The bedding plants will add splashes of bright, long-lasting summer colour among the more permanent plants. A low-growing perennial, such as sedum, can be used as a neat year-round edging that requires at the most an annual trim to keep it looking tidy. The centre of the bed can then be filled with spring bulbs and summer bedding plants.

> **TROUBLE-FREE SUMMER BEDDING PLANTS**
>
> *Begonia semperflorens*
> *Impatiens*
> *Lavatera trimestris*
> *Osteospermum*
> *Pelargonium*
> *Petunia*
> *Tagetes patula*

If you choose bedding plants such as begonias or petunias that flower prolifically over a long period without much attention, you will further cut down on the amount of work involved. The plants listed above will continue to flower for many months without requiring deadheading, regular attention or watering. They are some of the most trouble-free and spectacular bedding plants you can use.

Below: Impatiens *and* Begonia 'White Devil' *(right) are two long-flowering and reliable summer bedding plants.*

PLANTING A PERMANENT EDGING

If you want to add small permanent plants at the front of a border that will give seasonal splashes of colour rather than temporary bedding plants choose from the wide range of miniature bulbs or creeping plants.

1 Dig over the ground at the front of the border and clear it of weeds. Rake in a general fertilizer if planting in spring to encourage vigorous early growth and help the plants to knit together. (Wait until spring to do this if planting in autumn or winter.)

2 Space the plants out in their pots and adjust them to go evenly around the bed. About 15cm (6in) apart is suitable for most plants if you want quick cover, further apart if you don't mind waiting a little longer. Plant using a trowel.

3 Firm in to remove large pockets of air, then water thoroughly. The bed may be planted immediately with bulbs or spring or summer bedding plants as appropriate.

Above: Cyclamen *form a clump of varie-gated leaves, with bright flowers in late winter. They are particularly suited to the front of a shady border.*

PLANTS AND BULBS FOR PERMANENT EDGING

Creeping willow
Cyclamen
Dianthus
Grape hyacinth
Lavandula 'Munstead Dwarf'
Miniature box
Salvia officinalis

Above: Creeping willow is an excellent plant for permanent edging with its delicate, glossy green foliage and attractive yellow flowers.

SELF-SUFFICIENT SHRUBS

Some of the most popular shrubs, like roses and buddlejas, require a lot of attention. Regular pruning is necessary for many of them to remain looking good, and others may be prone to pests and diseases, which require time and effort to prevent or eliminate. Fortunately, there are many low-maintenance shrubs that are just as attractive and almost trouble-free.

You can choose from hundreds of well-behaved compact shrubs that will not require frequent pruning or hacking back. Check with your local garden centre to make sure the shrubs you select won't need regular pruning, won't become bare and leggy at the base with all the flowers at the top, and aren't susceptible to diseases.

Viburnum tinus is useful for its autumn and winter flowers, but it can

Above: Easy to grow Elaeagnus *is an ideal low-maintenance shrub. Its silvery foliage is set off by* Erysimum.

grow tall and require pruning to keep it compact. Many hebes are naturally compact and so require little pruning; most have pretty flowers, but some need protection during cold winters.

Above: Choose evergreen heucheras for attractive leaves all year round.

LOW-MAINTENANCE SHRUBS

Flowering
Cistus
Escallonia
Hibiscus syriacus
Hypericum
Mahonia
Olearia x *hastii*
Yucca

Foliage
Aucuba japonica
Berberis thunbergii
Choisya ternata
Elaeagnus pungens 'Maculata'
Euonymus fortunei
Ruscus aculeatus
Viburnum davidii

Above: Choisya ternata *has the benefit of a strong shape, pale green foliage and delightfully scented white flowers.*

PLANTING SHRUBS

Your choice of shrubs will be in position for many years, so plant them carefully and take time to prepare the ground thoroughly.

Water the pots and let them drain. Position them where you think they should be in the border. Check the likely size on the label or in a book, then revise your spacing if necessary. If the spacing seems excessive initially, leaving large gaps, you can always plant a few extra inexpensive shrubs between them to discard when they become crowded.

If planting in spring or summer, apply a balanced fertilizer according to the manufacturer's instructions; if planting at any other time, wait until spring to apply. Hoe or rake it into the surface then water thoroughly.

1 Dig a hole large enough to take the rootball. Stand the plant in the hole and use a cane or stick to check that the plant will be at the same depth as it was in the pot. Add or remove soil as necessary.

2 Carefully tease out some of the roots if they are tightly wound round the inside of the pot. This will encourage them to grow out into the surrounding soil and become quickly established.

3 Return the soil and firm it well around the roots to steady the shrub in wind and to eliminate large pockets of air that might allow the roots to dry out. Keep it watered during dry periods to begin with; once established, it should rarely require watering.

LOW-MAINTENANCE BULBS

Producing flower colour for virtually any time of the year, bulbs make a valuable contribution to the low-maintenance garden. Many bulbs will flower reliably year after year, with the clumps improving all the time, and once they have been planted they need very little attention.

Most summer-flowering bulbs, such as alliums and lilies, are best planted in groups in a border, but the easiest way to grow many spring- and autumn-flowering bulbs is to naturalize them in grass. This eliminates the need for annual replanting and means that you don't have to cut that part of the lawn until the leaves have died down naturally. It is better to keep naturalized bulbs to one small area of the lawn so that the rest can be cut normally and it won't look too untidy.

Caring for Bulbs

Naturalized bulbs and those left in a border for many years will eventually need dividing to prevent overcrowding, which would lead to deteriorating results. Lift large clumps when the leaves have just died back, or any time when the bulbs are dormant. Separate the clump into smaller pieces and replant. You do not have to separate into individual bulbs.

Above: A sunny border aglow with yellow tulips will give pleasure year after year.

Left: Daffodils naturalized in a small area of lawn look charming in the early spring.

NATURALIZING LARGE BULBS

1 To create a natural effect, scatter the bulbs on the grass and plant them where they fall. Make a hole for each, roughly three times their own depth, using either a trowel or a bulb planter, which pulls out a neat plug of grass and soil. Insertion will be easier if the ground is moist rather than dry.

2 Place a bulb in the hole. Crumble some soil from the bottom of the plug and let it fall around the bulb to make sure it will not be left in a pocket of air. Press the plug back into position.

Above: Autumn-flowering Colchicum *extend the interest in a bulb-filled lawn.*

EASY BULBS

Allium
Colchicum
Crocus
Cyclamen
Galanthus nivalis
Lilium
Muscari
Narcissus
Tulipa

NATURALIZING SMALL BULBS

1 For small bulbs and corms it is sometimes easier to lift and then replace the grass. Use a spade to slice beneath the grass, then roll it back for planting.

2 Loosen the soil with a fork, and work in a slow-acting fertilizer such as bonemeal. Scatter the bulbs randomly as a uniform pattern will look unnatural in grass. Small ones can be left on the surface; larger ones are best buried slightly.

3 Aim to cover the bulbs with twice their own depth of soil under the grass. Roll back the grass, firm it well with your hands and water thoroughly.

181

TIME-SAVING GROUND COVER

Plants that cover bare ground with a carpet of colour are invaluable in the low-maintenance garden, not least for their ability to suppress weeds. They are ideal for softening the hard edges of a path or the front of borders and for filling in gaps.

Ground-cover plants usually grow no more than 45cm (18in) in height, but many shrubs and sub-shrubs are compact enough to be used as ground cover as well. Heathers and conifers make pleasing ground cover, although the latter may be slow growing. Prostrate cotoneasters make excellent ground-hugging cover in front of other shrubs. Many prostrate thymes are also good ground covers.

Some herbaceous plants make a carpet of lush foliage in summer, as well as flowers in many cases. Hostas, for instance, have a wide range of leaf

Above: *Hostas make excellent ground cover in moist, shady areas.*

colour and delicate spears of pale lilac or white flowers, while cranesbills bloom for a long period.

Some ground-covering shrubs, such as *Hypericum calycinum*, are normally too aggressive for a small garden and will quickly take over. But this hypericum is ideal for a sloping bank that is difficult to cultivate. (If you plant it elsewhere you will need to contain it with paving.)

Left: Euonymus fortunei '*Emerald 'n' Gold' makes a striking ground cover in sun or shade. Its brightly variegated leaves will provide winter colour.*

Left: Lamium maculatum *is quick to become established and makes an effective and colourful ground cover in spring.*

GROUND-COVERING PLANTS
Ajuga reptans
Alchemilla mollis
Bergenia
Cerastium tomentosum
Convallaria majalis
Geranium endressii
Hypericum calycinum
Lamium maculatum
Pulmonaria
Tiarella cordifolia
Vinca minor

Filling Shady Locations

Fast-growing ivy is excellent for all types of shade, and *Pachysandra terminalis* 'Variegata' makes a green-and-white carpet in dry shade. Lily-of-the-valley, *Liriope muscari* and periwinkle also grow well below trees.

Maintenance of Ground Cover

Many ground-cover plants are quite tough, and once planted require little attention other than an annual feed. Heathers need an annual trim with shears after flowering to keep them looking neat. And plants like *Hypericum calycinum* can be clipped annually with shears or a nylon line trimmer to reduce their height and encourage bushiness.

Planting Ground-cover Plants

Ground cover will eventually suppress weeds, but initially needs protection from them. Before you start planting, clear the ground thoroughly of existing weeds.

Unless you are planting a ground cover that spreads by underground stems or rooting prostrate stems on the surface, it is best to plant through a mulching sheet to control weeds while the plants are becoming established. If you are planting large ground-cover plants, you may need to dig holes with a spade before laying the mulching sheet.

Above: Evergreen ivy is a fast-growing plant for ground cover.

183

MAKING THE MOST OF TREES

Trees make attractive features as specimens set in a lawn, or planted towards the back of a shrub border. Once they are established, most trees require no maintenance. Those in a border are generally less trouble because falling leaves drop almost unnoticed onto the soil, where they are quickly recycled.

Make your selection to suit the size of your garden and to give as much long-term interest as possible. Many small ornamental trees bear spring blossom, or have bright autumn foliage such as *Acer palmatum*, or they may have berries or fruit, including many varieties of *Malus*. Some have interestingly coloured or textured bark, which stands out in winter; the peeling bark of *Acer griseum*, for instance, is cinnamon-coloured.

SMALL GARDEN TREES
Acer palmatum
Crataegus
Malus
Prunus
Sorbus vilmorinii

Trees in Lawns

Leaves on a lawn usually have to be raked up, but a way around this problem could be to choose a tree with small leaves or an evergreen one. Mowing beneath a low-hanging tree or up to a trunk can also cause difficulties. Lawn trees are generally better planted in a bed cut into the grass, which can either be planted with attractive ground cover or covered with a decorative mulch to suppress weeds and retain moisture.

Trees in Borders

The best way to cover the ground beneath trees in a border is with ground-cover plants that will tolerate shade and dry soil. If the tree is very large or has large leaves you may have to rake the leaves off the plants when they fall, but most of them usually work their way between the plants and soon rot down. If you use a ground cover that dies down in winter, falling leaves will not matter.

Left: Mulch around the base of a specimen tree to prevent weed growth. Large pebbles have been used here but you could also choose chipped bark or gravel.

184

PLANTING A LAWN TREE

1 Mark a circle on the grass about 90–120cm (3–4ft) across. Lift the grass with a spade, and remove about 5cm (6in) of soil with it. Dig a planting hole, and fork in plenty of garden compost or well-rotted manure.

3 Place the tree in the hole and use a cane to check that the final soil level – about 5cm (2in) below the grass – will be the same as in the container (or with bare-root trees the soil mark on the stem).

2 Insert a short but sturdy wooden stake before you plant the tree, placing it on the side of the prevailing wind. Place it off-centre, to allow space for the large rootball.

4 With bare-root trees, spread out the roots; with container-grown ones, gently tease some out. Return the soil, and firm in well. Water thoroughly, secure with a tree-tie, and mulch the bed.

Above: This magnificent magnolia is underplanted with grape hyacinths. The colours look stunning when both are in flower.

185

Ideas for Special Features

SOME OF THE MOST POPULAR GARDEN FEATURES CAN ALSO BE LOW-MAINTENANCE IF SELECTED WISELY AND CAREFULLY ESTABLISHED. HERE ARE SOME SUGGESTIONS FOR INSTALLING AND MAINTAINING A SELECTION OF ATTRACTIVE ADDITIONS TO YOUR GARDEN.

EASY-CARE CONTAINERS

The main task with containers is watering, which in summer often needs to be done more than once a day. However, an automatic watering system can take care of this.

Alternatively, choose tough plants such as shrubs, rather than bedding plants. They will still need watering, but will survive limited periods of neglect. There are also perennial plants that can remain in their containers for several years. These will provide less of a summer show than brightly coloured bedding plants, but can be successful as focal points.

Mixed Collections

Try a mixed planting of perhaps three small shrubs, with different foliage shapes and colours. If you really want the brightness of bedding plants, plant just a couple of these and have permanent plants in other containers.

Decorative Containers

Some flowering evergreens can look a bit boring when not in bloom. A frost-proof decorative pot will make sure such plants always remain a feature.

EASY-CARE PLANTS
FOR CONTAINERS

Azalea
Bergenia
Dwarf conifers
Erica hyemalis
Euonymus fortunei
'Emerald 'n' Gold'
Fatsia japonica
Gaultheria
Hebe
Phormium
Rhododendron
Santolina chamaecyparissus
Skimmia

Left: A collection of shrubs, conifers and bergenia has plenty of impact. They won't die if left unwatered for a day or two.

WATER FEATURES

If you like water features, installing a fountain or pond are simple ways to create an interesting low-maintenance garden. A large pond may be less demanding than a flowerbed.

How to Make a Pond

Make your pond as large as possible. Fish and wildlife will be happier, and the water will stay clearer. You can dig out a pond and line it in a weekend, but you may prefer to get someone else to excavate it for you. Leave a shallow ledge 23cm (9in) down around part of the pond for marginal plants, and to allow wildlife access.

Planting a Pond

The best time to plant aquatics is spring and early summer, so that they

> ### TROUBLE-FREE PLANTS FOR PONDS
> *Acorus graminens* 'Variegatus'
> *Aponegeton distachysos*
> *Iris laevigata* (Japanese iris)
> *Myriphyllum aquaticum*
> *Pontederia cordata*

can become established. Use a planting basket designed for aquatic plants, line it with a special basket liner and use aquatic soil.

Maintenance

Overcrowded plants benefit from division and replanting in spring, and in autumn it's best to cut down dead foliage that might pollute the water, and to rake out the leaves. Every few years the pond should be emptied and cleaned – the only big task.

Above: *A pond can become a strong focal point, yet the amount of maintenance required is modest.*

HEDGES

Well-clipped hedges are excellent plants for defining and giving structure to a garden, and for many gardeners a hedge is preferable to a fence or wall. However, hedges can be tedious and time-consuming to trim. Nonetheless with imagination you may be able to overcome some of the problems.

Down-sizing

Many established hedges will respond well to quite severe height or width reduction, which will cut down considerably on the amount of trimming required. Cut back to about 30cm (12in) lower or in from the final height or width, to allow for new growth. Improving the shape of a straight-sided hedge by sloping the sides will marginally reduce the amount to be cut and make pruning easier.

> **LOW-MAINTENANCE HEDGES**
>
> Beech
> *Carpinus betulus*
> *Ilex*
> Laurel
> *Ligistrum*
> *Taxus Baccata*

Alternative Plants

Think about using low-maintenance plants if you are planting a new hedge. It may even be worth replacing a rather boring or very formal hedge with a more easily maintained and attractive alternative. Informal flowering hedges only need cutting back once a year after flowering, whereas formal hedges usually require clipping two or three times a year to look good. A beech or hornbeam hedge requires only one clip a year, in late summer.

Above: A mature beech hedge will need trimming only once a year.

Above: A Clematis 'Bees' Jubilee' scrambling over a rhododendron will flower after its host has finished.

CLIMBERS

Although climbers are popular for softening walls and fences, many require regular pruning, training or tying which can be time-consuming. However, many climbers are self-clinging or twining, so do not need tying in. Roses do need regular pruning to flower well, and many plants benefit from dead-heading, but most

climbers will perform well if simply pruned when they outgrow their allotted space.

Planting a Climber

1 Make the planting hole at least 45cm (1½ft) away from a wall or fence, to avoid the "rain shadow" that will prevent moisture reaching young roots. Work plenty of moisture-holding material such as garden compost or manure into the soil.

2 Plant at an angle so that the stems grow towards the wall. Leave in any cane that was used as a support while in the pot, but if there are several stems untie them and spread them out.

3 To help start off newly planted self-clinging plants, use small ties that you can fix to the wall by suction or a special adhesive.

4 Water thoroughly after planting and whenever the ground is dry during the first season. Once the plant is well established, watering should seldom be necessary.

SELF-CLINGING AND
TWINING CLIMBERS
Ceropegia sandersonii
Clematis
Hedera
Lonicera periclymenum
Manettia leteorubra
Parthenocissus quinquefolia
Tropaeolum
Wisteria sinensis

189

A Simplified Kitchen Garden

Kitchen gardens are usually labour-intensive, with many hours spent digging, watering, feeding and weeding. If you want to grow fruit and vegetables in a low-maintenance garden, choose those that demand the least attention and try some of the techniques described here.

Watering Edible Plants

Vegetables and salads need plenty of water, so a sprinkler will be essential. To save more time, you could add a time switch to make the system automatic. Seep hoses are ideal for rows of vegetables as the water goes directly to where it is needed at the roots (see Easy Garden Maintenance).

Above: French beans need a rich soil but require little after-care, apart from regular harvesting to maintain production.

Above: Planting fruit and vegetable seedlings through a mulching sheet will avoid the need for weeding.

Eliminate Weeding

By using a mulching sheet that will keep out light yet let through water, you can almost eliminate weeding on beds. Always make sure the soil is enriched with well-rotted manure or garden compost and fertilizers before you lay the mulching sheet. Secure the sheet edges, then cut crosses in the sheet with a knife and plant through the holes, folding the sheet back after planting. Water thoroughly. Later, feeding is best done by applying a liquid fertilizer, rather than compost, so that it will penetrate the mulch to reach the plant roots.

> ### GARDENER'S TIP
> If you find spacing seeds by hand difficult, one of the proprietary seed-sowers might help. These are available for both seed trays and drills. For sowing in the ground, you can choose a long-handled version, to avoid the need for bending.

GROWING FRUIT

Concentrate on soft fruit such as blackcurrants and raspberries. Gooseberries are trouble-free in themselves but are prone to pests and diseases. Rhubarb is completely trouble-free. You can leave it for years, to flourish without any attention at all.

Avoid troublesome fruit such as apricots, which are demanding, and apples and pears, which are prone to problems and require careful pruning if trained to one of the systems popular in small gardens.

If you really want to grow apples, try one of the flagpoles that grow upright and form the fruit on natural short spurs along the upright stem. Apart from cutting out the odd wayward shoot, pruning is not required.

Above: This eye-catching herb and salad garden is easy to maintain.

GROWING VEGETABLES AND SALAD

There are many vegetables and salads that are easy to grow and are not overly troubled by pests and diseases. Many can now be bought as plugs from the garden centre if you do not want to sow them from seed. Try courgettes, French beans, sweetcorn, perpetual spinach, lettuces and rocket. If you enjoy the taste of home-grown new potatoes, but do not want all the hard work of earthing up several times and heavy digging to harvest, you can grow them beneath black polythene.

Above: Potatoes grown under black polythene are easy to cultivate and harvest as they do not require earthing up.

GROWING HERBS

After the initial soil preparation to provide well-drained conditions, many herbs are easy to grow. If you stick to perennials such as chives, sage, rosemary, thyme, French tarragon and winter savory, the only maintenance required is regular picking to prevent flowering and cutting down in the autumn or early spring to encourage new growth.

191

Easy-care Plants

USE THIS LIST OF EASY-CARE PLANTS TO PLAN YOUR GARDEN SO THAT
IT REQUIRES MINIMUM MAINTENANCE.

Plant Name	When to Plant	Season of Interest
Acer palmatum (s)	autumn	autumn foliage
Ajuga reptans (ps, fs)	autumn, spring	year-round
Allium (s)	autumn	summer, autumn
Anemone x *hybrida* (s, ps)	spring	late summer to mid-autumn
Anthemis tinctoria (s)	autumn, spring	summer
Aquilegia (s, ps)	autumn, spring	late spring, early summer
Artemisia absinthium (s)	autumn, spring	late summer
Astilbe (s)	autumn, spring	summer
Aucuba japonica (s, ps, fs)	autumn	year-round
Azalea * (ps)	autumn	spring
Begonia semperflorens ñ (ps)	late spring	summer
Berberis (s, ps)	autumn	spring, autumn
Bergenia (s, ps)	autumn, spring	spring
Buxus sempervirens (ps)	autumn	year-round
Calendula officinalis (s, ps)	sow in situ, spring	summer to autumn
Calluna vulgaris * (s)	autumn, spring	summer, autumn
Carex (s, ps)	autumn, spring	year-round
Chamaecyparis, dwarf cultivars ñ to slightly ^ (s)	autumn, spring	year-round
Chamaemelum nobile 'Treneague' (s)	sow in situ or divide in spring	year-round
Choisya ternata (s)	autumn, spring	year-round
Cistus (s)	autumn, spring	summer

Allium

Calendula

Colchicum autumnale (s)	summer	autumn
Cortaderia selloana (s)	autumn, spring	late summer
Cotoneaster (s, ps)	autumn	year-round, autumn berries
Crataegus (s, ps)	autumn	spring flowers, autumn fruits
Crocus (s)	autumn, summer	spring, autumn
Cyclamen (ps)	late summer	autumn, winter, early spring
Cytisus (s)	autumn	summer
Deschampsia ñ to * (s, ps)	autumn, spring	late spring, early summer
Dianthus ñ to ^ (s)	autumn, spring	summer
Dicentra spectabilis ñ to ^ (ps)	autumn, spring	summer
Digitalis purpurea (ps)	autumn	late spring, early summer
Echinops ritro (s, ps)	autumn	early summer
Elaeagnus pungens (s, ps)	autumn	summer
Erica cultivars * (s)	autumn	winter, spring
Erigeron (ps)	autumn	spring, summer
Eryngium (s)	spring, autumn	summer
Eschscholzia californica (s)	sow in situ, spring	summer to autumn
Euonymus fortunei (s)	autumn	year-round
Euphorbia (s)	autumn	summer
Fatsia japonica (s, ps)	autumn	year-round
Festuca glauca (s)	autumn, winter	year-round
Galanthus nivalis (ps)	autumn	late winter, early spring
Gaultheria (syn. Pernettya) * to ñ (ps)	autumn	year-round
Geranium (s, ps)	spring, autumn	summer
Hakonechloa (s, ps)	spring, autumn	year-round
Hebe (s, ps)	autumn	year-round, summer flowers
Hedera (s, ps, fs)	autumn	year-round
Helichrysum ñ to ^ (s)	autumn	summer, autumn
Hemerocallis (s)	autumn	summer
Hosta (ps, fs)	autumn	summer

Deschampsia

Erica *cultivars*

Houttuynia cordata (s)	autumn, spring	spring, summer
Hypericum calycinum (s, ps)	autumn	summer
Ilex aquifolium (s)	autumn, spring	year-round, autumn berries
Impatiens (ps)	autumn, spring	spring to autumn
Juniperus horizontalis (s)	autumn	year-round
Kniphofia hybrids (s, ps)	autumn, spring	summer
Lamium maculatum (ps, s)	spring, autumn	summer to autumn
Lavandula (s)	autumn	summer, early autumn
Lavatera trimestris (s)	autumn, spring	summer
Laurus nobilis (s, ps)	autumn	year-round
Lilium * (s, ps)	autumn, spring	summer
Limnanthes (s)	sow in situ, spring	summer
Liriope muscari (fs)	autumn	autumn
Lonicera periclymenum (s, ps)	autumn	summer
Lupinus slightly * (s, ps)	autumn, spring	summer
Mahonia (fs)	autumn, spring	autumn, winter, spring
Malus (s, ps)	autumn	spring, autumn fruits
Miscanthus sinensis (s)	autumn	spring to autumn
Muscari (s)	autumn	spring
Narcissus (s)	autumn	spring
Olearia x *haastii* (s)	autumn	year-round, summer flowers
Origanum vulgare ^ (s)	autumn	summer
Osteospermum (s)	spring	summer
Parthenocissus quinquefolia (s, fs)	autumn, spring	spring to autumn
Pelargonium (s)	spring	summer
Persicaria affinis (s, ps)	spring	summer to autumn
Petunia (s)	spring	summer to autumn
Phormium (s)	autumn, spring	year-round
Pyracantha (s, ps)	spring, autumn	autumn berries
Rhododendron *(ps)	autumn, spring	late spring
Rosmarinus officinalis (s)	autumn	year-round

Lavandula

Juniperus horizontalis

Rudbeckia (s)	autumn, spring	summer to autumn
Salvia officinalis (s)	autumn	year-round
Santolina chamaecyparissus (s)	autumn, spring	year-round, summer flowers
Schizostylis coccinea (s)	spring, autumn	summer, autumn
Sedum spectabile (s)	autumn	late summer
Sorbus vilmorinii (s)	autumn	autumn berries
Stipa (s)	autumn	year-round
Tagetes patula (s)	autumn, spring	summer to early autumn
Taxus baccata (s, ps, fs)	autumn	year-round, autumn berries
Thuja orientalis 'Aurea Nana' (s)	autumn, spring	year-round
Thymus ñ to ^ (s)	autumn, spring	year-round
Tropaeolum speciosum ñ to ^ (s, ps)	autumn	summer
Tulipa (s)	autumn	spring
Veronica spicata (s, ps)	autumn, spring	summer
Viburnum davidii (s, ps)	autumn	year-round
Vinca minor (s, ps)	autumn, spring	year-round
Waldsteinia ternata (ps, fs)	spring	mid- to late spring
Wisteria sinensis (s, ps)	autumn	summer
Yucca gloriosa (s)	spring	year-round

Stipa

Tulipa

SYMBOLS

Plants marked with * require acid soil;

Plants marked with ^ prefer alkaline soil;

Plants marked with ñ prefer neutral soil.

(S) = sun

(PS) = partial shade

(FS) = full shade

PRUNING SUCCESS

Many plants benefit from some form
of regular pruning, either to keep them
to size or to increase the amount of
flowers. Knowing which plants benefit
from the treatment and how and when
to prune is the key. The pruning notes
in this chapter cover general
techniques and details for all the main
types of plant, while a seasonal chart
enables you to identify exactly when
and how to prune particular plants.
Different types of hedging plants
are included.

Left: *Annual pruning helps to create prolific
flowering, especially lower down the stem.*

What is Pruning?

PRUNING IS A TECHNIQUE USED TO RESTRICT THE GROWTH OF PLANTS,
INCREASE THE YIELD OF FLOWERS AND FRUIT AND GENERALLY KEEP
PLANTS IN GOOD HEALTH. IT CAN ALSO BE USED TO ENHANCE THE
DECORATIVE EFFECT OF LEAVES AND STEMS.

PRUNING CONCERNS

Amateur gardeners are often more baffled by pruning than by any other aspect of gardening; this may be partly due to conflicting advice in publications, and on television and radio pro-

grammes. Even many experienced gardeners approach the subject with caution. The main concerns are that pruning incorrectly will result in the failure of plants to flower or fruit, or that the shape will be spoilt or, in the worst scenario, that the plant will be killed. However, take comfort from the knowledge that you are unlikely to kill a plant by pruning it, as plants are surprisingly resilient. The worst that can happen is that you may lose a season's flowers or fruit,

and even then, you will probably find that the plant will perform better than ever the following year.

Once you have learned a few basic principles, it's a good idea to watch your plants to discover how they grow and flower. Different techniques will yield different results, so adopt the approach that best suits you and your style of gardening.

Some gardeners like the garden to look tidy with everything tightly controlled and clipped to shape. This can be

Above: Shrub roses are usually quite large and bushy but they still benefit from pruning.

Right: Clematis 'Barbara Dibley' needs selective pruning in early spring for a flush of flowers in late spring and summer.

rewarding but is also time-consuming. Others take a more relaxed approach, often through necessity. The overall appearance of their gardens may be less regimented, but the plants will still be healthy and will perform well.

BUILDING CONFIDENCE

The best way to learn to prune is to do it, then to observe the results. You will soon discover which methods produce the effect you want. You can then apply the same technique to other similar plants.

Always remember that pruning is not always strictly necessary. If a plant pleases you exactly the way it is, you can often leave it alone as long as it remains healthy and productive. However, this does not mean that you

should allow your plants to grow unchecked for years, and then attack them with the shears only when they have got out of hand.

Prune a plant indiscriminately at the wrong time and in the wrong way and it may well regrow with redoubled vigour, making it much more of a problem than it was in the first place. If you have any serious doubts, prune lightly; you can always do a little more trimming later if the plant responds well. Alternatively, prune the plant in stages, perhaps a quarter of the growth one year, then, after checking the response, tackling the remainder in the following year.

Above: Pruning climbing roses in spring will encourage stronger growth.

Left: A healthy camellia at its peak.

What is Pruning?

WHY WE NEED TO PRUNE

We prune plants for a variety of reasons: one is to control size and shape. This is especially important in a small garden where space is at a premium. However, the number of plants that you can control in this way is relatively small.

It is better to think of pruning as a means of refreshing the plant, so that it will produce a large proportion of young growth. Young wood flowers and fruits better, provides good, strong material for taking cuttings, and is healthier than the old.

If allowed to build up, old, dead wood can harbour disease. Thinning stems is also a good means of improving air circulation within the body of the plant. If the growth is dense and congested, damp air tends to settle

around the stems, encouraging mildew and other fungal diseases which can only be eliminated with fungicides. These days, gardeners try to keep their use of chemicals in the garden to the absolute minimum, and correct pruning can mean you will not need them.

You can also prune to enhance a particular decorative effect, for example, to give larger leaves, or to encourage a mass of brilliantly coloured young stems. Remember, however, that these techniques usually bring some losses as well as gains. Prune a dogwood hard for its vivid winter stem effect, and you will lose that summer's flowers, because the plant does not have time to grow and ripen sufficiently for flowering. The choice is yours.

Fruit trees and bushes usually have quite specific needs, in order to help them produce the biggest crop. Turn to any pruning manual and you will find a number of complicated procedures, most of which have been developed by professional fruit-growers whose livelihood depends on a large crop. There is no need to worry about those methods as you can easily

Left: Pruning a late-flowering clematis in late winter produces abundant blooms.

achieve yields good enough for the average family using the simplified methods described in this book.

WHEN TO PRUNE

The important thing to remember is that pruning always stimulates new growth, from the point at which you cut. For this reason, it is unwise to prune after midsummer and into autumn. The plant will put on a spurt of fresh, sappy growth that will not have time to harden before the onset of winter, and will probably die back.

NEW WOOD OR OLD?

The first rule in pruning is to make the cut on the correct part of the stem, so it is important to be able to recognize new and old wood. Sometimes also called the current season's growth new wood is supple and bright green in colour, gradually turning brown in summer as it becomes progressively less pliable. One-year-old wood is usually brown. Older wood tends to be grey.

MAKING THE CUTS

Depending on the plant, growth buds either lie opposite each other on the stem or are arranged alternately.

In both cases, you need to cut back to just above a growth bud. In the case of plants with opposite buds, two new shoots will grow, making a bushier

Right: Rambling roses flower once on old wood.

This year's growth – greener and flexible

Last summer's growth – darker and less flexible

Two-year-old wood – darker, thicker and more rigid

plant. With alternate buds, a new shoot will emerge growing in the direction the bud was pointing. This is why you often hear about cutting back to an outward-facing bud, a method that creates a vase-shaped plant with an open centre through which air can circulate freely.

201

MAKING A GOOD CUT

1 Cut about 5mm (¼in) above a bud, angled so that moisture runs away from the bud and not into it. If the plant has buds lying opposite one another, cut straight across the stem, just above a strong pair of buds.

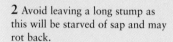

2 Avoid leaving a long stump as this will be starved of sap and may rot back.

3 Avoid cutting too close to the bud as this may allow infection to enter.

4 Blunt secateurs (pruning shears) or careless use may bruise or tear the stem instead of cutting through it cleanly. This is an invitation for disease spores to enter. The stump is also too long.

5 If the cut slopes down-wards towards the bud, the excessive moisture that may collect in the area could cause the stem to rot.

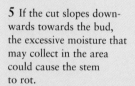

6 Shrubs with opposite leaves should be treated in a different way to those with leaves that form an alternate leaf arrangement. Cut straight across the stem, just above a strong pair of buds.

HOW TO USE THIS CHAPTER

The chapter is arranged so that the basic principles of pruning various well-known and popular plants are explained in detail. Drawings are included for each pruning method showing clearly how the cuts should be made. Read the chapter through and you will soon discover that many of the techniques are similar – because the principles of pruning remain the same whatever type of plant you are dealing with.

Roses and clematis have specific needs depending on the variety. Use a good rose catalogue if you are unsure which type of rose you have. Clematis are divided into three groups, and this information is usually stated on the plant label when you buy your plant. If in doubt, the section on clematis will help you ascertain to which group your plant belongs.

The chapter begins with details of basic pruning equipment that you will need. At the end of the chapter, a quick reference chart provides appropriate pruning methods for each plant, with the exception of roses, clematis and fruits, which have specific needs. The chart also gives the time of year that each plant should be pruned.

This book does not deal with tree pruning. If you have a large tree that needs attention, it is best to contact a qualified professional. Ask at your local nursery or garden centre for their recommendations.

Saws & Power Tools

GOOD-QUALITY TOOLS ALWAYS MAKE THE JOB EASIER. SHARP BLADES
MAKE CLEAN CUTS THAT HEAL RAPIDLY.

GRECIAN SAW

This is a good general-purpose pruning saw. It has a curved blade that nar-
rows towards the tip, making it easy
to use among congested branches. It is
also easy to use above head height,
because the backward-pointing teeth
cut on the pull stroke.

STRAIGHT PRUNING SAW

This is a general-purpose tool for
cutting through thicker branches.
Choose one with teeth on just one side
of the blade.

BOW SAW

Because this saw is designed to cut on
both the pull and push strokes, it cuts

fast and is useful for making horizontal cuts low down on a plant.
However, it is difficult to use in a confined space.

POWERED HEDGE TRIMMERS

Electrically powered models are suitable for most gardens. They can be
mains or battery powered, but mains-
driven types can be used for longer
periods of time. Always carry the
cable over your shoulder to avoid
accidents. Battery-driven models are
useful for a small or remote hedges,
where access is difficult with a cable;
the charge may not last long enough
for a long hedge without recharging.
If you have a long stretch of hedge to
cut, use a petrol- (gasoline-) driven
model, which can be be hired.

SAFETY TIPS

• Electrically powered tools must be
used with a circuit breaker.

• Wear goggles to protect your eyes and
(if necessary) ear defenders to protect
your ears.

• Take extra care with power tools
when standing on a stepladder as your
balance will be affected.

• Do not use electrical equipment
during or just after rain.

Small Hand Tools

ALTHOUGH MOST OF US CAN MANAGE WITH A GOOD PAIR OF
SECATEURS (PRUNING SHEARS OR PRUNERS), LONG-HANDLED PRUNERS
(LOPPERS OR LOPPING SHEARS) AND HAND SHEARS, THERE ARE TIMES
WHEN MORE SPECIALIST TOOLS ARE REQUIRED.

BYPASS SECATEURS
(Pruning shears)
Good secateurs (pruning shears) are
suitable for a range of pruning jobs.
Bypass secateurs have a broad concave or square blade that cuts against
a narrower, hooked blade that holds
the branch while the cut is made.

*Bypass secateurs
(pruning shears)*

ANVIL SECATEURS
(Pruning shears)
These have a straight blade that cuts
against a flat anvil, often with a
groove cut in it through which sap can
drain away. Ensure that the blade is
sharp to avoid crushing the stems.

*Anvil secateurs
(pruning shears)*

If you have a weak grip, ratchet
shears may be more appropriate. The
ratchet device enables you to cut
through the stem in several small
movements that require less effort.

Most secateurs will cut stems up to
1cm (½ in) thick.

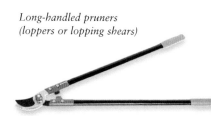

*Long-handled pruners
(loppers or lopping shears)*

LONG-HANDLED PRUNERS
(Loppers or lopping shears)
These can be used to cut through
stems that are too thick to be cut with
secateurs. They are useful for reaching
high or low, congested branches.

Pruning knife

Hand shears with a straight blade

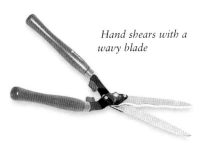

Hand shears with a wavy blade

TREE PRUNERS

(Tree loppers or pole pruners)
For tall shrubs, these will make the job easier. Long-handled pruners do not reach as high and can be tiring to use above shoulder level.

The mechanism by which these work varies with the make: they may be operated by rope, metal rods, or fixed or telescopic handles. The small lever mechanism in the handle transfers the cutting action to the cutting head. The hooked end makes it easier to position and steadies the tool.

PRUNING KNIFE

These knives have a curved, folding blade that ensures the blade cuts into the shoot as you cut towards yourself with a slicing motion.

Because of the temptation to use the thumb as an anvil, such knives must be used with great care.

SHEARS

Mainly used for hedge trimming, shears can also be used for cutting through branches on shrubs and trees that are too thick for secateurs or loppers, provided there is a notch at the base of the blades. They can also be used to trim low-growing shrubs. Some models have blades with wavy edges that help trap and hold the shoots while cutting.

Choose shears of a weight you feel comfortable with; cutting a hedge by hand can be tiring work.

Coppicing & Pollarding

THESE METHODS, CARRIED OUT IN EARLY SPRING TO DOGWOODS AND SOME WILLOWS, ARE USED TO ENHANCE THE COLOUR OF ORNAMENTAL STEMS OR THE LEAVES, OR TO RESTRICT TREE SIZE.

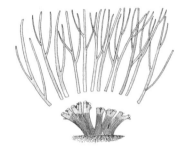

Left: To coppice, cut back all the recent growth in late winter to early spring, leaving a low woody mound (or 'stool').

Below: Rubus cockburnianus, *coppiced for winter effect.*

PLANTS TO TRY

Catalpa bignonioides
Cornus sibirica
Cornus stolonifera
Eucalyptus gunnii
Paulownia tomentosa
Rubus cockburnianus
Salix alba vitellina

1 For coppicing, pruning is severe. Cut back stems to near ground level leaving a low, woody framework. Do this early every spring or every other spring if the plant is still young.

2 A coppiced shrub will look like this at the start of the growing season. The technique is a useful means of restricting the size of plants that could otherwise grow too big.

206

Above: The stems of a pollarded Salix alba vitelina *'Britzensis' in full winter glory.*

1 For pollarding, allow the plant to grow until the trunk has reached the desired height.

PLANTS TO TRY

Catalpa bignonioides
Eucalyptus gunnii
Paulownia tomentosa
Robinia pseudoacacia
Tilia

2 In late winter or spring, cut the stems back hard near to the top of the trunk to leave short stubs. The new shoots produced over the summer will create a colourful winter effect.

3 Over time the pollarded head becomes more stubby and will produce fine colourful stems annually.

4 If possible, feed immediately after pruning to give the plant a boost and to achieve the desired growth.

207

Cutting Back to a Framework

SHRUBS THAT FLOWER ON SHOOTS PRODUCED IN THE CURRENT YEAR WILL BECOME INCREASINGLY STRAGGLY UNLESS THEY ARE PRUNED ANNUALLY. PRUNING WILL PROMOTE BLOOMS CLOSER TO THE GROUND.

Left: Prune hard annually to a low framework of old, darker wood to encourage a mass of new shoots and a bushy habit.

Below: Buddleja davidii *produces masses of flowers when pruned this way.*

PLANTS TO TRY

Buddleja davidii
Caryopteris
Hydrangea paniculata
Sambucus racemosa

1 In late winter to early spring, before new growth starts, cut back to a low framework no higher than 90cm (3ft).

2 You can also prune harder, cutting the thicker stems flush with the ground. If you delay pruning until early spring, new growth from the base of the plant will be clearly visible.

Cutting to the Ground

THIS TECHNIQUE IS OFTEN USED ON LATE-FLOWERING SHRUBS OF BORDERLINE HARDINESS THAT TEND TO DIE BACK IN WINTER. LEAVE THE STEMS OVER WINTER TO PROVIDE FROST PROTECTION.

Left: Cut back all the previous year's growth just above the ground each spring.

Below: Fuchsia 'Tom Thumb' benefits from a pruned framework after the winter.

PLANTS TO TRY

Ceratostigma willmottianum
Cestrum parqui
Fuchsia (hardy varieties)
Perovskia atriplicifolia

1 In spring, as soon as new growth is visible, cut the old stems back hard, flush with the ground or close to it.

2 The plant will grow strongly, having more access to the light. This will create a bushy, compact plant.

209

Deadheading with Shears

REMOVING FADED FLOWERS IS A FORM OF PRUNING. IN THE CASE OF HEATHERS (*CALLUNA*, *DABOECIA* AND *ERICA*) IT IS EASIEST TO SHEAR THEM OFF IN ONE GO.

Above: *Trim back heathers as the flowers begin to fade, being careful not to cut back into the darker, old wood.*

Above: *Pruning to keep heathers compact will give you a neat heather bed.*

1 Shear over your plants, cutting just below the flower spike. Heathers will not regenerate from cuts made into old, bare wood. Prune winter-flowering heather in spring to ensure you do not damage tender growth.

2 Some heathers are grown for their coloured foliage, not their flowers. In winter, lightly trim back the developing flowers before they have the chance to open. This will encourage further leaf growth.

210

Clipping

MANY EVERGREENS RESPOND WELL TO BEING CLIPPED TO SHAPE, EITHER WITH SHEARS OR (IF THE LEAVES ARE LARGE) WITH SECATEURS (PRUNERS). WITH PRACTICE YOU CAN CREATE UNUSUAL TOPIARY.

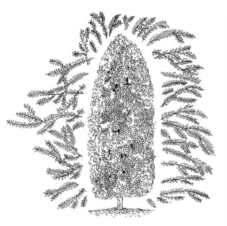

Above: Trim new growth to shape in spring and midsummer.

Above: Yew is the classic shrub to clip into interesting shapes.

1 Trim off the new growth as necessary, but avoid cutting into old wood. Shear the plants twice in the growing season to produce a smooth surface. Practise on quick-growing plants such as *Ligustrum vulgare* before progressing to ambitious schemes.

PLANTS TO TRY

Berberis
Buxus sempervirens
Ligustrum vulgare
Lonicera nitida
Osmanthus decorus
Phillyrea angustifolia
Prunus lusitanica
Taxus baccata

Large-leaved Evergreens

MOST EVERGREEN SHRUBS GROW HAPPILY WITHOUT ROUTINE PRUN-
ING, BUT IF YOU HAVE A SMALL GARDEN YOU MAY WANT TO RESTRICT
THE SIZE OF LARGER SHRUBS.

Above: Prune out awkwardly placed stems and some of the older growth. You can also shorten stems that have flowered, cutting back just above a growth bud.

Above: Most larger leaved evergreens only need pruning when they need restricting.

1 If a shrub produces a shoot that spoils the outline of the plant, cut it back to its point of origin, reaching right into the plant if necessary. This will restore its uniform shape.

Variegated evergreens sometimes pro-
duce plain green shoots. These are always more vigorous than the typical growth and should be cut out entirely as soon as you spot them.

The 'One-third' Method

THIS SIMPLE TECHNIQUE WORKS ON A WIDE VARIETY OF ORNAMENTAL FLOWERING SHRUBS. IT IS A GOOD WAY TO KEEP THEM COMPACT AND FRESH, AND IT ENCOURAGES HEALTHY BLOOMS.

Above: Cut out one-third of the oldest stems close to ground level.

PLANTS TO TRY

Cornus (grown for foliage effect, e.g. *C. alba* 'Elegantissima' and 'Spaethii')
Cotinus coggygria
Forsythia
Hypericum
Kerria japonica 'Pleniflora'
Kolkwitzia
Leycesteria
Philadelphus
Potentilla (shrubby types)
Ribes sanguineum
Spiraea

1 Immediately after flowering, cut back a third of the oldest stems, cutting some back to strong buds low down and removing others at or near ground level. Remove any weak or badly placed branches and shorten any damaged stems. Use this technique for established plants, not for any under three years old.

Above: Kolkwitzia amabilis *pruned by one-third will stay compact.*

213

Shortening New Growth

A LIGHT TRIMMING WILL ENCOURAGE A BUSHIER HABIT ON PLANTS SUCH AS *CYSTISUS* AND *GENISTA* THAT OTHERWISE CAN EASILY BECOME GAUNT WITH LONG, BARE BRANCHES.

Above: Trim back the new growth by half after flowering. Be careful not to cut back into older wood.

GARDENER'S TIP

Use this method on young plants only. Old, neglected plants will not respond well and are best replaced.

Below: This Genista lydia *is covered with flowers the year following pruning.*

1 Immediately after flowering, shorten last season's growth, which will be pale and supple, by about half. Take care not to cut back into old wood.

2 A light trimming is all that will be necessary on some of the stems. Ensure that you cut recent growth only, that made last summer.

214

Shortening Side Shoots

SHRUBS THAT FLOWER ON THE PREVIOUS YEAR'S SHOOTS OFTEN BENE-
FIT FROM A LIGHT PRUNING AFTER FLOWERING. THIS WILL ENCOUR-
AGE MORE BLOOMS THE FOLLOWING YEAR.

Above: *Trim back shoots that have flowered (shown here in yellow) by between a half and two-thirds of their length.*

PLANTS TO TRY
Cistus
Convolvulus cneorum
Helianthemum
Kalmia latifolia

Below: *A* Cistus *in full flower.*

1 Immediately after flowering, trim back only the shoots that have flowered. Shorten the current season's growth, which will still be soft and pliable, by up to two-thirds. Do not cut into older, darker wood.

Plants in this category keep a good shape whether you prune or not, but a trimming results in more shoots which will all be flower-bearers.

215

Grey-leaved Foliage Plants

MANY GREY-LEAVED PLANTS LOOK UNATTRACTIVE IF ALLOWED TO BECOME STRAGGLY. ANNUAL PRUNING WILL KEEP THEM LOOKING FRESH AND WELL-CLOTHED WITH FOLIAGE.

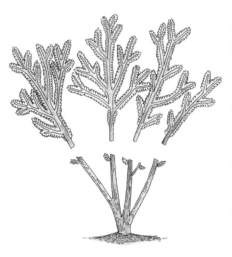

PLANTS TO TRY

Artemisia (shrubby types)
Helichrysum italicum
Lavandula
Santolina chamaecyparissus

Above: *Cut back grey-leaved plants to as low down on the stem as possible, just above a new growth bud.*

Above: *A* Santolina chamaecyparissus *that has become leggy.*

1 In early spring, as the new growth emerges, prune back last year's growth, cutting just above a new shoot or a developing bud. The plant will look sparse.

2 The plant will soon be well-clothed with new leaves. Start this regime early in the life of the plant: most grey-leaved plants will not regenerate well if you cut into very old wood.

Rejuvenating the Neglected

OLD AND NEGLECTED SHRUBS OFTEN NEED TO BE REPLACED, BUT IT IS
WORTH TRYING SOME DRASTIC PRUNING FIRST. IF THE SHRUB DOESN'T
RESPOND, THEN REPLACE IT.

Above: Staggering drastic pruning is often effective. Here, the central stem has been left unpruned. Two stems pruned hard last year have produced fresh growth, so it is safe to cut back the two old branches as shown to encourage further growth.

Above: New shoots will soon appear.

1 In late winter to early spring, cut back all the stems to just above ground level. Alternatively, cut the shrub back in stages. Prune back one-third of the stems in the first year, a second third in the next. Cut back the remainder the following year.

2 Trim any ragged edges with a pruning knife or rasp to prevent infection entering the wound. If the shrub shows no sign of life in the first year after pruning, dig it up and replace it.

217

Floribunda Roses

SOMETIMES CALLED CLUSTER-FLOWERED ROSES, FLORIBUNDAS ARE
NOTED FOR THEIR PROLIFIC BLOOMING.

Above: Cut out damaged, badly placed,
and weak shoots, then shorten the
remainder by between a half and two-
thirds of their length.

Above: Rosa 'Sexy Rexy'.

1 In early spring, cut back all dead,
diseased and damaged stems, cutting
them back to their point of origin,
if necessary.

2 Remove any crossing or awkwardly
placed shoots that are growing into
the centre of the bush.

3 Shorten the remaining stems by up
to two-thirds of their length, cutting
back to healthy buds that are pointing
outwards. Prune vigorous varieties
lightly, weaker-growing plants harder.

4 During the flowering season,
remove spent flower trusses to encourage the plant to flower further.

Hybrid Tea Roses

ALSO KNOWN AS LARGE-FLOWERED ROSES, HYBRID TEAS HAVE LARGE, FULLY DOUBLE FLOWERS WITH A HIGH CENTRE. THEIR BEAUTIFUL BLOOMS ARE PERFECT FOR FLORAL DISPLAYS.

Above: Cut out badly placed, diseased or dead wood to the base. Shorten all other stems by about half.

Above: Rosa 'Savoy Hotel'.

1 In early spring, cut out any diseased or dead shoots, as well as any stems that are badly placed. Most of these can be cut back to their point of origin, but if growth is sparse, cut to just above a healthy bud.

2 Prune the remaining stems to within 20–25cm (8–10in) of the ground. Always cut to an outward-facing bud.

3 During the flowering season, remove spent flowers to prolong the display.

Shrub Roses

WILD ROSES AND OLD-FASHIONED VARIETIES OF ROSES THAT
PRE-DATE HYBRID TEAS AND FLORIBUNDAS ARE KNOWN AS SHRUB
ROSES. THEY GENERALLY FLOWER FOR A FAIRLY SHORT PERIOD.

Above: Shorten main stems by about a quarter to a half, side shoots by up to two-thirds. Cut out weak and badly placed stems entirely.

Above: Rosa 'Frühlingsgold'.

1 Pruning prevents congestion, improves the shrub's appearance and increases the number of blooms. In early spring, thin congested growth by cutting back old stems at ground level.

2 Shorten main shoots by up to a half. Some need only light trimming.

3 Side shoots can be shortened by up to two-thirds.

Standard Roses

PRUNE STANDARD ROSES IN EARLY SPRING TO FORM AN ATTRACTIVE, ROUNDED HEAD. WEEPING STANDARDS ARE PRUNED IN SUMMER TO RETAIN THEIR FLOWING APPEARANCE.

Above: Shorten the previous season's growth by about a half (left). On a weeping standard, cut back the trailing shoots to new buds in the crown when flowering has finished (right).

Above: Standard roses need staking to keep them upright.

1 In early spring, shorten the previous year's main stems to about six buds from the base, cutting to outward-facing buds. Aim for a balanced shape, but do not prune too hard or new shoots may spoil the shape.

2 Shorten side shoots to a couple of buds. To prevent congestion cut back dead or diseased wood.

3 Remove the flowers as they fade to prolong the display.

221

Climbing Roses

PROLIFIC CLIMBING ROSES ARE USUALLY REPEAT-FLOWERING, OFTEN ON A COMBINATION OF THE OLD AND NEW WOOD. THEY ARE FREQUENTLY HIGHLY SCENTED AS WELL AS IMPRESSIVE TO LOOK AT.

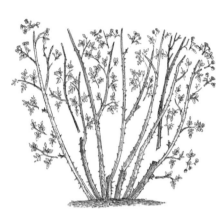

Above: Cut some of the oldest stems back to strong new shoots near the base or where there is a suitable replacement. Shorten laterals by up to two-thirds.

Above: The magnificent wall-mounted Rosa 'Climbing Iceberg'.

1 In the first few years after planting, the aim is to build up a framework of branches. In spring, cut back any unproductive shoots, but not more than one-third of the stems or flowering will suffer next year.

2 In summer, tie in vigorous shoots as they grow, using soft string. Do not tie too tightly – you may chafe the stems.

3 Cut back the faded flowers to encourage further flowering.

Rambling Roses

THESE ROSES FLOWER ONCE, ON THE OLD WOOD. THEY THEN PRO-
DUCE A MASS OF NEW GROWTH NEAR TO THE BASE.

Above: Remove very old or diseased stems
entirely. Cut back old canes that have
flowered to a point where there is
vigorous replacement growth.

Above: Ramblers, such as Rosa 'Rambling
Rector', should be pruned after flowering.

1 In late summer, after flowering, cut
out all dead or damaged shoots, as
well as any that are weak and spindly.

2 Shorten older canes that have flowered to vigorous new shoots. You will
be able to leave some unpruned.

3 Tie in the new shoots to the support.
Try to pull them to the horizontal –
they will produce more flower-bearing
laterals for next year.

4 On the canes that remain, shorten
the side shoots to two or three leaves.

223

Clematis

THESE POPULAR CLIMBERS ARE DIVIDED INTO THREE GROUPS, EACH FLOWERING AT DIFFERENT TIMES OF THE YEAR. THE GROUPS ALSO HAVE DIFFERENT PRUNING REQUIREMENTS.

Clematis climb by curling leaf stalks, and are attractive against walls or on fences (fitted with trellis supports), over pergolas, or growing through other plants. Vigorous species look spectacular growing through trees.

For pruning purposes, clematis are divided into three groups, depending on when they flower. Most clematis on sale will state on the label to which group they belong.

Group 1 clematis flower from late winter to spring on wood made the previous year. Usually small-flowered, several of this group are species.

Group 2 consists of large-flowered hybrids that flower in late spring and early summer, on wood made the previous year, then again in mid- to late summer on the new wood. The group includes some species with double flowers. However, the flowers in the second flush are always single.

Group 3 clematis flower from midsummer to autumn on the current season's growth. The group includes many large-flowered hybrids, as well as texensis and viticella types. There are also several notable species: the yellow-flowered *C. tibetana* subsp. *vernayi*, and *C. flammula* and *C. rehderiana*.

Above: C. *'Fireworks' is one of the most spectacular clematis with large luminous violet flowers.*

GARDENER'S TIP

Training is vital and should begin early. Tie the stems to the horizontal as far as is possible as they grow, but take great care: the stems are brittle and are easily broken.

Group 1 Clematis

THIS GROUP COMPRISES THOSE CLEMATIS THAT FLOWER BEFORE MID-SUMMER, ON SHOOTS PRODUCED THE PREVIOUS YEAR. PRUNE ONLY TO KEEP THE PLANT WITHIN BOUNDS.

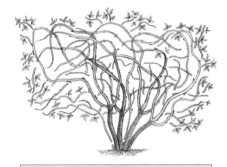

Left: *Shorten only those stems that have outgrown their allotted space and cut out a proportion of the remainder to relieve congestion. Otherwise, this group can be left unpruned.*

GARDENER'S TIP

If a group 1 clematis has been allowed to get out of control, has tangled stems and is bare at the base, you can renovate it by cutting it all back to near ground level. Regeneration can be slow, however, and it might be a couple of years before the plant is flowering freely again.

Above: C. montana *var.* rubens 'Continuity' *requires only light pruning.*

1 Immediately after flowering, when necessary, cut back to their point of origin any stems that have outgrown their allotted space.

2 Thin congested growth if necessary. After pruning, the plant will look neater at the edges but overall few shoots will have been removed.

Group 2 Clematis

THESE CLEMATIS FLOWER TWICE: IN LATE SPRING OR EARLY SUMMER ON WOOD MADE THE PREVIOUS YEAR, AND IN MID- TO LATE SUMMER ON THE CURRENT SEASON'S GROWTH.

Above: *Prune selectively in early spring. Cut out old, damaged and weak shoots, thin tangled growth, but leave a good proportion unpruned.*

GARDENER'S TIP

You can also prune group 2 clematis as for group 3. You will lose the first crop of flowers, but the second will be more spectacular. Double-flowered types will only produce single flowers, however.

1 Cut back any dead or damaged stems to near ground level. Shorten any that have outgrown their space.

2 Leave some of the growth unpruned, respacing the shoots. These will carry the first crop of flowers.

Above: *Group 2 Clematis 'Royalty' produces glorious, rich purple flowers twice each year.*

Group 3 Clematis

THESE CLEMATIS FLOWER FROM MIDSUMMER TO AUTUMN. THE
GROUP INCLUDES SEVERAL SPECIES, MANY LARGE-FLOWERED HYBRIDS
AND THE TEXENSIS AND VITICELLA TYPES.

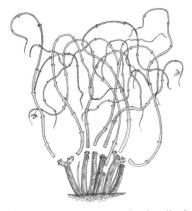

Left: Pruning a group 3 clematis is basically a matter of renovation. In late winter, cut back all the previous year's growth to the lowest set of strong buds on each stem to leave a woody framework.

> **GARDENER'S TIP**
> For a late crop of flowers, delay pruning until mid-spring.

1 In late winter, cut back all the growth to a pair of strong buds low down on the stem. Any dead stems can be cut off at ground level.

2 If you want the flowers high up the plant, for example to cover the top of a pergola, cut back higher on the stem. This method particularly suits vigorous species and the stunning yellow-flowered C. 'Bill MacKenzie'.

Above: The enduringly popular C. 'Jackmanii Superba'.

227

Honeysuckle

LONICERA (HONEYSUCKLES) NEED LITTLE PRUNING WHEN YOUNG, BUT WITH AGE CAN EASILY DEVELOP A TANGLE OF UNPRODUCTIVE STEMS THAT FLOWER ONLY ABOVE EYE LEVEL.

Above: Shortening congested stems will control the spread of a honeysuckle.

Right: Regular pruning of honeysuckles will ensure an even distribution of flowers.

1 In late winter to early spring, when the stems are bare and you can see what you are doing, shear back dead and congested stems, cutting just above strong buds. You can be brutal. Honeysuckles are vigorous plants that seem to thrive on rough treatment.

2 If the plant is badly tangled, cut back all stems to a height of 30–60cm (1–2ft) from the ground. Flowering in the next season will not be prolific, but the plant will soon return to its full glory. You can train the new shoots to a support as they appear.

Wisteria

THIS IS A VIGOROUS PLANT THAT PRODUCES A VAST QUANTITY OF LEAFY STEMS ANNUALLY. CAREFUL PRUNING DIVERTS ITS ENERGIES INTO FLOWER PRODUCTION.

Above: After flowering, wisterias suddenly produce a mass of new stems. Cut back any that are not needed to extend the framework. Shorten this growth further in winter.

Above: A wisteria in full flower.

1 Throughout the growing season, train in the new stems that are needed to extend the framework. Once this is established, in late summer shorten the new growth to between four and six leaves to restrict the plant's spread.

2 In late winter, shorten the pruned stems further to two or three buds. This usually means reducing the summer's growth to 7.5–10cm (3–4in). Over time the plant develops a system of spurs that carry the flowers.

229

Other Climbers

MANY CLIMBERS ARE VIGOROUS PLANTS THAT CAN EASILY BECOME CONGESTED. PRUNING IS EASIEST TO DO WHEN THE STEMS ARE BARE IN WINTER AND YOU CAN SEE WHAT YOU ARE DOING.

Above: When pruning climbers, cut out older, unproductive stems to the base and shorten other stems as necessary.

Right: Solanum crispum 'Glasnevin'.

1 In winter cut out old, dead wood completely. You may need to shorten long stems bit by bit if they are very congested. Shorten any overlong but otherwise healthy and supple stems.

2 Tie in the remaining shoots to create a balanced framework. Although the plant will probably occupy a similar area, the growth should look less congested and more evenly balanced.

Wall-trained Chaenomeles

SOMETIMES KNOWN AS ORNAMENTAL QUINCES OR JAPONICA, *CHAENOMELES* ARE VALUED FOR THEIR ATTRACTIVE FLOWERS IN LATE WINTER. WALL-TRAINED SPECIMENS NEED ANNUAL TRIMMING.

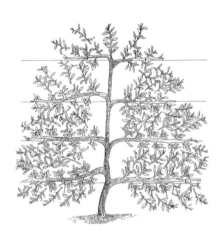

Above: Chaenomeles *should be trained espalier-fashion as shown. Once the shape of the espalier is established, shortening the side shoots in summer will help display the flowers.*

Above: The bright, waxy flowers of Chaenomeles speciosa *'Cardinalis'.*

1 As they grow, tie in strong shoots to the horizontal to extend the framework. This will help maintain a neat and controlled shape.

2 In summer, shorten sideshoots growing away from the main stem to five leaves. Remove any that are growing towards the wall.

231

Wall-trained Pyracanthas

PYRACANTHAS ARE POPULAR AS WALL-SHRUBS, EITHER TRAINED AS ESPALIERS OR MORE INFORMALLY TIED BACK, DEPENDING ON THE EFFECT YOU WISH TO CREATE.

Above: On wall-trained pyracanthas, shorten side shoots in midsummer to expose the berries.

Right: Pyracanthas are grown mainly for their brilliantly coloured berries.

1 Tie in new shoots to the wall to create an espalier or fan shape, or pin back the strongest shoots and let the others billow forward.

2 In midsummer, remove any awkwardly placed shoots as these will induce spur-like shoots. Shorten other side shoots to expose the berries.

Ornamental Vines

VINES, SUCH AS *VITIS COIGNETIAE* AND *V. VINIFERA* 'PURPUREA', ARE OFTEN GROWN OVER A FRAMEWORK. UNLESS YOU ADOPT A METHODICAL APPROACH TO PRUNING, THEY WILL BECOME TANGLED.

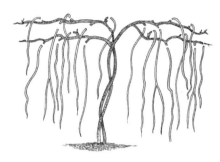

Above: A vine that has been trained over a pergola or similar support will produce stems that cascade downwards. Prune these back close to the main stem when the plant is dormant.

Right: A well-pruned ornamental vine provides neat and even coverage.

1 Train the stems horizontally over the support as required. Once established, each winter cut back the previous season's growth to within one or two buds of its point of origin, to keep the plant tidy.

2 Over the years, short spurs (stubs) will form along the main framework of branches. Cut new growth back to these each winter to produce a fresh curtain of new shoots each summer that is free of tangles.

233

Conifers

GENERALLY, CONIFERS ARE TROUBLE-FREE PLANTS THAT THRIVE
WITHOUT REGULAR PRUNING. HOWEVER, YOU MAY OCCASIONALLY
EXPERIENCE THE PROBLEMS DESCRIBED HERE.

*Above: Conifers with a spreading habit
may grow so wide that they begin to
encroach on a path or surrounding plants.
Cut back offending branches to a point
where the cuts are hidden by other
branches that cover them.*

Right: *A group of dwarf conifers.*

REMOVING A COMPETING LEADER

1 To ensure a straight, single stem,
where two or more leaders have
formed, leave the strongest unpruned.
Cut the other back to its point of origin to prevent further competition.

2 If the remaining leader is not growing strongly upright, tie a cane to the
main stem. Tie the leader to the cane
to encourage vertical growth. Once
established, remove the cane.

CUTTING BACK UNCHARACTERISTIC GROWTH

Conifers have two types of foliage: juvenile and adult. Sometimes a conifer retains its juvenile form but may produce adult shoots. If the conifer throws out a stem that is uncharacteristic, it will spoil the overall appearance of the plant. Cut back the stem to its point of origin, reaching into the heart of the plant if necessary.

Below: This Cedrus atlantica *'Glauca Pendula' has a naturally arching habit. Removing the leader has encouraged it to spread far and wide. The horizontal branches will need support as they age.*

SHAPING CONIFERS

Though most conifers achieve a pleasing profile unaided, you can clip them, provided you do this regularly and do not cut back into old wood. In spring or summer, lightly trim the conifer with shears or secateurs (pruners).

REMOVING DEAD PATCHES

Dead patches occasionally appear on conifers, sometimes as the result of drought or very cold winds. Prune out the dead growth, cutting back to live wood. If this results in an unsightly gap, loosely tie in some of the surrounding stems to cover the gap.

New Hedges

IF THEY ARE TO PROVIDE A THICK, EVEN BARRIER, HEDGES NEED PRUNING FROM THE VERY START. CUT THEM BACK WHEN YOU PLANT THEM TO ENSURE THEY BRANCH NEAR TO THE BASE.

Above: Shorten the stems on newly planted hedges by up to a half to encourage branching close to the base (left). Once the new growth appears, shorten this as well, to make bushier plants (right).

> ### GARDENER'S TIP
> When buying hedging material, young plants make sense. They are not only very cheap, but also establish much more quickly than the more expensive larger ones.

1 Hedges are best planted in spring or autumn. They are usually purchased as young plants with a single straight stem. To ensure they bush out properly, cut them back by up to one-half of their length when you plant them.

2 The following summer, trim the new shoots back by about a half to encourage further branching from near to the base of the plant. This will encourage a thick, bushy habit.

Above: Box is an excellent hedging plant.

236

Formal Hedges

CLASSIC FORMAL HEDGES GIVE STYLE AND ELEGANCE TO A GARDEN.
THE SIMPLE TECHNIQUES DESCRIBED HERE WILL KEEP THEM LOOKING
WELL SHAPED AND SMART.

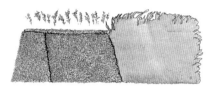

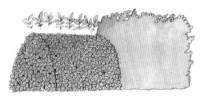

> PLANTS TO TRY
>
> *Buxus sempervirens*
> *Buxus sempervirens* 'Suffruticosa'
> x *Cupressocyparis leylandii*
> *Taxus baccata*

Above: *Cut the sides so that they slope towards the top. A flat top is easier to clip than a curved one (top). A rounded top is attractive, but you need a good eye to keep it even (bottom).*

Above: *A carefully clipped yew.*

1 Clip established hedges twice a year, in mid-spring and midsummer. To cut the top straight, run a string between two uprights and check the level with a spirit level. Hold the shears flat and horizontal when trimming the top.

2 Shear over the surface of the hedge, holding the blades flat against the surface. Using power tools (see inset) can speed up the job considerably. Use an even, wide, sweeping motion, keeping the blade parallel to the hedge.

237

Informal Flowering Hedges

FLOWERING HEDGES NEED PRUNING AT THE RIGHT TIME IF THE FLOWERS ARE NOT TO BE LOST. A CRISP OUTLINE IS NOT EXPECTED, SO PRUNING IS AIMED MAINLY AT RESTRICTING SIZE.

Above: Restrict pruning to shortening the shoots that have grown since the last prune to maintain a reasonably compact habit. Prune early-flowering hedges immediately after flowering and late-flowering hedges in early spring.

Above: Fuchsia makes a delightful informal hedge when it flowers in late summer.

A hedge of rugosa roses will not need extensive pruning like those used in rose beds, but it is worth cutting damaged, old, tired and woody shoots back to ground level periodically. This will avoid congested growth occurring.

An early-flowering hedge, such as this spiky berberis, can be lightly trimmed immediately after flowering. Shear back the flowered growth. The aim is to keep the plants compact and dense rather than to create a formal outline.

238

Rejuvenating a Neglected Hedge

IT IS SOMETIMES WORTH SALVAGING A NEGLECTED HEDGE THAT WOULD TAKE YEARS TO REPLACE, BUT CONIFER HEDGES (APART FROM YEW) WILL NOT RESPOND WELL TO THIS TECHNIQUE.

Above: Cut back all the growth on one side of the hedge to near the base of the shoots. Leave the other side uncut (left). The following year, once new growth has appeared on the cut stems, cut back the other side (right).

Above: A neglected hedge after pruning.

1 This hedge has been neglected and is a mass of tangled shoots. In winter, cut back the top of the hedge by up to 1m (3ft) below the desired height.

2 Trim back all the shoots to one side of the hedge, using loppers or a pruning saw, if necessary.

3 Lightly trim new growth that arises from the cut stems once it has reached about 15cm (6in) in length to encourage bushiness. Tackle the other side of the hedge the following year.

GARDENER'S TIP

If individual plants within the hedge do not regenerate well, dig them up and replace with young specimens.

239

Dwarf Bush Apple

FOR A SMALL GARDEN, A DWARF BUSH IS USUALLY THE MOST POPULAR OPTION. THIS GIVES YOU A TREE WITH BRANCHES CLOSE TO GROUND LEVEL, MAKING IT EASY TO HARVEST AND PRUNE.

Left: Cut out completely any badly placed or crossing branches close to the point of origin. Then shorten all side shoots to leave a couple of buds on each.

Below: A well-pruned bush apple.

GARDENER'S TIP
It is best to buy a tree ready trained that has been grafted onto a dwarfing rootstock.

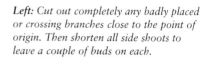

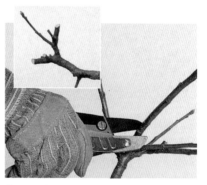

1 Young trees may not need pruning. Only prune if they begin to look congested or bear less fruit. In winter, when the tree is dormant, remove any congested or crossing branches to keep the centre of the bush open.

2 Cut the previous year's growth by two-thirds. On mature specimens, you can cut some back harder to within one or two buds. Shorten any side shoots on the pruned branches to leave just a couple of buds (see inset).

240

Espalier Apple

COMPACT ESPALIER APPLES ARE PRACTICAL IN CONFINED SPACES AND CAN BE TRAINED ON HORIZONTAL WIRES AGAINST WALLS OR FENCES. THEY CAN BE BOUGHT READY TRAINED.

Above: Espalier apples need pruning towards the end of the growing season to control their shape. Cut back side shoots from the main stems to about three leaves above the basal cluster. Side shoots growing from shoots pruned the previous year can be cut back to just one leaf.

Above: A productive espalier apple.

1 Once the main stem has reached the desired height, cut it back to a bud just above the top wire. Growth is directed into the horizontal branches.

2 In summer, cut shoots from the main branches that are over 23cm (9in) to three leaves above the basal cluster.

3 In winter, when the tree is dormant, cut back any shoots that have grown since the summer prune to about 5cm (2in), to develop a system of short spurs (see inset). Shorten all other long shoots to buds close to the main stem, cutting back to one or two buds. These will bear the next crop of fruit.

241

Cordon Apple

ANGLED CORDONS ALLOW YOU TO GROW A NUMBER OF DIFFERENT VARIETIES IN A LIMITED SPACE, BUT REGULAR PRUNING IS ESSENTIAL TO STOP THEM OVERLAPPING EACH OTHER.

GARDENER'S TIP
Prune cordon pears in the same way as apples.

Above: Prune cordons in summer by cutting the current season's growth back to two or three leaves above the basal cluster of leaves (and side shoots on these back to one leaf).

Right: Cordons are economic with space.

1 Between late spring and midsummer, prune back the main stem if it has outgrown its allotted space, to within 1–2.5cm (½ –1in) of the old wood. Repeat annually with any new leaders that form to prevent leggy growth.

2 In mid- to late summer, shorten side shoots from the main stem that are over 23cm (9in) long, so that only three leaves remain above the basal cluster. Cordons can also be pruned in winter in the same way as espaliers.

242

Raspberries

PRUNING RASPBERRIES DEPENDS ON WHETHER THEY FRUIT ON SHOOTS PRODUCED THE PREVIOUS YEAR (SUMMER-FRUITING) OR IN THE CURRENT YEAR (AUTUMN-FRUITING).

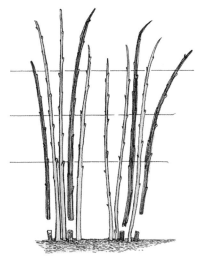

PLANTS TO TRY
Summer-fruiting raspberries:
'Glen Coe'
'Glen Moy'
'Leo'
'Malling Admiral'
'Malling Delight'
'Malling Jewel'
'Malling Promise'
Autumn-fruiting raspberries:
'Autumn Bliss'
'Heritage'
'September'
'Zeva Herbsternte'

Above: On summer-fruiters, cut out the shoots that fruited the previous summer and tie in the new canes to replace them.

SUMMER-FRUITING VARIETIES

1 In spring, prune back the old canes, which are darker than the new ones, cutting right back to the base.

2 Tie the new canes to the support. If the clump is very congested, thin the new canes to 7.5cm (3in) apart.

AUTUMN-FRUITING VARIETIES

When dormant in winter, cut all the stems back to just above soil level.

Right: The autumn-fruiting 'Zeva Herbsternte'.

243

Gooseberries

THESE FRUITING PLANTS ARE USUALLY GROWN ON A SHORT LEG OR AS BUSHES. THE MAIN PRUNING IS IN WINTER, BUT YOU CAN THIN THE GROWTH IN SUMMER TO KEEP THE BUSHES OPEN.

Above: Shorten the summer's growth at the ends of the main stems by between one-third and a half, then shorten side shoots growing from the main stems to two buds.

Right: A gooseberry bush after pruning.

1 Gooseberries are thorny plants. Wearing gloves, reduce last season's growth at the end of each main shoot by between one-third and a half. You should also cut out any low, weak, badly placed or crossing branches.

2 Shorten side shoots arising from the main stems, cutting them back to two buds from the old wood. This makes the plant less congested. After fruiting, thin the new growth to improve air circulation and prevent mildew.

244

Black, Red & White Currants

PROLIFIC BLACKCURRANTS FRUIT BEST ON YEAR-OLD BRANCHES. RED AND WHITE CURRANTS FRUIT ON SHOOTS THAT ARE AT LEAST TWO YEARS OLD. ALL ARE PRUNED IN WINTER.

Below: White currants ready for picking.

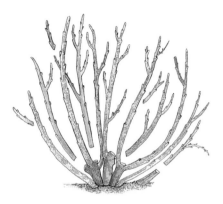

Above: On blackcurrants, cut out some of the oldest wood each year, close to the base where there is a younger shoot to replace it. Also prune any damaged or badly placed branches.

2 For red and white currants, remove one old stem only, pruning just above a bud near ground level.

1 For blackcurrants, remove branches that are too low or growing inwards. Cut back some of the oldest branches (usually the thickest and darkest) close to the base. Aim to remove one-third.

3 Shorten the wood produced the previous summer by half its length. Trim back overlong branches, cutting back to a replacement side shoot.

245

Blackberries & Hybrid Berries

THESE BERRIES (INCLUDING TAYBERRIES AND LOGANBERRIES) ARE
EASY TO PRUNE, SINCE MOST FRUIT ON YEAR-OLD CANES.

Left: *In winter or early spring, cut back the older shoots that have previously fruited. Tie in the greener shoots made the previous summer.*

Below: *Ripening blackberries.*

PLANTS TO TRY

Blackberries:
'Bedford Giant'
'Himalaya Giant'
'John Innes'
'Smoothstem'
'No Thorn'

Hybrid berries:
Boysenberry
Loganberry
Sunberry
Tayberry
Veitchberry

---

1 Prune out the darker, fruited canes, which grew the previous year, cutting as close to the ground as possible.

2 Untie the one-year-old canes that have yet to fruit and reposition them in an evenly spaced fan shape. Tie in new shoots as they grow.

246

Blueberries

THESE ARE SLOW-GROWING PLANTS THAT FRUIT ON BRANCHES TWO
TO THREE YEARS OLD. START PRUNING THEM LIGHTLY WHEN THEY
ARE THREE OR FOUR YEARS OLD.

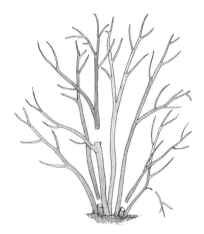

Above: On established plants, prune out older, unproductive wood in spring, cutting back to a vigorous side shoot.

Above: Blueberries when ripe have a whitish bloom which is safe to eat. It is better not to wash berries before eating them.

1 Cut back any unproductive shoots, either to a strong replacement shoot or to the ground. Do not remove more than one-quarter of the branches.

2 Remove any weak, spindly growth.

PLANTS TO TRY
'Berkeley'
'Bluecrop'
'Bluetta'
'Coville'
'Darrow'
'Earliblue'
'Goldtraube'
'Herbert'
'Ivanhoe'
'Jersey'
'Patriot'

247

Pruning Methods & Timing

USE THIS CHART TO CHECK WHEN AND HOW TO PRUNE YOUR PLANTS.

Name of plant	Type of pruning	Time to prune
Abeliophyllum	no routine pruning	
Abutilon	shorten side shoots	summer
Actinidia	as for ornamental vines	Winter
Akebia	no routine pruning	
Artemisia	cut back hard, if necessary	early spring
Aucuba	clip to shape	spring, summer
Berberis	one-third method	winter (deciduous); spring (evergreen)
Brachyglottis	prune to a framework	early spring
Buddleja	prune to a framework	early spring
Buxus	clip to shape	spring, summer
Callicarpa	no routine pruning	
Calluna	deadhead with shears	after flowering
Camellia	no routine pruning	
Campsis	no routine pruning	
Carpenteria	one-third method	early spring
Caryopteris	prune to a framework	early spring
Catalpa bignioides	coppicing	early spring
Ceanothus, deciduous	trim previous year's shoots	spring
Ceanothus, evergreen	shorten side shoots	after flowering
Ceratostigma	prune to a framework	early spring
Cestrum parqui	prune to the base	early spring
Chaenomeles, wall-trained	trim previous year's shoots	after flowering
Chimonanthus	one-third method	spring
Choisya	no routine pruning	

Berberis

Erica

Cistus	shorten side shoots	after flowering
Clematis	see clematis section	
Clerodendrum	no routine pruning	
Clethra	no routine pruning	
Colutea	one-third method	early spring
Convolvulus	shorten side shoots	late summer
Cornus alba (most cvs)	one-third method	mid-spring
C. alba 'Sibirica'	prune hard	early spring
C. controversa, C. florida	no routine pruning	
C. kousa	no routine pruning	
C. stolonifera 'Flaviramea'	prune hard	early spring
Corylopsis	no routine pruning	
Corylus	one-third method	spring
Cotinus	one-third method	spring
Cotoneaster	one-third method	winter (deciduous); spring (evergreen)
Cytisus	shorten new growth	after flowering
Daboecia	deadhead with shears	after flowering
Daphne	no routine pruning	
Deutzia	one-third method	after flowering
Elaeagnus	no routine pruning	
Enkianthus	no routine pruning	
Erica	deadhead with shears	after flowering
Escallonia	one-third method	late spring
Eucalyptus	prune to a framework	early spring
Euonymus	no routine pruning	
Fallopia	one-third method	spring
Fatsia	no routine pruning	
Forsythia	one-third method	after flowering
Fothergilla	no routine pruning	
Fremontodendron	shorten side shoots	spring
Fruits	see individual sections	
Fuchsia, hardy	prune to the base	early spring
Garrya	one-third method	spring
Gaultheria	one-third method	spring
Genista	shorten new growth	late summer
Griselinia	no routine pruning	
x *Halimiocistus*	shorten side shoots	late summer
Hebe	no routine pruning	
Hedera	clip to shape	summer
Helianthemum	shorten new shoots	after flowering
Helichrysum	cut back close to old wood	early spring
Hibiscus	prune out old wood	early spring
Hippophae	one-third method	spring

Hydrangea macrophylla	cut back thin shoots; shorten flowered stem	spring
H. paniculata	prune back to a framework	early spring
H. petiolaris	no routine pruning	
Hypericum	one-third method	spring
Ilex	clip to shape	spring, summer
Indigofera	cut back to a framework	late summer
Jasminum nudiflorum	one-third method	after flowering
J. officinale	thin, as necessary	after flowering
Kalmia	one-third method	after flowering
Kerria	one-third method	early summer
Kolkwitzia	one-third method	after flowering
Laurus	clip to shape	spring, summer
Lavandula	trim previous year's growth	early to mid-spring
Lavatera	prune to a framework	spring
Leycesteria	one-third method	after flowering
Ligustrum	clip to shape	spring, summer
Lonicera, climbing	thin tangled stems	after flowering
Lonicera, shrubby	no routine pruning	
L. nitida	clip to shape	spring, summer
Mahonia, bushy	one-third method	early summer
Mahonia, groundcover	cut to 15–30cm (6–12in) above ground level	spring, alternate years
Mahonia, tall	shorten flowered stems	after flowering
Olearia	one-third method	after flowering
Osmanthus	no routine pruning	
Paeonia	cut out dead wood	early summer
Parthenocissus	as for vines	winter
Passiflora	thin tangled stems	spring
Paulownia	no pruning necessary, but can be cut back to a framework	early spring
Perovskia	prune to the base	early spring

Convolvulus

Fuchsia

Philadelphus	one-third method	after flowering
Phlomis	cut back side shoots	spring
Phormium	remove dead leaves	late spring
Potentilla	one-third method	after flowering
Pyracantha, wall trained	shorten side shoots	midsummer
Ribes	one-third method	after flowering
Robinia pseudoacacia	pollarding	late winter
Rosa	see rose section	
Rosmarinus	clip to shape	spring, summer
Rubus (most)	one-third method	midsummer
R. cockburnianus,		
R. thibetanus	cut back to ground level	early spring
Ruta	trim previous year's growth	spring
Salix	no pruning necessary, but some can be cut back hard	
Sambucus	one-third method,	mid-spring
	or cut back to a framework	early spring
Santolina	trim previous year's growth	mid-spring
Skimmia	no routine pruning	
Sorbaria	one-third method	late winter to mid-spring
Spiraea, spring-flowering	one-third method	after flowering
Spiraea, summer-flowering	trim previous year's growth	mid-spring
Symphoricarpos	one-third method	midsummer
Syringa	remove a quarter of the oldest stems	winter
Tamarix	no routine pruning	
Tilia	pollarding	late winter
Ulex	clip to shape	early summer
Viburnum	no routine pruning	
Vinca	shear back to near ground level	early spring
Vitis	shorten to stubs	winter
Weigela	one-third method	midsummer
Wisteria	cut back new growth	after flowering

Syringa Peony

251

SEASONAL
TASKS

Keeping up with the gardening year is
essential if you want to get the most
out of your garden; running a few
weeks behind in some cases could
mean missing a whole season's results.
To help you keep on track, this
chapter divides the year into 12 time
frames; refer to it regularly to see
what you should be doing and when.

Left: *Having the right tools to hand helps make
the seasonal tasks easier.*

Jobs for Each Season

KEEPING A GARDEN LOOKING GOOD ALL YEAR ROUND SHOULD NEVER BECOME A BURDEN. SPREADING ESSENTIAL TASKS THROUGHOUT THE SEASONS, SO THAT THE GARDEN IS ALWAYS UNDER CONTROL, WILL ENSURE THAT IT REMAINS A PLEASURE EVEN AT THE BUSIEST TIMES.

Good gardeners are always thinking about the future, and forward planning is important if the garden is always to look its best. However, with the busy lives that most of us lead these days, it is easy to overlook some of the simple gardening tasks that will save time in the long run – hence the value of a mini season-by-season guide to gardening activities.

No gardening calendar can ever be followed rigidly, of course, because not only does the climate vary from one place to another, but the weather is never the same two years running. In one year a bumper crop of slugs will wreak havoc on your young plants, but in another you may hardly be troubled by them; and disease attacks vary considerably from year to year, also largely depending on the weather. Fruit crops may be delayed to early or mid-autumn by late spring frosts or may be ready for harvesting in late summer. Nevertheless, even given the vagaries of the weather, it is

Above: Successional sowing of vegetables in spring will ensure that your kitchen garden plots are well filled and productive all summer long.

254

possible to list the main tasks in the general order in which they should be done so that you can complete them when you have time and when the weather permits you to get into the garden to carry them out.

WORKING WITH THE SEASONS

Fortunately, many plants are forgiving and allow you a certain amount of leeway if certain tasks are mis-timed. A mild, damp winter, for example, might mean that your roses burst into growth, persuading you that they need pruning early. If a sudden cold spell kills off the resulting new growth, you can simply prune them again and reconcile yourself to the fact that flowering may be a bit later than usual. The plants don't seem to mind.

It's a good idea to make staggered sowings of vegetables or summer bedding plants, so that you always have reserve stock should any early sowings fail. If you do not have a greenhouse, you can make use of your kitchen windowsill to start seeds into growth several weeks earlier than if you wait to sow them outdoors.

HOW TO USE THIS CHAPTER

This chapter is organized by season, with each season further subdivided into early, mid and late to coincide broadly with the months of the year. Within each mini-season, tasks for the ornamental garden, kitchen garden

Above: Give a summer hanging basket a head-start by planting it in spring and keeping it in a greenhouse until there is no more fear of late frosts.

and greenhouse or conservatory are described, with handy, at-a-glance checklists of the main jobs to be done. The more important tasks are dealt with in greater depth, with pictures showing the correct techniques.

Below: A good crop of apples is largely dependent on the weather.

Early Spring

THE BEGINNING OF THE NATURAL YEAR IS AN EXCITING TIME IN THE
GARDEN, EVEN IF WINTER CANNOT YET BE ENTIRELY FORGOTTEN.
MANY PLANTS ARE BEGINNING TO WAKE UP FROM THEIR WINTER
DORMANCY AND TO PUT OUT FRESH GREEN SHOOTS.

THE ORNAMENTAL GARDEN

Despite the cold, early spring is a good
time to make a start on many outdoor
jobs. The soil is starting to warm up
and spring rains will help plants establish well and get off to a good start.

Planting

As long as the soil is not waterlogged
or frozen, early spring is one of the
best times to plant new shrubs and

Above: A welcome sight in early spring,
Muscari armeniacum 'Blue Spike' forms
clumps that can be divided in summer.

perennials. Prepare the ground first,
digging over the whole area thoroughly and removing any perennial weeds,
such as couch grass and bindweed.
Fork in plenty of well-rotted garden
compost or farmyard manure and add
a handful of a slow-release granular
fertilizer or some bonemeal. Dig a
hole twice the width of the plant's
container, slide the plant out of the
pot, carefully tease out its roots and
set it in the centre of the hole. Backfill
with the excavated soil, firming it in
well, and water thoroughly.

Sowing Hardy Annuals

Hardy annual seeds, such as hawks-
beard (*Crepis rubra*), poached-egg
plant (*Limnanthes douglasii*) and
love-in-a-mist (*Nigella damsascena*),
can be sown where the plants are to
flower. Weed the ground and rake it
level, then sow the seeds in rows
(which makes weeding easier) or by
sprinkling (broadcasting) it over the
ground. Cover the seed lightly and
water in dry weather. When the
seedlings are large enough to handle,
thin them to the distances recommended on the seed packets.

LAYING TURF

Early spring is a good time to make a new lawn, either by sowing grass seed or by laying turf. Although turf is the more expensive option, it does provide an instant result. However, after a few years you will not be able to tell the difference between a seed-raised lawn and bought-in turfs.

1 Mark out the area of the new lawn. Dig over the area, removing any large stones and all traces of perennial weeds. Taking very small steps, tread over the area to consolidate the soil, then rake the surface level. Lay the first strip of turf along a straight edge.

2 Place a plank on top of the first strip of turf and stand on this when positioing subsequent rows, moving it as necessary. Place the second row of turfs tight against the first, but stagger any joints between the strips like the bonds in brickwork.

3 Tamp down each row of turf using the back of a rake. Trim the edges, after the turf is laid, using a half-moon edger. In dry weather, water the new lawn frequently until it is established.

THE KITCHEN GARDEN

Now is your best opportunity to improve the soil in the kitchen garden, which can become impoverished over time. To improve its structure and moisture-retentiveness, dig in plenty of organic matter such as well-rotted farmyard manure or garden compost. A general fertilizer such as bonemeal, or a granular fertilizer, will break down gradually as the crops grow. Use organic or chemical formulations as you wish, but follow the quantities recommended by the manufacturer.

Above: Space onion sets about 15cm (6in) apart and cover with soil, leaving just the tips of the bulbs protruding.

This is also a good time to plant onion sets in a shallow drill, made with the corner of a hoe or rake. If birds disturb the sets, simply push them back into the ground.

Above: With careful planning, even a small border can accommodate both ornamental plants and vegetables.

THINGS TO DO
IN THE KITCHEN GARDEN

Apply fertilizers
Warm up the soil with cloches or fleece
Plant new strawberries
Chit seed potatoes
Plant onion sets or shallots
Sow vegetable seeds (in mild areas only)

Keeping Seedlings Warm

Sowing seed can be a gamble, because a sudden cold snap can cause vulnerable seedlings to rot or run to seed, but if you cannot wait to get busy, cover the seeds with horticultural fleece, which is a virtually foolproof way of ensuring a good crop. It will warm up the soil as well as providing protection from frost and pests. It allows light and moisture through to keep plants growing but will not squash them.

Perforated plastic film is an alternative to fleece. A cloche – a sheet of film stretched over wire supports – can be used to protect larger seedlings.

The Greenhouse

You can steal a march on other gardeners by raising new plants from seed under glass before the weather has really warmed up. Even if your greenhouse is not heated, the extra shelter will make it possible for you to sow the seed of half-hardy annuals and tender vegetables, which can be potted up as they germinate. Don't forget, however, that a bright windowsill can be just as useful.

Using a Propagator

You can speed up the germination of early sowings using a propagator. A heated propagator will give you even more options, especially if it is thermostatically controlled.

1 Use different containers for different seeds. Square or oblong seed trays that fit snugly into the propagator make the most economical use of the space. The modules on the right are useful for small seedlings, or for seeds that are large enough to sow individually.

> ### THINGS TO DO
> ### IN THE GREENHOUSE
> Start begonias and gloxinias into growth
> Pot on cuttings of
> pelargoniums and fuchsias
> Prick out tender seedlings
> Ventilate the greenhouse on warm days

2 An unheated propagator should be placed in a warm position in the greenhouse. Adjust the ventilation as soon as the seeds have germinated.

Keeping Hippeastrums

If you have grown hippeastrum bulbs for winter flowers, instead of discarding the bulbs when the flowers are over, you can try building them up for flowering next year.

Keep the plants growing in a warm, bright spot and feed and water them regularly as long as the leaves are growing strongly. Stop watering as the leaves start to turn yellow and die back, and store the bulbs in dry potting mix until the winter. Flowering cannot be guaranteed, but it is worth the attempt.

Starting off Begonias

Tuberous begonias can be started into growth now. Set the tubers on the surface of the potting mix, in either individual pots or trays. Look for emerging shoots or place the concave surface of each tuber uppermost. Keep them in a warm, light place and water as the shoots develop.

Mid-spring

THE GARDEN WILL BEGIN TO FILL WITH COLOUR AS THE WEATHER WARMS UP AND THE DAYS LENGTHEN. MID-SPRING IS THE BEST TIME FOR MOVING AND DIVIDING PLANTS AND FOR SOWING SEEDS IN READINESS FOR THE JOYS OF SUMMER DISPLAYS TO COME.

THE ORNAMENTAL GARDEN

As the sap rises with the warmer weather, work in the garden can begin in earnest. This is a great time for pruning shrubs, either to revive neglected specimens or to keep vigorous species within bounds. You also need to plan for the big events of summer in the herbaceous border by setting stakes and ties in position.

Pruning Bush Roses

The old, rather rigorous rules for rose pruning have been reappraised and relaxed in recent years, but some long-established principles remain. Cut out any damaged and diseased wood completely, then assess the rest of the bush. Spindly shoots are unlikely to bear flowers, so cut them back hard to stimulate stronger growth. Shoots that are already growing strongly need cutting back only lightly, if at all. If the centre of the bush is overcrowded, with lots of crossing branches, thin these out. Feed the rose with a special rose fertilizer and water it in, then apply a generous mulch of well-rotted organic matter.

Supporting Summer Climbers

Climbing plants, such as sweet peas (*Lathyrus odoratus*), look sensational rising above smaller plants in summer borders. Although you can buy ready-made obelisks and tripods, it is easy to make your own using bamboo canes,

Above: This old rose needs little more than a general tidy up. Old wood should be cut out completely.

THINGS TO DO
IN THE ORNAMENTAL GARDEN
Plant aquatic plants
Sow sweet peas and other annuals
Stake border plants
Take softwood cuttings
Prune early-flowering shrubs
Trim winter-flowering heathers

Above: Make a support for sweet peas by driving bamboo canes into the soil in a circle. Bind at the top with wire or string.

Above: Plants with large flowers, such as Paeonia lactiflora 'Bowl of Beauty', will benefit from staking.

held together at the top with garden twine. You can also buy special plastic grips, which are designed to hold the canes securely at the top. Put one plant at the base of each cane.

Staking Plants

Some border plants that have large, heavy flowers, such as peonies and delphiniums, need staking if the weight of the flower is not to bring the stem crashing down. Stakes should be set in position before the stems grow too tall, so that new growth can be fastened to the supports as it develops.

There are a number of ways of supporting plants, depending on their habit. In an informal, cottage garden border, twigs can be pushed into the ground around the plants; they will soon be hidden by the leafy growth.

Bamboo canes are best for tall, single-stemmed plants like delphiniums, but shorter, clump-forming plants, such as some peonies, can be effectively supported with a ring stake, which can be raised as the stems grow.

Above: Set up proprietary supports early so that herbaceous plants can grow up through the framework.

261

THE KITCHEN GARDEN

Although the weather is still unpredictable, the soil should be warming up sufficiently for you to consider planting out seedlings of cabbages, broccoli and cauliflower when they have been hardened off. You should also make further sowings of onion sets and shallots to give a longer cropping season.

Remember, however, that late frosts can kill tender young shoots, so be prepared to cover vulnerable plants with horticultural fleece, cloches or even sheets of newspaper if frosty weather is forecast.

Protecting Blossom

A spell of warm spring weather will encourage fruit trees to produce blossom, but an air frost at this time can do untold harm. This occurs when the temperature of the air about 1.2m (4ft) above ground level falls below freezing point at night, freezing the moisture in the blossom and in other tender shoots. When the temperature rises in the morning, the cell walls of the plant tissue often burst, damaging the blossom so that it never sets fruit. Pears are particularly badly affected by this problem, as they tend to flower early.

**THINGS TO DO
IN THE VEGETABLE GARDEN**
Sow maincrop vegetables
Plant potatoes
Transplant cabbages and cauliflowers
Apply a mulch of well-rotted compost to fruit bushes
Protect early strawberries
Protect blossom on fruit trees

Above: Sowing vegetables in rows makes subsequent weeding of the plot easier, as it allows annual weeds to be quickly removed with a hoe.

Wall-trained fruit trees can be protected most easily by draping sheets of plastic or even fine netting over a framework. Free-standing standard trees are more difficult to protect, although horticultural fleece can be used. If you use plastic sheeting, make sure it is held above the plant and cannot touch the young shoots, which might otherwise rot. Remove the protection during the day so that insects can pollinate the blossom.

Planting Potatoes

You will get the best results if you chit the potatoes before planting. Chitted potatoes get off to a quicker start than unchitted tubers, and this is a useful method of staggering crops. Chitted tubers are those that have begun to sprout, and to encourage this you should place the tubers in a light, frost-free position – a windowsill indoors is ideal.

Potatoes can be planted through a heavy-duty black plastic sheet, which saves the trouble of having to earth (hill) them up. Cultivate the soil, then cover the area with the sheet, holding it down around the edges with soil. Cut X-shaped slits in the sheet at regular intervals and plant the tubers through these.

If you prefer to plant your potatoes in the traditional way, cover the soil with a cloche for a week or two before planting to warm it up.

1 In prepared soil, make broad drills 10–13cm (4–5in) deep and 50–75cm (20–30in) apart, using a draw hoe.

2 Space the tubers 30–45cm (12–18in) apart in the drill, making sure that the buds (eyes) or shoots face upward.

3 Cover the tubers with the excavated soil or use a sheet of heavy-duty black plastic, held down in the soil.

> **GARDENER'S TIP**
>
> If you want larger potatoes, once you have chitted the tubers rub off all but three of the shoots before planting.

THE GREENHOUSE

This is the time of year when most gardeners wish they had a larger greenhouse. Not only are all the seedlings from earlier sowings now ready to be pricked out or potted up, but tender vegetables, including outdoor tomatoes and runner beans, can be sown under glass now.

PLANTING A HANGING BASKET

Hanging baskets are associated with high summer and are planted up in late spring, usually at the time when it is safe to put tender plants outdoors. However, if you have a greenhouse or conservatory that provides protection from frost, or, better still, one that is heated, you can get your baskets off to a flying start now and have a mature display earlier in the season.

Above: The trailing habit of the tender fuchsia 'Dark Eyes' makes it an ideal subject for a hanging basket.

1 Rest the basket in a bucket or large pot to keep it steady and line it with moss or a hanging basket liner. Half-fill with a suitable potting mix.

2 Set trailing plants around the sides of the basket. Add more potting mix to cover the rootballs.

3 Place larger plants in the centre, fill any gaps with potting mix and water well. Hang in a light, sheltered place.

GARDENER'S TIP
Use water-retaining crystals in hanging baskets to reduce the likelihood of the contents drying out in summer.

Sowing Tender Vegetables

For early crops of tender vegetables, such as marrows, courgettes (zucchini) and outdoor cucumbers, sow now in small pots, filled with seed potting mix to within about 2.5cm (1in) of the rim. Water the potting mix and allow it to drain before sowing the seed, which should be lightly covered with sieved potting mix. Keep in a warm, light place until the seeds germinate, then grow them on under cover until

Above: Courgette (zucchini) plants germinated in the greenhouse need to be hardened off in a cold frame before they can be planted outside.

all risk of frost has passed. Transfer them to a cold frame to acclimatize before planting them out in their final positions in the garden.

Above: Sow two or three seeds of outdoor cucumbers in each pot, setting them on edge, and lightly cover with potting mix.

THINGS TO DO
IN THE GREENHOUSE
Sow tender vegetables
Prick out or pot up seedlings
Take leaf cuttings of flowering
houseplants, such as *Saintpaulia* and
Streptocarpus
Decrease the water given to cyclamen
Take cuttings of tender perennials
Check for vine weevil grubs when
repotting plants

Late Spring

THIS IS MANY PEOPLE'S FAVOURITE SEASON IN THE GARDEN, WHEN
PLANTS ARE GROWING STRONGLY BUT WITH ALL THE FRESHNESS OF
YOUTH STILL UPON THEM. YOU SHOULD STILL BE ALERT FOR LATE
FROSTS AND GIVE ANY FROST-PRONE PLANTS ADEQUATE PROTECTION.

THE ORNAMENTAL GARDEN

Unseasonal weather, in the form of
late frosts or extremely wet or windy
weather, can still cause problems, so
keep an eye on forecasts and be ready
to protect vulnerable plants. After
especially strong winds, check that all
newly planted shrubs and perennials
are still firmly bedded into the soil and
have not been affected by wind rock.

Bedding Plants

Half-hardy annuals that you have
raised under glass can now be hardened off – that is, acclimatized to outdoor conditions. Place them outdoors
in a spot that is sheltered from strong

*Above: Many gardeners regard waterlilies,
such as this* Nymphaea 'Attraction', *as the
most desirable of all water plants.*

sun and wind for increasingly longer
periods during the day. Move them
back under cover at night, either
indoors or into a cold frame. They can
be planted out in their final positions
once all danger of frost has passed.

> THINGS TO DO
> IN THE ORNAMENTAL GARDEN
> Plant hanging baskets
> Harden off bedding plants
> Clip evergreen hedges
> Prune *Clematis montana* after flowering,
> if necessary
> Deadhead flowered bulbs

266

Planting a Waterlily

This is the best time of year to plant waterlilies, which should now be producing signs of fresh growth. Waterlilies should be planted as soon as possible after purchase to ensure that the rhizomes do not dry out. Plant them in baskets specially designed for aquatic plants; those with a fine mesh do not need lining, but open-sided baskets should be lined with coarse hessian (burlap).

1 If necessary, line the aquatic planting basket and half-fill with garden soil or specially formulated potting mix. Place the waterlily rhizome on top and cover with more soil, leaving the buds exposed.

2 Place a layer of stones or gravel on top so that soil does not float out of the basket. Hold under the surface of the pool to flood it with water, then lower it to the appropriate depth, depending on the variety of waterlily. Support it on bricks if necessary.

Above: If necessary, prune the vigorous Clematis montana *'Elizabeth' when it has finished flowering.*

Hedges

Evergreen hedges should be given their first trim about now. To make sure the top is level, run a string between two uprights as a guide. If you are using power tools (possibly on loan from a hire shop), make sure you follow any safety advice and remember to wear gloves, goggles and ear protectors.

Above: As well as clipping hedges, now is the time to neaten up topiary specimens, such as this spiral bay (Laurus nobilis).

267

THE KITCHEN GARDEN

When you are planting out in the kitchen garden, remember that successional sowing and planting will reduce gluts and give you a continuous supply of vegetables and fruit over a longer period.

Intercropping

One of the best ways of making good use of every available scrap of ground is to grow some quick-growing plants, such as cut-and-come-again lettuces or radishes, in the spaces between larger, slower-growing plants, such as Brussels sprouts and parsnips. Not only will this give you two crops in the space of one, but it will also help to keep down weeds by covering what would otherwise be bare soil. Do not overcrowd plants, however, or they will compete with each other for available light, air and nutrients, and all the crops will suffer.

Although combining a variety of different plants in your vegetable plot can minimize the incidence of pests and diseases, there are some crops that should not be grown close together. Onions and garlic, for example, do not grow well alongside beans and peas, and potatoes should not be combined with cucumbers, marrows and courgettes (zucchini).

There are also some herbs that can be invasive. Mint is the most notorious but you might also consider growing tansy *(Tanacetum vulgare)* and woodruff *(Asperula odorata* syn. *Galium odoratum)* in pots too.

*Above: Mints, including the variegated applemint (*Mentha suaveolens *'Variegata'), are vigorous plants that can be divided now. Restricting the roots by growing them in containers or a separate bed will stop them becoming too invasive.*

THINGS TO DO
IN THE KITCHEN GARDEN

Sow sweetcorn (corn)
Sow root crops such as beetroot (beets),
carrots and parsnips
Plant outdoor tomatoes
Plant runner (green) and pole beans
Lift and divide mint
Hoe around vegetables to keep
weeds down

PLANTING RUNNER BEANS

Runner (green) beans are twining climbers that need support, and a wig-wam of canes works well in a small space. In warm areas, simply plant a seed at the base of each cane. In cold districts, it is better to raise seedlings under cover and delay planting out until the threat of frosts has gone.

1 Crossing pairs of canes in rows is a good method of supporting beans if your plot is rectangular.

2 Plant one bean plant at the base of each support and water in well. As they grow, twine the stems around the canes.

Growing Outdoor Tomatoes

Many gardeners find outdoor tomatoes an easier proposition than indoor ones, because they need less maintenance, although the crops will be smaller and the season is shorter. The plants must still be raised from seed under cover. If you don't want to sow seed, you can usually buy small plants for growing on from garden centres. Harden them off first, before planting them out in containers or growing bags. Wait until all risk of frost has passed before planting them out.

Above: Outdoor tomatoes are often tastier than those grown under glass, particularly if the summer has been hot and the fruit is able to ripen well.

THE GREENHOUSE

It is not too late to sow tomatoes, marrows, melons, ridge cucumbers, courgettes (zucchini), pumpkins, sweetcorn (corn) and half-hardy annuals.

On warm, sunny days make sure that the greenhouse is well ventilated. Humid, still air will encourage fungal diseases, and seedlings will die. A common problem in a poorly ventilated, overcrowded greenhouse is damping off, a disease that causes seedlings to collapse at soil level. Use sterile pots and new potting mix for seeds and do not overwater. If you do not mind using chemicals in the greenhouse, apply a fungicidal drench to the potting mix before sowing.

Above: Melons need a sturdy framework to support the growing plants. Nets slung above the containers hold the fruit.

GROWING INDOOR TOMATOES

Indoor tomatoes, either raised from seed or bought in as young plants, can now be planted. Because tomatoes cannot be grown in the same soil year after year, it is best to use growing bags or large containers. To support the growing plants (unless you are growing the bush or dwarf types), erect a cane next to each of the plants or train them on strings.

1 Cut holes in the growing bags according to the instructions on the bag. Most growing bags will accommodate three plants, but make sure that when you plant the tomatoes they are the recommended distance apart.

2 Fix a horizontal wire across the greenhouse, as high above the plants as possible. Fix a second length of wire parallel to the first but near ground level. Tie a length of string between the wires in line with each plant. Loop the string around the growing tip of each plant.

Plant indoor tomatoes
Plant and train cucumbers
Sow half-hardy annuals for autumn
display outdoors
Make further sowings of courgettes (zucchini), cucumbers, melons, squashes,
pumpkins and sweetcorn (corn)
Sow seed of ornamental cabbages
and kales

Above: Control greenhouse pests by
introducing natural predators such as
parasitic wasps, effective against whitefly.

Biological Controls

The warm, humid atmosphere of a greenhouse is the perfect environment for insect pests, but increasing numbers of these can be controlled with other insects so that you do not have to use chemicals. The beneficial insects are released on to the susceptible plants in order to attack the pest.

Whitefly, spider mites, soft scale insects and thrips can be controlled by this method. Remember that once a biological control has been introduced, you should not use pesticides of any kind (or you will also kill the predators) and you should also remove any sticky traps that you put up earlier in the year.

Above: Peppers are increasingly popular as a greenhouse crop. They appreciate the extra heat and humidity that the enclosed environment provides.

271

Early Summer

EVERY TIME YOU STEP INTO THE GARDEN AT THIS TIME OF YEAR YOU ARE GREETED BY A MASS OF FRESH NEW FOLIAGE AND FLOWERS. THE KITCHEN GARDEN IS COMING INTO ITS OWN NOW, PROVIDING A FEAST OF HOME-GROWN PRODUCE FOR THE TABLE.

THE ORNAMENTAL GARDEN

Early summer is a transitional period in the flower garden, and there may be a week or two between the spring-flowering plants and bulbs dying down and the summer bedding coming into flower. Focus attention on the patio and create an instant display by planting up pots and troughs that will provide colour and interest now and for the rest of the summer.

PLANTING A CONTAINER

By now it is safe to leave tender plants outdoors, and because these are usually long-flowering, they make ideal subjects for a container planting.

1 Line a large container with crocks and half-fill with potting mix.

2 Place a feature plant in the centre of the arrangement. An osteospermum will carry on flowering until well into the autumn.

3 Position other flowering plants and trailers around the container to soften the edge, then fill the gaps with more potting mix. Water well.

Pruning Shrubs

Now is the time to tidy up any early-flowering shrubs, which will be putting on rapid growth. Remove all faded flowers, then cut back any damaged branches and remove the thick, old growth entirely, reaching into the base of the plant with loppers if necessary. Shorten the remaining stems to

Above: Inspect lilies, such as these Asiatic hybrids, for signs of the bright red lily beetle, a serious pest of lilies and fritillaries.

produce an open, well-balanced plant, cutting back thin shoots hard but trimming vigorous ones only lightly.

Above: As soon as lilacs finish flowering, deadhead them by cutting back to the first pair of leaves below the flowerhead.

**THINGS TO DO
IN THE ORNAMENTAL GARDEN**

Sow hardy annuals for late flowers
Move hanging baskets outdoors
Check lilies for signs of lily beetle
Plant containers for summer interest
Layer climbers to increase your stock
Prune early-flowering shrubs
Feed lawns
Deadhead rhododendrons

GARDENER'S TIP

Choose containers that are as large as possible. Not only will they dry out more slowly, but they will also provide the most impressive display. Move the container into position before filling it with potting mix and plants: it will be too heavy to move when it is full.

273

THE KITCHEN GARDEN

Keep an eye on newly planted-out seedlings so that you can take prompt action to prevent pests and diseases from building up and becoming a serious problem.

Earthing up Potatoes

An important aspect of potato growing, earthing (hilling) up protects potato tubers that are near the soil surface. If they are exposed to light, the tubers turn green and become inedible. When the green shoots are about 15cm (6in) tall, draw the soil up with a hoe on either side of the plants. Continue to do this as the potatoes grow, until the soil is mounded up to about 15cm (6in).

> **GARDENER'S TIP**
> Spray cuttings in a propagator with a fungicide to prevent mould.

> **THINGS TO DO**
> **IN THE KITCHEN GARDEN**
> Thin the fruit on gooseberry bushes
> Check gooseberry foliage for
> sawfly caterpillars
> Check strawberries for grey mould
> (botrytis)
> Feed asparagus plants after harvesting

Thinning Seedlings

Unless they are thinned now, vegetable seedlings will crowd each other out and crop poorly. The recommended distance for each crop will vary depending on the variety; check the seed packet for details. The uprooted seedlings of some crops can be used in salads.

Thin the emerging crops in stages. The first thinning should leave the plants twice as close as the final recommended spacing. Simply pull up the surplus plants with your finger and thumb and discard.

Above: *Use a hoe to draw soil up around the developing potatoes without damaging the delicate root system.*

Above: *Thin seedlings to the distance recommended on the seed packet to give them space to develop properly.*

THE GREENHOUSE

Summer is a time when you need to keep a watchful eye on your greenhouse and conservatory plants, which can easily overheat as the temperature rises outdoors.

If you have time and if there is space in the greenhouse, this is a good time to take softwood cuttings of shrubs from the open garden.

TAKING SOFTWOOD CUTTINGS

Softwood cuttings usually root readily, but need the warm, protected environment that glass provides. The method is suitable for many garden shrubs as well as conservatory plants.

1 Cut a sideshoot just above a bud. Trim just below a leaf joint, and trim the tip leaving a stem 10cm (4in) long.

2 Insert up to two-thirds of the stem in a pot of cuttings potting mix.

3 Place a clear plastic tent over the pot supported on canes. Keep in shade, in the warmth of a heated propagator. Softwood cuttings root in 4–6 weeks.

THINGS TO DO
IN THE GREENHOUSE

Feed and water pot plants
Use biological controls to eliminate pests
Divide congested pot plants

SHRUBS TO INCREASE BY
SOFTWOOD CUTTINGS

Abutilon
Aloysia
Cotoneaster
Cytisus
Daphne
Fuchsia
Hydrangea
Philadelphus

Midsummer

For most gardeners this is the peak of the gardening year, when all your earlier efforts are rewarded. The flower borders are a riot of colour and scent and the vegetable plot is filled to overflowing with fresh young crops.

The Ornamental Garden

On the hottest days of summer you will want to sit back and relax and enjoy your garden, but there are still plenty of jobs to be done if the garden is to continue looking good.

Above: Iris *'Blue Eyed Brunette' is one of the large number of rhizomatous irises that can be divided in midsummer.*

> ### THINGS TO DO
> ### IN THE ORNAMENTAL GARDEN
> Divide flag irises
> Take semi-ripe cuttings
> Plant hardy cyclamen
> Prune wisteria
> Watch for and treat roses
> for disease
> Top up ponds in hot weather
> Thin oxygenating plants in ponds

Planting Autumn Crocuses

Corms of autumn crocus (*Colchicum autumnale*) can be planted in lawns, borders or even in the light shade of a deciduous tree. They will flower after two or three months, but the leaves will not appear until the following spring.

1 For an informal look, scatter the bulbs over grass and plant them where they land.

2 Use a bulb planter to take out a plug of soil. Place a corm in the base of each hole. Remove a little soil from the bottom of the plug. Replace the plug and firm in.

Above: Autumn crocuses, such as Colchicum *'The Giant', are not in fact crocuses, but resemble the spring flowers.*

DIVIDING IRISES

Rhizomatous irises can be divided immediately after they have flowered.

1 Lift the clump and cut away the old, unproductive parts of the rhizome. Sections for replanting should have at least one growing point.

2 Replant the cut sections, ensuring the upper surface of the rhizome is above the surface. Trim the topgrowth into a V-shape to minimize wind rock.

PLANTS TO INCREASE BY LAYERING

Aucuba
Campsis
Chaenomeles
Clematis
Erica
Humulus
Laurus
Lonicera
Magnolia
Rhododendron
Skimmia
Solanum
Wisteria

LAYERING

Woody shrubs and climbers with flexible stems can be increased by layering. This is a reliable method because the new plant remains attached to the parent while rooting takes place, but it is not usually practicable for producing more than a couple of plants. Layers can take up to a year to root, after which they can be severed from the parent plant.

1 Bring a flexible, low-growing branch down to ground level about 15–30cm (6–12in) from the tip.

2 Dig a shallow hole where the stem meets the ground and peg the stem in place. Cover with soil. Bend the tip of the stem as near to the vertical as possible and tie loosely to a supporting cane, to encourage upright growth.

GARDENER'S TIP

Conserve water by installing water butts and mulch around plants to reduce evaporation from the soil surface.

THE KITCHEN GARDEN

This is a busy time in the kitchen garden. Plants must be watered regularly so that their growth is not checked, and weeds, which will compete for nutrients, must be removed as soon as they are noticed. If you are an organic gardener, this is a good time to apply a dilute seaweed foliar feed as a spray.

CONTROLLING WEEDS

Effective weed control is important throughout the growing season, but especially so now, when any weeds missed earlier on will be growing strongly, flowering and setting seed. Once you have got on top of the problem, use mulches to prevent weed seeds blown in from neighbouring gardens from germinating.

1 Chemical weedkillers are useful for clearing a large area quickly. Choose a still day to prevent them blowing on to neighbouring ornamental plants. Repeated applications may be necessary for tough weeds.

2 To remove deep-rooted weeds by hand, loosen the soil around the weed with a fork first. With perennial weeds, make sure you remove every piece of root, or they will regrow.

3 Covering the soil around vegetable crops with black plastic is unsightly, but it will suppress weeds.

4 A layer of bark chippings or crushed cocoa shells is easier on the eye and can be spread around plants once all the weeds have been eliminated. Any weeds that germinate in the mulch itself should be removed promptly.

THINGS TO DO IN THE KITCHEN GARDEN

Pinch out tips of runner beans when they reach the required height
Cut back foliage on fruited strawberries
Sow autumn and winter salads
Earth (hill) up celery
Harvest onions, garlic and shallots
Water vegetables during dry weather

The Greenhouse

As the temperature rises in the greenhouse, you may need to provide shade, either in the form of purpose-made blinds or by applying a special wash to the glass. On hot, sunny days, damping down by spraying the floor and staging first thing in the morning will improve the atmosphere.

Cultivating Indoor Tomatoes

As they come into flower, the tomatoes growing in the greenhouse need regular attention if they are to produce the best crop. Look out, too, for early signs of pests and diseases and deal with these promptly.

1 If you are growing tall varieties, snap off any sideshoots as soon as they appear. Do not remove sideshoots from bush varieties.

2 To ensure pollination in the greenhouse, shake the tomato plants each day or spray the flowers regularly with water to disperse the pollen.

3 Remove any yellowing leaves from the base of the plants.

4 After the plant has set between four and seven fruit trusses, stop the top of the plant by removing the growing tip. (The warmer the environment, the more trusses you can allow to ripen.)

Other Indoor Crops

Pinch out the growing tips on aubergine (eggplant) plants once they are about 30cm (12in) tall. Allow only one fruit to develop on each shoot. Count three leaves beyond the fruit then pinch out the tip of each shoot. Keep the atmosphere around the plants humid by regular misting.

Train the sideshoots of melon plants on to horizontal wires. To pollinate the flowers, transfer the pollen from the male to the female flowers using a small paintbrush. Pinch back the sideshoots to two leaves beyond each fruit that develops.

Pinch out male flowers on cucumbers to prevent pollination (which affects the flavour of the fruits). Many modern varieties have exclusively female flowers.

**THINGS TO DO
IN THE GREENHOUSE**
Care for tomato plants and other crops under glass
Damp down the floor on hot days
Ventilate on hot days

Late Summer

SUMMER TRAVELS MAY MEAN THAT YOU HAVE TO BE AWAY FROM THE GARDEN WHEN IT NEEDS DAILY CARE. IT'S WORTH ASKING A NEIGHBOUR TO TAKE ON SOME OF THE LIGHTER TASKS, ESPECIALLY WATERING, AND OFFERING TO RETURN THE FAVOUR.

THE ORNAMENTAL GARDEN

This is often the hottest time of year, and you won't want to tackle a heavy workload. Above a certain temperature, plant growth stops anyway, and this year's growth on woody plants is now starting to firm up.

You need to keep a close eye on containers and hanging baskets, which can dry out all too quickly. Water them every day – twice a day if necessary – and remember that an evening watering is more economical, since the moisture will evaporate more slowly. You might also consider moving the containers to a position that is shaded at midday, to avoid leaf scorch.

Plants are rapidly forming seeds at this time, so remember to remove faded flowers promptly to keep up the flower power in containers and hanging baskets. In the open garden, however, this is a good time of year to harvest seed from any perennials and bulbs that you wish to increase. Cut off the flowerheads as soon as the seeds ripen but before they fall, and shake them into a paper bag for storage. Species are easily raised from seed (*Lilium regale* is especially rewarding) but hybrids will not come true.

Above: Grouping containers together helps to shade the pots, keeping them cooler and conserving moisture.

THINGS TO DO
IN THE ORNAMENTAL GARDEN

Collect seed from annuals and perennials
Take cuttings of tender perennials
Dig up spent annuals
Layer carnations and pinks
Remove shed leaves from roses
Prune rambling roses
Trim hedges

Above: Collect seed by shaking it off the seedhead (here of an allium) into a paper bag. Store in a cool, dry place.

The garden can easily start to look tired after a prolonged hot spell. Cutting back flopping foliage on perennial plants such as artemisias and achilleas will usually promote a flush of new leaves, restoring freshness to your borders.

Rambling Roses

By now, rambling roses will have finished flowering and there should be plenty of vigorous shoots appearing near the base. Cut out the older stems and tie in the new ones while they are still flexible, training them horizontally to promote plenty of sideshoots.

This is a time of year when ramblers often fall victim to mildew and other fungal diseases, caused by poor air circulation through the plant and dryness at the roots. Keep plants well watered, especially if they are next to a wall where the soil may be dry.

PRUNING RAMBLERS

Opening up the topgrowth by pruning can help to revive congested ramblers and prevent disease.

1 Cut old flowered stems back to near ground level, reaching in to the base of the plant with loppers if necessary.

2 Tie in new shoots close to the horizontal, for flowering next year.

GARDENER'S TIP

Stop feeding roses and other shrubs, as a rush of new, lush growth will be susceptible to frost damage.

281

The Kitchen Garden

Regular watering and weeding will ensure that all your fruit and vegetables produce good crops.

Watering Systems

Although they can seem expensive luxuries, automatic watering systems that deliver water to the ground rather than spraying it around indiscriminately can save time, money and effort. They are especially useful if your vegetable plot is any distance from your outdoor tap and if your water is metered.

A simple seep or drip hose, which can be laid along a row of plants, will water the ground immediately under it and supply water to the roots of nearby plants. More sophisticated systems allow you to attach T-junctions so that several rows can be watered. Attaching a water timer or even a computer to the tap will give a completely automatic system.

**THINGS TO DO
IN THE KITCHEN GARDEN**
Summer-prune fruit trees
Support heavily laden fruit tree branches
Watch for viral diseases
Lift ripening marrows, pumpkins and squashes on to straw
Pinch out tops of tomato plants

GARDENER'S TIP
Don't store damaged or thick-necked onions – use them straight away.

Harvesting Onions

When the foliage on onion plants has withered, the bulbs can be lifted. Choose a warm spell of weather and allow the onions to ripen for a few days in the sun. They will harden and store better.

1 Allow the foliage to die back naturally; do not bend it over as this can lead to disease in storage.

2 Gently ease the onions out of the ground, and place them on racks until the skins are completely dry. In wet weather, bring them under cover.

3 Onions can be hung up to dry through. Store good specimens in a dry, frost-free place.

THE GREENHOUSE

As you empty plant pots and seed pans, make a point of washing them thoroughly before you store them. It is all too easy to put the used containers to one side and then to forget about them: they will be an ideal breeding ground for pests and diseases.

Bringing Cyclamen into Growth

Tender cyclamen (hybrids of *Cyclamen persicum*) that have been resting over summer can now be brought back into growth. Gently remove the tuber from its pot and rub off the old potting mix. Using fresh potting mix, pot the tuber on, so that the top is just above the potting mix surface. Put the pot in a well-lit position (but out of direct sunlight) no warmer than around 16°C (61°F). Water sparingly around the tuber, increasing the amounts as the plant comes into growth.

Above: The many unnamed hybrids of Cyclamen persicum *can be started into growth now to give a good winter display.*

PLANTING HYACINTHS FOR FORCING

Specially prepared hyacinth bulbs that will flower indoors in winter should now be appearing for sale. They will have been kept in controlled conditions that persuade the plants that winter is already well advanced. Plant them in specially formulated bulb fibre, which contains extra bark.

1 Plant the bulbs in a shallow container, close together but not touching.

2 Pack potting mix around the bulbs, leaving the tops exposed. Water gently. Keep in a cool, dark place and water just to keep the potting mix moist until the shoots are about 5cm (2in) high. Then bring them into a light position, out of direct sunlight.

**THINGS TO DO
IN THE GREENHOUSE**

Bring cyclamen into growth
Sow seed for flowering pot
plants, such as *Calceolaria*
and *Schizanthus*

283

Early Autumn

AUTUMN IS THE SEASON FOR HARVESTING FRUITS FROM THE GARDEN. THE DAYS ARE GETTING COOLER AND SHORTER NOW, AND THIS IS A TIME TO PRESS ON WITH SEVERAL IMPORTANT TASKS.

THE ORNAMENTAL GARDEN

Traditionally, autumn is the time to plant hardy shrubs and trees, and conditions are usually ideal. The soil is still warm, but the days are shorter and cooler, making plants less likely to dry out. And the first frosts are still some weeks away.

THINGS TO DO
IN THE ORNAMENTAL GARDEN

Take cuttings of tender perennials
Sow hardy annuals for spring flowers
Clear summer bedding
Disbud dahlias and chrysanthemums
Lift gladioli and other tender bulbs

Above: The autumn display of Rosa *'Buff Beauty' is often even better than the summer one.*

Planning for Spring

Good gardeners are always looking ahead, and as soon as one group of plants starts to die back, they begin to think about what is going to replace them. Spent summer bedding plants can now make way for fresh plantings in preparation for the following spring. The soil is likely to be exhausted, so once the bed is cleared work in some general fertilizer and some organic matter to improve structure.

Planting Spring Bedding

Early-flowering bedding plants such as wallflowers (*Erysimum*) and forget-me-nots (*Myosotis*) can be interplanted with bulbs such as tulips for a colourful spring display.

1 Spring bedding plants are often sold at this time of year in modules, or you may have grown your own. Space them evenly across the bed.

2 Once all the bedding plants are in, drop the bulbs among them and plant them, using a trowel, so that they are covered with twice their own depth of soil.

Lifting Gladioli

In mild areas gladioli may still be flowering in early autumn, but in colder districts you will need to lift the corms for storage over the winter before they can be nipped by the first hard frosts.

As the topgrowth starts to die back, lift the corms with a fork. Trim off most of the foliage to leave just a stub. Dry the corms off for a few days in a well-ventilated place.

Snap off the tiny new corms that you will find around the base of the main corm. You can either discard these or keep them for growing on (they will take several years to reach flowering size). Dust the large corms with fungicide and store them in paper bags in a dry, frost-free environment for re-planting next spring.

Above: After flowering, lift gladioli corms and store in a dry, frost-free place. This is Gladiolus 'Charming Beauty'.

285

THE KITCHEN GARDEN

There are a number of leafy vegetables that can be sown now for winter crops. Look for lettuce varieties that have been bred for autumn sowing, and try sowing lamb's lettuce (mâche), rocket (arugula) and winter purslane as cold month crops. Spring cabbages sown now will provide spring greens early next year. Cover seedlings with a cloche if the weather turns cold.

Above: Beetroot, here grown in a raised bed, is best harvested while still quite small, about seven weeks after sowing.

Lifting Root Vegetables

Beetroot (beets), carrots and turnips can be lifted now for storing over winter. Only undamaged roots are suitable for storing. Twist off the leaves and pack the roots in wooden boxes filled with sand. Keep the root vegeta-

bles in a cool, frost-free place. Parsnips and swedes (rutabagas) should be left in the ground until after the first frosts, as this improves their flavour.

Above: Globe artichokes will be ready for harvesting in early autumn of the second year after planting. They should be eaten as soon as possible after cutting.

PROTECTING OUTDOOR TOMATOES

It is likely that outdoor tomatoes will still be ripening. Green fruits can be picked and ripened indoors provided they are reasonably mature, but for the best flavour it makes sense to ripen as many as possible on the plant. They will benefit from some protection, particularly if frosts are forecast. Plants trained to vertical stakes can be tented with horticultural fleece. Alternatively, the plants can be untied and rested on the ground.

1 Untie the plants from their stakes. To avoid damaging the fruit and provide a little extra insulation, spread a layer of dry straw on the ground and gently lower the plants on to this.

2 Cover the tomatoes with a rigid plastic cloche, which will warm the air around them – thus speeding up ripening – as well as keeping off frost.

3 Alternatively, cover the plants loosely with horticultural fleece. This protects against frost but will not warm up the air as a rigid cloche does.

**THINGS TO DO
IN THE KITCHEN GARDEN**

Protect outdoor tomatoes
against frost
Plant strawberries
Stake Brussels sprouts
Divide herbaceous herbs

GARDENER'S TIP

Sow a crop of green manure (such as mustard) to use up nutrients left in vacant ground after harvesting. It will be recycled when the crop is dug in.

THE GREENHOUSE

Before the first autumn frosts, take time to make sure that any heating system in your greenhouse is in good working order. Check that all extension leads are in good condition and take any heaters to be serviced if you are not confident of your own abilities to look after them.

Plants now need all the light they can get, so remove greenhouse blinds or shading. If you applied a shading wash earlier in the year, it can usually be rubbed off with a cloth when the glass is dry.

Sowing Hardy Annuals

If you want an early display of flowers next season, hardy annuals can be sown now for planting out next

Above: Continue to keep the greenhouse well ventilated. Even in autumn the temperature under the glass will rise sharply on a sunny day.

spring. They can also be grown on in pots to provide flowering pot plants for the conservatory. Compact forms of pot marigolds (*Calendula*) are easy and rewarding, or try cornflowers, godetias or stocks (*Matthiola*).

Protecting Early-flowering Shrubs

If you grow early-flowering shrubs, such as daphnes, skimmias or camellias, in pots, move them under cover for earlier, perfectly formed flowers. Keep them well-watered and in good light, but check that they do not scorch on the odd sunny day when the temperature can rise dramatically.

Bringing in Houseplants

Many winter- and spring-flowering houseplants, such as zygocactus, solanums grown for their winter berries and even orchids, benefit from spending the summer outdoors, but they must be brought inside before the first frost threatens. Remove any fallen leaves and debris from the soil surface and clean the pots carefully to avoid contaminating the greenhouse. Check for any signs of disease and look under the leaves for snails and other pests before bringing them in.

REPOTTING CACTI

Cacti and succulents can be repotted at any time of year, but it is often convenient to do so either in spring or autumn. Cacti benefit from a specially formulated potting mix that allows very free drainage while supplying the correct nutrients. They also demand special handling.

1 Wrap the cactus in thick paper to protect your hands from the spines. Ease it from the container.

2 Centre the plant in the new container and fill with cactus potting mix.

3 Top-dress with grit to improve drainage and to protect the collar of the plant from excess damp. Withhold water for several days to allow any damaged roots to form calluses.

> ### THINGS TO DO
> ### IN THE GREENHOUSE
> Bring in houseplants that have spent
> the summer outdoors
> Sow seed of spring-flowering
> tender perennials
> Clean off summer shading washes
> Pot up and pot on seedlings of pot
> plants as necessary
> Check greenhouse heating system

Mid-autumn

AT THIS TIME OF YEAR SUDDEN CHANGES IN THE WEATHER CAN AFFECT THE GARDEN. IN A BALMY SPELL, PLANTS WILL CONTINUE TO GROW, BUT A COLD NIGHT WILL HAVE AN IMMEDIATE EFFECT.

THE ORNAMENTAL GARDEN

If you need to lay a new lawn and did not do so in spring, consider ordering turfs or sowing seed now. The soil will still be warm enough to encourage the roots to grow strongly and there will be plenty of autumn rain.

If your established lawn is looking rather tired and bedraggled, autumn is the time for tasks such as scarifying, to remove an accumulation of clippings, and spiking, to aerate the soil. Sweep up all fallen leaves, which can damage the lawn. They should be collected to make leaf mould, a precious organic substance that can be used either as a mulch or as a general soil improver.

Pond Care

Garden ponds – especially informal and wildlife ones – generally look after themselves, but most repay a little extra attention at this time of year. There is always the danger that leaves shed by deciduous shrubs and trees, as well as other plant debris, will find their way into the water. If left there, they will rot and create poisonous gases. Either net the pond to catch any debris, or rake the surface to collect any fallen leaves.

Above: Osteospermums are not reliably hardy, but they have a long flowering season and will bloom until the first frosts. This is Osteospermum 'Lady Leitrim'.

Pruning Deciduous Shrubs

Although hard pruning should be left until spring, you can cut back whippy growth on tall deciduous shrubs, such as buddleias and some roses, to prevent wind rock. Reduce the topgrowth by up to one third.

Beds and Borders

Plants of doubtful hardiness, such as fuchsias, osteospermums, busy Lizzies and *Begonia semperflorens*, can be dug up now for storage over winter. Fuchsias should be kept dry, but the others can be kept growing in a warm, light place, where they will continue to flower for a few more weeks.

LIFTING AND STORING DAHLIAS

Dahlias are not hardy, but they should be left in the ground until a hard frost has blackened the topgrowth. The tubers can then be lifted for storage over winter.

1 When the foliage turns black, cut back the topgrowth to about 15cm (6in) above the ground and remove any stakes. Lift the tubers with a fork.

2 Carefully rub off as much soil as possible. Leave the tubers to dry off in an airy place such as a shed or unheated greenhouse. Store in paper bags in a cool but frost-free place over winter.

Planting a Root-balled Conifer

Root-balled conifers are lifted from the nursery field in autumn, and should be planted as soon as possible. Prepare a planting hole of the correct depth and width to accommodate the roots (check the depth with a cane) and remove the covering from the roots. Backfill with the excavated soil and firm in well. Keep the conifer well watered during dry spells and shelter it from winter gales, which could dry out the foliage.

Above: Place a cane across the hole to make sure that trees and shrubs are planted to their original depth.

THINGS TO DO IN THE ORNAMENTAL GARDEN

Plant spring bulbs (except tulips)
Plant bare-root roses and other shrubs
Lift and store dahlias
Plant spring bedding
Divide herbaceous plants
Bring tender perennials under cover
Plant new hedging
Scarify and spike established lawns

THE KITCHEN GARDEN

Taking steps to protect your plants from frost will keep them in good condition in case it turns cold before you are ready to harvest them. The stems of vegetables such as celery and beetroot (beets) can be protected with straw. Bend the surrounding leaves over the heads of late cauliflowers. Other vulnerable vegetables can be sheltered under cloches.

LIFTING AND STORING POTATOES

Late potatoes are mainly grown for use during the winter, and should now be ready for harvesting and storing. Small crops can be kept indoors, but if space is at a premium, consider making a potato clamp in a sheltered spot in the garden.

2 Sort the potatoes by size, as the largest tubers are the most suitable for winter storage. The tiniest potatoes should be used immediately, otherwise they can be discarded. You should be able to sort the remainder into three groups: small, for early consumption, medium and large, for storing indoors or in a potato clamp in the garden.

1 Once the foliage has died down, lift the potatoes with a fork – they can be left longer if there is no frost. Leave on the soil surface for a few hours to harden off the outer skins.

3 Place in sacks and store them in a dark, cool, frost-free place. Paper sacks are best, but if you cannot obtain these, use plastic sacks, making slits to provide some ventilation.

4 To make a potato clamp, excavate a shallow depression in bare soil and line it with a thick layer of dry straw. Pile the potatoes on top. Heap another layer of straw over the top of the potatoes to provide good insulation. Mound the excavated earth over the straw, but leave a few tufts protruding to ensure adequate ventilation in the clamp. The tubers will be protected from all but the most severe weather.

Caring for Fruit Trees

Pick apples when they are ripe, which is usually when the fruit comes away easily with a quick twist. Store unblemished fruit in a cool, dark place, ensuring the fruits do not touch.

Clear away fallen fruit and leaves from around fruit trees. If it is left on the ground it tends to harbour pests and diseases ready to attack the trees next spring. Fasten grease bands around the trunks of fruit trees so that wingless female codling moths cannot climb up the trunks to lay eggs.

> ### THINGS TO DO
> ### IN THE KITCHEN GARDEN
> Plant spring cabbages
> Earth (hill) up celery and leek plants
> Lift and store potatoes
> Protect vulnerable vegetables
> with cloches
> Pot up herbs for winter use
> Harvest and store apples
> Cut spent canes of summer-fruiting
> raspberries to the ground
> Protect late-fruiting strawberries
> from frost
> Apply grease bands to apple trees

Protecting Herbs

You can keep some of your herbs, including parsley, cropping throughout the winter if you protect them from frosts with a rigid plastic cloche. Make sure the end pieces are tightly secured to keep out the cold, but remove the cloche on warm, dry days.

Above: Rigid plastic cloches are ideal for protecting herbs such as parsley throughout winter.

293

THE GREENHOUSE

As the weather turns damper, you need to keep a look out for fungal problems, such as grey mould (botrytis). Good ventilation should minimize the risk, but this becomes less easy as the outdoor temperature drops. Remove dead, faded or diseased-looking leaves from plants and burn them. Spray the plants with copper fungicide solution. If you decide to use fumigation to control any pests and diseases that are lingering, read the manufacturer's instructions before use because some types can be used only in completely empty greenhouses.

Above: If you can empty the greenhouse completely, you can make sure that you rid it of all lurking pests and diseases by fumigating it.

Below: Good ventilation, particularly in the warmer months, will ensure that greenhouse crops don't suffer the effects of intense heat.

Forcing Lily-of-the-valley

For fragrant early flowers, force some lily-of-the-valley (*Convallaria majalis*) under glass. Dig up or buy a few rhizomes (sometimes known as pips) and pot them up. The more heat you can provide, the earlier they will flower. Although they can be planted out after flowering, they may take a season or two to regain their vigour and to flower as usual. Do not try to force the same rhizomes again.

2 Trim the longest roots and shorten the shoots to about 10cm (4in).

STORING PELARGONIUMS

Pelargoniums that have flowered their hearts out in summer borders will now be performing less well. They can be lifted from the ground this month and stored over winter, either for replanting next year or to provide material for early cuttings.

3 Pot up the plants in 15cm (6in) deep trays or pots of sowing compost. Water well initially, but sparingly over winter, just to prevent the soil from drying out. New shoots will emerge in spring, from which you can take cuttings.

1 Lift the pelargoniums from the ground before the first frost – they will often survive a light frost if you take them in promptly afterwards. Shake off the soil from the roots.

THINGS TO DO IN THE GREENHOUSE
Continue to ventilate in mild weather
Install a thermometer to check minimum temperatures at night
Remove and burn any dead or diseased leaves from plants
Clean and disinfect work areas

Late Autumn

THIS TIME OF YEAR OFTEN SPRINGS A SURPRISE: ALTHOUGH COLD, THE DAYS CAN BE CLEAR AND SUNNY. TAKE A STROLL ROUND THE GARDEN AND NOTE ANY DESIGN FEATURES THAT NEED IMPROVEMENT. NOW IS THE TIME TO GET THE GARDEN READY FOR WINTER.

THE ORNAMENTAL GARDEN

If you like a tidy garden, begin to cut back herbaceous perennials to about 15cm (6in) above the ground as the foliage and flowers die back.

Some gardeners prefer to leave the dead topgrowth in place until spring because it protects the crowns from winter cold. In addition, many plants, especially grasses, look attractive when their dry leaves and flowerheads are touched with frost. Seedheads left on plants such as teasels (*Dipsacus fullonum*) provide valuable winter food for birds, as do the insects that overwinter inside dead stems. However, garden pests, including slugs and snails, will also overwinter among the dead plant material, and it can be difficult to avoid damaging the tender new growth when you are cutting back the old topgrowth in spring.

Bulbs in Beds and Borders

As nerines start to die back after flowering, mulch them with straw or some other dry material if you live in a cold area. This is a good time to divide congested clumps, but do this only if the plants have ceased to flower well.

Above: Spiraea japonica *'Goldflame' is one of the shrubs that can be propagated from hardwood cuttings taken about now.*

Nerines are best left well alone as far as possible, but some other tender bulbs, such as gladioli, should be lifted so that they can be stored in a dry, frost-free place until next spring. There is still time to plant spring-flowering bulbs, including tulips.

GARDENER'S TIP

If you plan a bonfire, either warn your neighbours or light it in the evening when you are least likely to cause inconvenience.

Taking Hardwood Cuttings

You can increase your stock of a wide range of trees and shrubs by taking hardwood cuttings. They occupy little space, and aftercare is minimal, though they take up to a year to root.

1 Dig a narrow trench about 20cm (8in) deep. If the soil is heavy, line the base with a 2.5cm (1in) layer of grit. Take cuttings from the plant, each with four or more buds. Trim the base of each cutting just below a bud and the top just above a bud.

2 Insert the cuttings in the trench. Two or three buds should protrude above the ground, although if you are taking cuttings from a single-stemmed tree, you should insert them to their full length so that the topmost bud is just below the soil surface.

3 Firm in the cuttings, label them and water them in well. Leave them undisturbed until the following autumn, by which time they should have rooted.

SHRUBS TO INCREASE BY HARDWOOD CUTTINGS
Aucuba
Berberis
Buddleja
Buxus
Cornus
Cotoneaster
Escallonia
Forsythia
Kerria
Philadelphus
Rosa
Salix
Spiraea
Weigela

Above: Plant tulip bulbs to a depth of 8–15cm (3–6in). Tulipa praestans 'Fusilier' has up to six flowers on each stem.

THINGS TO DO IN THE ORNAMENTAL GARDEN
Cut back perennials
Burn woody garden debris
Plant bare-root roses and other shrubs
Plant tulip bulbs
Take hardwood cuttings
Plant hedges
Collect and compost fallen leaves
Protect vulnerable plants by packing around them with straw

THE KITCHEN GARDEN

As you clear the vegetable plot of the last of the summer crops, dig over the soil and leave it so that winter frosts can break down large clods. This is especially important if your soil is heavy. Continue to protect vulnerable plants with cloches or straw.

PLANTING SOFT FRUIT

Traditionally, soft fruit bushes are sold at this time of year as bare-root plants, and they should be planted as soon after purchase as possible, while they are dormant. Container-grown plants can be planted at any time of year when the weather is suitable and the ground is not waterlogged or frozen, although these, too, are best planted at this time of year.

1 Dig a large hole for each plant and work organic matter into the base. Soak the plant roots in a water for an hour and then place them in the centre of the hole. Use a cane to make sure you are planting at the original depth.

2 Backfill with the excavated soil and firm in well with your foot to eliminate pockets of air. Hoe around the plant, then water the plant well.

3 Soft fruits that grow on stems that sprout from the base are pruned hard. Cut back the topgrowth to 23–30cm (9–12in) from ground level to stimulate new shoots from the base.

> **THINGS TO DO**
> **IN THE KITCHEN GARDEN**
> Protect vulnerable vegetables
> with cloches
> Plant bare-root fruit bushes and trees
> Prune soft fruit bushes
> Pot up herbs for winter use

Pruning Soft Fruit

Once established, soft fruit bushes need pruning while dormant to maintain their vigour. Blackcurrants should be pruned only once they are fruiting reliably. Cut back one third of the shoots to the base, choosing the oldest. Red and white currants fruit on wood that is two or more years old, so pruning should concentrate on removing overcrowded shoots. Shorten sideshoots to one or two buds, and on main shoots cut back last summer's growth by half. Gooseberries also benefit from annual pruning to keep an open shape.

Autumn-fruiting raspberries bear fruit on the new season's canes, so all canes can be cut to ground level during the dormant season. On summer-fruiting varieties, the old canes that have fruited should be removed and the new shoots tied in to replace them.

Planting Garlic

To grow successfully, garlic needs a period of cold and can be planted throughout the autumn until early winter. Although it is possible to grow garlic from cloves bought for cooking, you will get better results from specially produced bulbs.

Snap each bulb into its component cloves and plant them in a row in a sunny spot, up to 10cm (4in) apart and with the tips of the cloves just below the soil surface.

Above: *When frost is forecast, protect crops such as strawberries with a portable plastic cloche.*

> ### GARDENER'S TIP
> Pot up herbs such as mint, chives and marjoram and keep them in the greenhouse or kitchen to ensure a supply of fresh leaves throughout the winter.

Above: *Use a dibber to make holes for garlic cloves, spacing them about 10cm (4in) apart along the row.*

299

THE GREENHOUSE

As the temperature drops, you need to start thinking about heating and insulation. Most conservatories are heated by means of the domestic system, but if your greenhouse is free-standing and has no power supply, you may consider installing a small gas or paraffin heater. These can be used only in a properly ventilated environment, however, because of the risk of fire or a build-up of noxious fumes.

Good insulation will help save on fuel bills. Bubble plastic is cheap and can be fixed to the greenhouse roof with clips. If you installed blinds or netting for shade in summer, you may be able to use the same fixings to hold the insulation in place.

If you have a large greenhouse that would be costly to heat, you may be

Above: An electric fan heater, especially if it is fitted with a thermostat, is an efficient way of heating a greenhouse.

able to group all the most tender plants together at one end and close this section off with a curtain of bubble plastic. Heat this area only.

Hygiene

If you have not already done so, take the opportunity to give the greenhouse a thorough clean before putting the insulation in place. If you used blinds or netting to shade the greenhouse during the summer, wash them before storing them away.

Clear away all dead and dying foliage and flowers so that grey mould (botrytis) cannot overwinter on the debris. Use hot water and a garden disinfectant or non-toxic detergent to clean the glass inside and out, taking particular care to clean between overlapping panes of glass, where algal growths tend to form. Also scrub down all wooden or metal frames and clean the staging.

Above: Insulate the greenhouse with sheets of bubble plastic fixed against the glass on the inside.

Before storing all your containers, plant pots and drip saucers over the winter, make sure they are clean, and wipe the outside of all containers used for long-term plants with a dilute solution of garden disinfectant.

Cold Frames

Although a cold frame is usually designed to store hardy plants, bear in mind that the plants will be young – and therefore more vulnerable than mature ones – and that their roots are above ground level: potting mix in pots can easily freeze in severe weather. On

Above: Clean the greenhouse glass inside and out to maximize light levels and prevent the build-up of algae.

the coldest nights, cover the frame with old carpet to protect from frost. Keep the carpet on in the daytime if the temperature stays below freezing. Excluding the light in very cold weather will do the plants no harm.

Above: Scrub all your plant pots and containers when not in use, so that they do not harbour disease.

> THINGS TO DO
> IN THE GREENHOUSE
> Clean all surfaces
> Clean greenhouse glass
> Insulate, if necessary
> Ventilate on mild days
> Check on indoor cyclamen and remove
> any dead leaves

301

Early Winter

THERE ARE STILL SOME ESSENTIAL GARDEN TASKS TO BE DONE IN WINTER, BUT THERE IS MUCH TO ENJOY AS WELL. AT THIS TIME OF YEAR THE VALUE OF EVERGREENS AND CONIFERS AS THE BACKBONE OF THE GARDEN CAN BE FULLY APPRECIATED.

THE ORNAMENTAL GARDEN

Continue to sweep up fallen leaves, especially from the lawn, and use them to make leaf mould.

One of the few perennials to be in flower at this time of year, the Christmas rose (*Helleborus niger*) can be difficult to keep looking its best. It often flowers during the worst of the winter weather, and it is worth protecting the emerging flower buds from rain and mud splashes. Alpines will also appreciate protection from winter wet, which is more likely to kill them than cold weather.

THE KITCHEN GARDEN

There will still be plenty of tidying up to do, as you clear away the last of this year's crops and dig over vacant beds to prepare for next season.

Pruning Apple and Pear Trees

Give some attention to apple and pear trees now that they are dormant. Pruning is largely a matter of tidying them up. Thin older branches to open up the crown and cut back any damaged branches entirely. If any growth shows signs of fungal disease such as mildew, cut back to firm, healthy

Above: *A sheet of glass placed over* Helleborus niger *will keep mud splashes off the pure white flowers.*

Above: *Established apple cordons should be pruned in both winter and summer, but standards can be pruned in winter only.*

wood and burn the prunings. Use a pruning saw with a serrated edge to deal with thicker branches. Take care that you do not prune too many branches too hard, as this will result in an excess of thin, sappy growth the following spring.

THE GREENHOUSE

On mild days make a point of opening the door or the roof lights to ventilate the greenhouse, and remove any fallen leaves or flowers. Reduce the water you give to plants that are being over-wintered in the greenhouse.

CHECKING STORED BULBS

If you are storing the dried bulbs, corms, tubers and rhizomes of such plants as freesias, gladioli, dahlias and begonias, it is worth checking up on them from time to time to make sure they are not showing any signs of rot.

1 About once a month, gently squeeze the bulbs (these are begonia tubers) to make sure they are still firm. Any that feel soft, or are showing signs of mould, should be discarded at once.

2 For extra protection, dust the healthy bulbs or tubers with a fungicidal powder, following the safety measures stipulated on the product label.

THINGS TO DO

Ornamental Garden
Sow seed of alpines
Put cloches over *Helleborus niger*
Protect alpines from winter wet
Install a pond heater

Kitchen Garden
Prune apple and pear trees
Force whitloof chicory

Greenhouse
Inspect bulbs in storage
Prune grape vines
Sow seed of pelargoniums

GARDENER'S TIP

Clean and oil your lawn mower now, as you are unlikely to have time when it is in regular use in summer, or take it to be professionally serviced before the busy spring season.

Midwinter

AT THIS TIME OF YEAR YOU NEED TO START LOOKING FORWARD. NO MATTER HOW COLD THE WEATHER, SPRING IS ONLY JUST AROUND THE CORNER. NOW IS THE TIME TO PLAN YOUR PLANTING SCHEMES, ORDER SEEDS AND CHECK THAT YOUR TOOLS ARE IN GOOD REPAIR.

THE ORNAMENTAL GARDEN

A job that is easily overlooked at this time of year is to knock off snow from the tops of hedges and specimen conifers. Evergreen hedges are usually trimmed so that the top slopes slightly, encouraging snow to slide off. Sometimes, however, heavy snowfall can lie on branches, causing permanent damage.

TAKING ROOT CUTTINGS

Root cuttings are an excellent way of increasing stocks of a number of perennials, but the plant must be fully dormant for the technique to be successful. Keep the cuttings in a cold frame or unheated greenhouse. New growth should appear in spring, when the young plants can be potted up individually and grown on for a season.

1 Dig up the plant when dormant, cut off some of the thicker roots close to the crown. Replant the crown.

2 Cut the roots into 5cm (2in) sections. Angle the cut at the base of each one to show the correct way up. Insert vertically in cuttings potting mix.

3 For plants with thin roots, such as border phlox, lay 5cm (2in) lengths of root in pots of potting mix. Cover with a fairly thin layer of potting mix.

PLANTS TO INCREASE BY
ROOT CUTTINGS

Acanthus
Echinops
Gaillardia
Phlox maculata
Phlox paniculata
Pulsatilla vulgaris
Romneya coulteri

THINGS TO DO
IN THE ORNAMENTAL GARDEN
Firm in new plantings lifted by frost
Check the stakes on trees
Prune wisteria
Aerate lawns
Melt ice on ponds

THE KITCHEN GARDEN

While most of the vegetable plot is bare, take the opportunity to test the soil. Most vegetables do best in slightly alkaline soil, so if necessary apply lime, in the form of calcium carbonate or calcium hydroxide (slaked lime), following the supplier's directions precisely.

Forcing Rhubarb

If you grow rhubarb, cover some of the crowns with a large bucket or a special rhubarb forcer that excludes light. This will encourage early growth that is pale, thin and tender – excellent for pies and fools in spring.

For a really early crop of rhubarb, lift the crown to expose the roots and leave it on the soil surface for a few weeks. This will persuade the plant that winter is more advanced than it really is and bring it into growth earlier. Replant the crown and cover the emerging shoots.

Above: Check stored apples regularly and promptly remove any fruits that show signs of rot.

Forcing Chicory

Chicory roots are sometimes sold at this time of year for forcing to produce chicons. Leave the roots on the soil surface for a few days to retard growth. Trim back the tops to leave stumps 2.5–5cm (1–2in) long and pot them up in threes, leaving the crowns exposed (trim the roots if necessary to fit in the pot). Cover with a second pot with the holes blocked to exclude light and keep at a temperature of 10–18°C (50–65°F). The chicons will be ready to cut in about three weeks.

**THINGS TO DO
IN THE KITCHEN GARDEN**

Net fruit bushes to protect emerging buds from birds
Force rhubarb and chicory
Sow broad (fava) beans and peas
(mild areas only)

THE GREENHOUSE

If you have a heated greenhouse or a heated propagator, it is not too soon to sow some summer bedding plants that need a long growing period, such as fibrous-rooted begonias *(Begonia semperflorens)*. Check seed packets to see if early sowings are needed.

It can be tempting to make early sowings of all half-hardy annuals and summer vegetables. However, remember that you will need plenty of space to keep the pricked-out and potted-on seedlings warm and well lit before they can be planted out. Seedlings that are kept in overcrowded, poorly ventilated conditions are susceptible to damping off, so in a small greenhouse it is more sensible to put off most early sowings for a few weeks.

Above: Now is the time to plan for next summer's chrysanthemum display. This is the early-flowering 'Primrose Allouise'.

PROPAGATING CHRYSANTHEMUMS

Chrysanthemums that are overwintered in a greenhouse or cold frame are generally used to produce new plants once they start into growth. In order to ensure large, robust plants for summer flowering, take cuttings from your stock plants now, once the new shoots reach about 5cm (2in).

1 Cut shoots growing from the base of the plant. Pull off the lower leaves and trim the base of each cutting.

2 Insert the stems in a pot containing a mixture suitable for cuttings.

3 Water and cover with a plastic bag, making sure it does not touch the leaves, or place the pot in a propagator.

Bringing Hippeastrums into Growth

Bulbs of hippeastrums, which are often, incorrectly, sold as amaryllis, can be obtained at this time of year for indoor display. Plant the bulbs in pots of bulb fibre or potting mix with the top half of the bulb above the surface. If the bulb is slow to start into growth, place the pot in a propagator for a week or so until the first green shoots appear.

GARDENER'S TIP

To make tiny seed like begonia easier to handle and see, mix it with a small quantity of silver sand and sprinkle the sand and seed mix over the surface of the tray.

THINGS TO DO
IN THE GREENHOUSE

Pick off and burn dead leaves
from pot plants
Check stored corms and tubers
for signs of rot
Continue to ventilate on mild days
Sow seed of annuals for early flowers

Above: Exotic-looking hippeastrums, such as this variety called 'Christmas Star', grow with phenomenal speed indoors and bloom in the depths of winter.

Late Winter

THIS IS OFTEN WHEN THE WORST OF THE WINTER WEATHER STRIKES, BUT THE DAYS ARE BECOMING PERCEPTIBLY LONGER AND MANY OF THE SPRING BULBS ARE BEGINNING TO SHOOT FROM BELOW GROUND. THE AIR OF ANTICIPATION IS ALMOST PALPABLE.

THE ORNAMENTAL GARDEN

There is plenty to do in the garden at this time of year – and plenty to enjoy. Magnolia buds are fattening up, and many winter-flowering shrubs are at their best. Several have bewitching fragrances, and a few cut stems will scent the whole house.

Prune late-flowering clematis hard back to a pair of strong, healthy buds. Thinner stems that show no signs of shooting can be cut down completely.

Above: When you prune a clematis, cut each stem back to a pair of strong buds near ground level.

Summer bulbs will be appearing for sale. If you are buying lilies, look for firm, plump bulbs that show no sign of disease and plant them as soon as possible, adding grit or sharp sand to the soil to ensure good drainage. Dahlia tubers should be stored until the weather warms up in late spring.

Above: One of the first bulbs to appear, Crocus tommasinianus *is ideal for naturalizing in grass.*

THINGS TO DO IN THE ORNAMENTAL GARDEN

Sow sweet peas
Plant snowdrops and winter aconites immediately after flowering
Prune clematis
Divide overcrowded snowdrops
Take root cuttings of perennials with thick, fleshy roots
Prepare ground for new lawns

The Kitchen Garden

Unless the soil is waterlogged or frozen, continue to dig over the vegetable plot, but take care that you do not compact wet soil by standing on it. Apply a mulch of well-rotted compost or manure to prevent weeds from germinating in the bare soil.

Sowing Early Crops

If you have a cold frame erected directly over garden soil, take advantage of the few extra degrees of warmth it provides to sow some early crops. In the open garden, you can warm up patches of soil for early sowings with cloches of various kinds.

2 Rigid cloches made of polycarbon are useful for warming up small areas of the garden. Butt the sections close together and firmly fix them in the ground. Close the ends with further sections of polycarbon to prevent the cloche becoming a wind tunnel.

3 You can warm up a larger area of soil with plastic sheeting stretched over hoops – an ambitious tunnel will have enough headroom to allow you to walk in and out of it. Pull the sheeting taut and secure it firmly at each end. Anchor the edges of the plastic to the ground by heaping soil over them.

1 If your cold frame stands on bare soil, prepare the ground by forking it over and adding as much organic matter as possible. Well-rotted farmyard manure is useful for enriching the soil for early crops. Powerful artificial fertilizers are not recommended. Rake the soil level and sow the seed thinly in shallow drills.

**THINGS TO DO
IN THE KITCHEN GARDEN**

Continue winter digging
Force young strawberry plants for
an early crop
Sprout early potatoes
Feed asparagus beds
Plant out Jerusalem artichokes
Sow vegetables under cloches
for early crops

THE GREENHOUSE

Make the most of your greenhouse, conservatory or kitchen windowsill to begin sowing seed of early vegetables and half-hardy annuals. To maximize the light that gets to your seedlings, make sure that the glass is clean. Don't forget to ventilate the greenhouse on warm days.

If you have stored dahlia tubers over winter, they can now be coaxed out of their dormancy. A good way of increasing your stock is to take cuttings from the emerging shoots. Provided you give them the appropriate care and attention, they should flower the same year.

For flowers in early summer, press on and sow seeds of annuals. A propagator can speed up germination, which is especially useful for half-hardy plants. To produce sturdy, healthy plants, prick them out as they grow. Early sowings can also be used to provide flowering pot plants for indoor displays.

Have a look at tender perennials you have overwintered, which will be mostly woody plants, such as fuchsias, pelargoniums, argyranthemums and felicias. Spraying them with water can help encourage them to push out fresh shoots. If the plants are old and straggly, any such shoots can be used as cuttings, if you didn't take cuttings the previous autumn.

Young plants need tender loving care. Keep them warm, in good light and out of draughts, and make sure they never dry out. If you need to keep

Above: Dahlia tubers that have been stored over the winter should be showing signs of growth now, and you can take cuttings to increase your stocks.

them in a closed environment such as a propagator, check regularly for signs of fungal disease, usually the result of excessive moisture.

Check that you have good supplies of clean pots and seed trays, potting mix for both seed and cuttings, and plant labels. You can save time later by stocking up now. Days that are too cold or wet for you to venture outside will be well spent washing old pots and sorting out seed packets.

GROWING CACTI FROM SEED

As a change, try growing cacti from seed, which is a gratifyingly easy way of producing large numbers of these fascinating plants. Use a heated propagator to start them off, then grow them on under normal greenhouse conditions but maintaining a minimum temperature of 10°C (50°F).

1 Fill small pots or a seed tray with potting mix specially formulated for cacti. Scatter the seed evenly and thinly over the surface.

2 Top-dress with a thin layer of fine gravel, water the pots or trays and stand them in a place that is warm and bright but out of direct sunlight.

3 Prick the seedlings out when they are large enough and pot them up. Most cacti do best in pots that are small in proportion to their topgrowth.

**THINGS TO DO
IN THE GREENHOUSE**

Take cuttings of dahlias
Bring overwintered tender perennials
back into growth
Sow tomatoes
Ventilate on mild days
Sow cacti

311

Common Names of Plants

aconite *Aconitum*
African daisy *Arctotis*
African lily *Agapanthus*
African marigold
   Tagetes erecta
Algerian iris
   Iris unguicularis
alyssum
   Lobularia maritima
annual pepper
   Capsicum annuum
auricula *Primula auricula*
   hybrids
autumn crocus
   Colchicum autumnale,
   Crocus nudiflorus
arum lily *Zantedeschia*
   aethiopica
avens *Geum*

baby blue-eyes
   Nemophila menziesii
baby's breath
   Gypsophila paniculata
balsam poplar
   Populus balsamifera
Barberry
   Berberis sargentiana
basil *Ocimum basilicum*
bay *Laurus nobilis*
bear's breeches *Acanthus*
beauty bush
   Kolkwitzia amabilis
bedding geranium
   Pelargonium
beech *Fagus sylvatica*
bellflower *Campanula*
bells of Ireland
   Moluccella laevis
bergamot *Monarda*

betony *Stachys*
black-eyed Susan
   Rudbeckia
bladder senna *Colutea*
blazing star *Liatris*
bleeding heart
   Dicentra spectabilis
blue daisy *Felicia*
blue fescue *Festuca glauca*
bluebell *Hyacinthoides*
borage *Borago officinalis*
Boston ivy *Parthenocissus*
   tricuspidata
box *Buxus sempervirens*
bridal wreath *Francoa*
broom *Cytisus, Genista*
bulrush *Typha latifolia*
burnet *Sanguisorba*
busy Lizzie *Impatiens*
buttercup *Ranunculus*
butterfly bush *Buddleja*
   davidii

calamint *Calamintha*
calico bush *Kalmia*
   latifolia
California lilac
   Ceanothus
Californian poppy
   Eschscholzia

campion *Silene*
candytuft *Iberis*
Canterbury bells
   Campanula medium
Cape figwort *Phygelius*
cardoon *Cynara*
   cardunculus
carnation *Dianthus*
castor oil plant *Ricinus*
catchfly *Lychnis*
catmint *Nepeta x faasseni*
chamomile
   Chamaemelum nobile
cherry *Prunus*
cherry pie *Heliotropum*
China aster *Callistephus*
   chinensis
Chinese pink *Dianthus*
   chinensis
chives *Allium*
   schoenoprasum
Christmas box
   Sarcococca
Christmas cactus
   Schlumbergera
cineraria
   Senecio cineraria
cinquefoil *Potentilla*
climbing hydrangea
   Hydrangea petiolaris
coleus *Solenostemon*
columbine *Aquilegia*
comfrey *Symphytum*
common bugle
   Ajuga reptans
coneflower *Echinacea,*
   Rudbeckia
contorted or corkscrew
   hazel *Corylus avellana*
   'Contorta'

coral flower *Heuchera*
cornflower *Centaurea cinerea*
cotton lavender *Santolina chamaecyparissus*
cowslip *Primula veris*
crab apple *Malus*
cranesbill *Geranium*
creeping Jenny *Lysimachia nummularia*
creeping zinnia *Sanvitalia*
cuckoo flower *Cardamine pratensis*
Cupid's dart *Catananche*
curry plant *Helichrysum italicum*

daffodil *Narcissus*
daisy *Bellis perennis*
daisy bush *Olearia*
dame's violet *Hesperis matronalis*
daylily *Hemerocallis*
deadnettle *Lamium*
dittany *Dictamnus*
dogwood *Cornus*
dog's tooth violet *Erythronium*
Dutchman's pipe *Aristolochia*

elder *Sambucus*
elephant ears *Bergenia*
evening primrose *Oenothera speciosa*

false castor oil plant *Fatsia japonica*
feather grass *Stipa*

fennel *Foeniculum vulgare*
feverfew *Tanacetum parthenium*
firethorn *Pyracantha*
flag *Iris germanica*
fleabane *Erigeron*
floss flower *Ageratum*
flowering currant *Ribes sanguineum*
flowering flax *Linum grandiflorum*
flowering quince *Chaenomeles*
forget-me-not *Myosotis*
foxglove *Digitalis purpurea*
French marigold *Tagetes patula*
fritillary *Fritillaria*
furze *Ulex*

garlic *Allium sativum*
gay feather *Liatris*
gentian *Gentiana*
geranium *Pelargonium*
giant thistle *Onopordum*
ginger mint *Mentha* x *gracilis* 'Variegata'
globe amaranth *Gomphrena globosa*
globe thistle *Echinops*
globeflower *Ranunculus ficaria*
godetia *Clarkia*
golden privet *Ligustrum ovalifolium* 'Aureum'
golden rod *Solidago*
gorse *Ulex*
grape hyacinth *Muscari*
guelder rose *Viburnum opulus*
gum *Eucalyptus*

harebell *Campanula rotundifolia*
Harry Lauder's walking stick *Corylus avellana* 'Contorta'
hart's tongue fern *Asplenium scolopendrium*
hawthorn *Crataegus*
hazel *Corylus*
heartsease *Viola tricolor*
heath *Erica carnea*
heather *Calluna vulgaris*
heliotrope *Heliotropium*
hellebore *Helleborus*
hemp agrimony *Eupatorium*
Himalayan poppy *Meconopsis*
holly *Ilex aquifolium*
hollyhock *Alcea rosea*
honesty *Lunaria annua*
honey bush *Melianthus*
honeysuckle *Lonicera*
honeywort *Cerinthe major*
hop *Humulus lupulus*
hornbeam *Carpinus betulus*
houseleek *Sempervivum*
hyacinth *Hyacinthus orientalis*

iceplant *Sedum spectabile*
Indian bean tree *Catalpa bignonioides*
ironweed *Vernonia*
ivy *Hedera*

Jacob's ladder *Polemonium*
Japanese anemone *Anemone x hybrida*
Japanese quince *Chaenomeles*
Japanese maple *Acer palmatum*
japonica *Chaenomeles*
jasmine *Jasminum*
Jerusalem cross *Lychnis chalcedonica*
jessamine *Jasminum*
Jew's mallow *Kerria japonica*

kaffir lily *Schizolstylis coccinea*
katsura tree *Cercidiphyllum*
king fern *Dryopteris pseudomas* 'Cristata'
kingcup *Caltha*
knapweed *Centaurea*
knotweed *Persicaria*
kolomikta vine *Actinidia kolomikta*

lad's love *Artemisia abrotanum*
lady fern *Athyrium*
lady's mantle *Alchemilla mollis*
larkspur *Consolida ambigua*
lavender *Lavandula*
lemon balm *Melissa officinalis*
lemon verbena *Aloysa triphylla*
leopard's bane *Doronicum*
lesser celandine *Ranunculus ficaria*
lesser stitchwort *Stellaria graminea*
Leyland cypress x *Cupressocyparis leylandii*
lilac *Syringa*
lily *Lilium*
lily-of-the-valley *Convallaria majalis*
lilyturf *Liriope muscari*
lime tree *Tilia*
loosestrife *Lysimachia*
love-in-a-mist *Nigella*
love-lies-bleeding *Amaranthus*
lungwort *Pulmonaria*
lupin *Lupinus*

Madonna lily *Lilium candidum*
mallow *Lavatera, Malva*
maple *Acer*
marguerite *Argyranthemum frutescens*

marjoram *see* pot marjoram, sweet marjoram
marigold *Calendula*
marsh marigold *Caltha palustris*
mask flower *Alonsoa*
masterwort *Astrantia*
meadowsweet *Filipendula*
medlar *Mespilus germanica*
Mexican orange blossom *Choisya ternata*
Mexican sunflower *Tithonia*
Michaelmas daisy *Aster*
mignonette *Reseda odorata*
mile-a-minute plant *Fallopia baldschuanica*
milk thistle *Silybum marianum*
mint *Mentha*
mock orange *Philadelphus*
money flower *Mimulus*
monkshood *Aconitum*
montbretia *Crocosmia*
morning glory *Ipomoea*
Mount Etna broom *Genista aetnensis*
moutan *Paeonia*
mullein *Verbascum*
meadow buttercup *Ranunculus acris*
meadow cranesbill *Geranium pratense*
milfoil *Achillea millefolium*
myrtle *Myrtus*

nasturtium *Tropaeolum majus*

New England aster *Aster novae-angliae*
New Zealand flax *Phormium*
night-scented stock *Matthiola longipetala*

old man *Artemisia abrotanum*
Oregon grape *Mahonia*
oregano *Origanum vulgare*
ornamental onion *Allium*
ornamental rhubarb *Rheum*
ornamental vine *Vitis*
ox eye *Heliopsis*

pampas grass *Cortaderia selloana*
pansy *Viola* x *wittrockiana* cultivars
parsley *Petroselinum crispum*
passion flower *Passiflora caerulea*
pennyroyal *Mentha pulegium*
peony *Paeonia*
periwinkle *Vinca major, V. minor*
Peruvian lily *Alstroemeria*
pimpernel *Anagallis*
pineapple broom *Cytisus battandieri*
pink *Dianthus*
plantain lily *Hosta*
plumbago *Ceratostigma willmottianum*
poached-egg flower *Limnanthes douglasii*
polyanthus *Primula*

poppy, field *Papaver rhoeas*
poppy, opium *Papaver somniferum*
Portugal laurel *Prunus lusitanica*
potato vine *Solanum crispum*
pot marigold *Calendula*
pot marjoram *Origanum*
prickly poppy *Argemone*
primrose *Primula vulgaris*
privet *Ligustrum*
purple coneflower *Echinacea purpurea*
purple loosestrife *Lythrum salicaria*
purple velvet plant *Gynura aurantiaca*
purslane *Portulaca*

quince *Cydonia oblonga*

red-hot poker *Kniphofia*
red orache *Atriplex*
red valerian *Centranthus ruber*
rock cress *Aubrieta deltoidea*
rock rose *Cistus, Helianthemum*
rose *Rosa*

rose of Sharon *Hypericum calycinum*
rosemary *Rosmarinus officinalis*
rue *Ruta graveolens*
Russian sage *Perovskia*

sage *Salvia officinalis*
saxifrage *Saxifraga*
scabious *Scabiosa*
scented geranium *Pelargonium fragrans*
scorpion weed *Phacelia*
sea buckthorn *Hippophäe rhamnoides*
sea holly *Eryngium*

shoo-fly flower *Nicandra physalodes*
Siberian wallflower *Erysimum* x *allioni*
silk tassel bush *Garrya elliptica*
slipper flower *Calceolaria*
smoke bush *Cotinus coggygria*
snake's-head fritillary *Fritillaria meleagris*
snapdragon *Antirrhinum*
sneezeweed *Helenium*
snowberry *Symphoricarpos*
snowdrop *Galanthus nivalis*
snowflake *Leucojum*
Solomon's seal *Polygonatum*
sorrel *Rumex acetosa*
southernwood *Artemisia abrotanum*
Spanish broom *Spartium junceum*
speedwell *Veronica*

315

spider plant *Chlorophytum comosum*
spiderflower *Cleome*
spindle *Euonymus*
spotted laurel *Aucuba japonica*
spurge *Euphorbia*
squirrel tail grass *Hordeum jubatum*
St John's wort *Hypericum*
stag's horn sumach *Rhus typhina*
star jasmine *Trachelospermum jasminoides*
statice *Limonium*
stock *Matthiola*
stonecrop *Sedum*
sun rose *Cistus, Helianthemum*
sunflower *Helianthus annuus*
Swan river daisy *Brachyscome iberidifolia*
sweet alyssum *Lobularia maritima*
sweet bay *Laurus nobilis*
sweet briar *Rosa eglanteria*
sweet box *Sarcococca*
sweet marjoram *Origanum majorana*
sweet pea *Lathyrus odoratus*
sweet rocket *Hesperis matronalis*
sweet rush *Acorus calamus*
sweet violet *Viola odorata*
sweet William *Dianthus barbatus*

tamarisk *Tamarix*
Texan bluebell *Eustoma grandiflorus*
thyme *Thymus vulgaris*
tickseed *Coreopsis tinctoria*
toadflax *Linaria*
tobacco plant *Nicotiana alata*
Torbay palm *Cordyline*
torch lily *Kniphofia*
tree mallow *Lavatera*
tree peony *Paeonia*
tulip *Tulipa*
turflily *Liriope*
turtle's head *Chelone*

velvet sumach *Rhus typhina*
Venus' navelwort *Omphalodes linifolia*
violet *Viola*
viper's bugloss *Echium vulgare*
Virginia creeper *Parthenocissus quinquefolia*
virgin's bower *Clematis flammula*

wake robin *Trillium grandiflorum*

wallflower *Erysimum cheiri*
wandering Jew *Tradescantia*
wattle *Acacia*
whitewash bramble *Rubus cockburnianus*
wild bergamot *Monarda fistulosa*
willow *Salix*
willow-leaved jessamine *Cestrum parqui*
windflower *Anemone*
winter aconite *Eranthis hyemalis*
winter cherry *Solanum pseudocapsicum*
winter green *Gaultheria procumbens*
winter heath *Erica carnea*
winter jasmine *Jasminum nudiflorum*
winter-sweet *Chimonanthus*
witch hazel *Hamamelis mollis*
woad *Isatis tinctoria*
wood anemone *Anemone nemorosa*
wood lily *Trillium*
wormwood *Artemisia*

yarrow *Achillea*
yew *Taxus baccata*

Index

Index

Index